THE
HERB GARDEN
month-by-month

THE
HERB GARDEN
month-by-month

BARBARA SEGALL

David & Charles

FOR PETER WAY
'We grew a garden'

With special thanks to Mary Lightfoot, whose designs appear on pages 58, 82, 106, 114 and 126;
Susan Conder, Susanna Longley, Gisela Mirwis, Isobel Moore, Linda Runnacles, Sue and Peter
Russell of Mills Farm Plants, John and Caroline Stevens of Sawyers Farm and Christine Walkden.
Many thanks also to my parents and to other garden writing friends and colleagues, who encouraged
me to keep going. Gardens: pp.11, 27 Barnsley House, Gloucestershire; p.75 Kenneth & Carla Carlisle of
Wyken Hall, near Bury St. Edmunds; p.99 Lower Severalls, Somerset; p.111 Bourton House, Gloucestershire.
Photographs: Sue Atkinson pp.3, 6, 87; Deni Bown p.63; David Cottle p.7; Clive Nichols pp.11, 27, 39,
99, 111; Derek St Romaine pp.19, 122, 131; Barbara Segall pp.2, 51, 75.
At David & Charles I would like particularly to thank Sarah Widdicombe and Jo Weeks.

A DAVID & CHARLES BOOK

Copyright © Barbara Seagall 1994
First published 1994
Reprinted 1994, 1996
First published in paperback 1997
Reprinted 1998

A catalogue record for this book is available from the British Library.

ISBN 0 7153 0060 1 (hardback)
ISBN 0 7153 0567 0 (paperback)

Illustrations by Avis Murray
Book design by Diana Knapp
Typeset by ABM Typographics Ltd, Hull
and printed in Scotland by Bath Press Colourbooks
for David & Charles
Brunel House   Newton Abbot   Devon

CONTENTS

INTRODUCTION

 My first encounter with herbs was very early in my childhood when I crawled out of the kitchen door to nose into a clump of mint. Since then my appreciation of herbs has grown, and so has the repertoire of herbs that I grow. I know, use and love herbs as they grow through each season. I have grown herbs in containers, in hanging baskets, on patios, allotments and now, in Suffolk, have a half-acre garden where herbs predominate. There is a circular culinary wheel, an informal herb potager, and through the rest of the garden herbs play an important role as attractive plants in herbaceous borders.

I love the taste of mint and have two collections of these aromatic but invasive plants. In an old enamel footbath, with holes drilled in it for drainage, I grow apple mint, curly mint and ginger mint. In a large round container sunk into the main herb garden, spearmint and peppermint compete with apple mint.

I also have upright pennyroyal growing in an ever increasing patch: its waywardness is always forgiven when its astonishing lavender-blue flowers appear. Creeping pennyroyal basks in a damp area near a small natural pond, that boasts a clump of watermint. The lowest-growing mint of all, Corsican

THE HERB POTAGER

I grow salad herbs, such as chervil, lambs' lettuce, landcress and chives, mixed in with tomatoes and lettuce, as well as fragrant and edible herb flowers in my herb potager. There are various sages including golden and purple sage and a lavender-scented one and also flax, costmary, thyme, sorrel, parsley, and dill. Here, too, angelica provides its own successors each year.

There are two shrub roses that make central features of two quarters of this garden. I have underplanted them with bronze and green fennel and French tarragon. In summer the herbs grow tall, hiding the bare, thorny stems of the roses.

Under and up to the stone seat a downy and fragrant path of creeping thyme and chamomile releases its heady scents as I walk along it. Twining through the wild plum arch, jasmine perfumes the air around me as I pause to admire the shape, leaf texture and flowers of the herbs in this informal herb and vegetable garden.

(opposite): *Calendula and feverfew;* (left): *meadowsweet*

THE BASIL COLLECTION

For years I have grown up to 15 different types of basil, including anise basil, bush basil, cinnamon basil, dark opal basil, Greek basil, Genovese basil, green ruffles, Holy basil, horapha or Thai basil, lemon basil, Neopolitana basil, purple ruffles, spice basil and sweet fine basil. They vary in size, fragrance, and size and shape of leaf and all are wonderful plants to grow in a hot, sunny border, in pots in the greenhouse, or, sown late in the season, to grow potted up specially, indoors in autumn and winter. I nip off most buds to encourage leaf formation, but let some go to flower, so I can enjoy their fragrance. I also harvest some for pot-pourri.

NOTE TO NORTH AMERICAN READERS

Not all these monthly projects will be appropriate for every region and will have to be adapted to your area.

SEASONS AND MONTHS

Under average conditions, the terms 'early', 'mid' and 'late' season as used throughout the book correspond to the following months:

SPRING
Early: March
Mid: April
Late: May

SUMMER
Early: June
Mid: July
Late: August

AUTUMN
Early: September
Mid: October
Late: November

WINTER
Early: December
Mid: January
Late: February

mint, fills cracks in the paths of the main herb garden.

Edged with brick, my herb circle has an old glazed chimney for its central feature. The herbs once grew in wedge shapes: sage, thyme, salad burnet and fennel, with large clumps of chives, garlic chives, lavender and lemon balm. Some, including thyme, salad burnet, fennel and sage are still in their wedge shapes. In spring there is a lovely display from the variegated lemon balm, hyssop provides pretty blue flowers, while the garlic chives have heads of starry white. There are also some asparagus crowns, rescued from other parts of the garden, and angelica regularly sows itself here. These give the circle height in late summer.

From a herb garden there are many rewards: for most gardeners the idea of creating and running a herb garden is one of the dearest dreams. It appeals to the herbalist, cook and gardener in us all.

USING THE BOOK

In *The Herb Garden Month-by-Month* there are practical activities to undertake each month in the herb garden, as well as projects, many of which allow you to enjoy the plants indoors. Create the herb garden, with paths, benches, arches, even statuary. Then fill it with plants that will delight visual and aromatic senses as they grow – and still have more to offer as you use them in the kitchen, or preserve them for cosmetic, decorative, culinary and fragrant use later.

Each month is introduced by a scene-setting picture of the herb garden and an outline of the month's activities. In the sections which follow are set out the principal tasks for the month, such as seed sowing, taking cuttings, harvesting and preserving herbs, or maintaining the herb garden. In each chapter there are herb profiles, each providing a full

description of the plant, how to grow it, maintain, harvest and preserve it. Here, too, you will find general information on how to use the herb. On page 139 there is an additional list of plants traditionally grown in the herb garden.

To find out more about a herb that is mentioned in the general text, look it up in the index, and you will be referred to its profile. Included in the herb profiles are one or two that might seem unusual. For example, Norway spruce, our familiar Christmas tree, is included, because I wanted to use its branches as backing for a festive herbal wreath and for garlands. (But it has other herbal uses too – if you buy a small, rooted tree in a pot, when you plant it outdoors after Christmas, it will soon begin to grow new shoots, and you can harvest these to make your own spruce beer for summer drinks!)

In the winter and early spring months there are indoor planning projects, while all through the summer there are activities centred around particular types of herb gardens. Grow a tea garden, for example, and learn how to harvest and use herbs to make relaxing teas, or grow a fragrant cosmetic garden and use its produce to make gentle home cosmetics.

Traditionally, herbs have many uses for remedying everyday ailments, both minor and major. There are specialist books available on herbal remedies, but if you are seriously interested it is wise always to consult a professional herbalist.

In this book, I have set out to look at herbs as intensely rewarding garden plants – culinary, decorative and cosmetic – that we can all enjoy throughout the year.

USEFUL HERBS

FRESH FROM THE GARDEN
Hyssop
Rosemary
Sage
Salad burnet
Thyme
Winter savory

FRESH FROM THE KITCHEN WINDOWSILL
Chervil
Chives
Parsley
Winter savory

IN THE GREENHOUSE
French tarragon
Lemon verbena
Liquorice
Mint
Scented pelargonium

PLEASE NOTE
Any mention of herbal remedies is intended for reference only. Plant substances, whether used as foods, remedies or cosmetics, used externally or taken internally, can cause allergic reactions in some people. Neither the author nor the publishers can be held responsible for claims arising from the mistaken identity of any herbs or their inappropriate use. Do not try self-diagnosis or self-treatment for serious or chronic medical conditions without consulting a medical practitioner or a qualified medical herbal practitioner. Do not take herbal remedies if you are undergoing any other medical treatment. Always seek professional medical advice if symptoms persist.

JANUARY

If you are a first-time herb gardener, you are embarking upon one of gardening's greatest pleasures. What better time than mid-winter to start thinking about the aroma and fragrance of herbs in the spring or summer garden, as well as the household pleasures they provide throughout the year?

A herb garden offers a special combination of plants, which can be enjoyed in different ways. They can be admired simply for their decorative effect and overall shape, as they grow into the plan you have created. In addition, you can appreciate the scents, aromas and colours of their flowers and foliage.

Herbs can be raised from seed, grown from cuttings or bought in containers from garden centres or nurseries. During winter, in an established herb garden, fresh herb leaves are still available from many evergreen plants such as rosemary, thyme and sage. You can also grow a selection of herbs indoors on a sunny kitchen windowsill. Winter savory, chives, parsley, chervil, sage and thyme will all provide flavour for soups, stews, sauces and vegetable dishes through the winter season.

If you are new to herb gardening, use the calm and relative inactivity of this 'in-between' season to choose the site for your herb garden and the plants that you will use and enjoy. Then settle down to create a planting plan for the herb garden. Herbs are versatile plants that look equally attractive whether they are grown in formal, shaped beds such as squares, rectangles and circles, or informal borders. If space is at a premium, plan a herb garden using containers on a balcony or patio, or even a windowbox.

Whether you are growing a herb garden for the first time, extending an existing one or adding a new herb feature to your garden, now is the time to choose or reassess the site and to make the right plant choices.

tasks

FOR THE

month

HERB THEMES FOR THE GARDEN

LEMON-SCENTED LEAVES
Balm • Lemon mint •
Lemon thyme • Verbena

ORNAMENTAL DYE PLANTS
Coreopsis • Dyer's chamomile •
Safflower

EDIBLE FLOWERS
Bergamot • Borage •
Garlic chives • Hyssop •
Lavender • Mallow •
Pot marigold • Rose • Sage •
Viola

ENGLISH CULINARY
Chives • Mint • Parsley (curled) •
Rosemary • Sorrel

FRENCH CULINARY
Bay • Chervil • Fennel •
Garlic • Parsley • Tarragon •
Thyme

ITALIAN CULINARY
Basil • Bay • Oregano •
Parsley (flat-leaved) • Sage

POT-POURRI HERBS: FLOWERS
Lavender • Rose • Sage •
Sweet rocket • Thyme

POT-POURRI HERBS: LEAVES
Basil • Bergamot • Mint •
Scented pelargonium •
Rosemary • Sage • Thyme •
Wild strawberry

CHECKLIST

- Plan a new herb garden or bed
- Select herbs to grow
- Order seeds

STARTING A HERB GARDEN

If you begin a herb garden in midwinter, most of your activity will be comfortably achieved indoors – drawing plans; ordering seeds and imagining the non-stop pleasure of harvesting throughout the following seasons. Now is the time to get to know the plants on paper; discover what conditions suit them best and check that you have the right soil and site for them. Then decide on the shape of the herb garden and the range of plants you want to grow.

NOTE

- *Before making a formal plan, ask yourself the following questions about your garden. Is the soil a heavy clay? Is it a light, infertile sandy soil? Is the garden sheltered from wind? Is it shady or sunny?* ■

Herbs are adaptable plants that will grow in most conditions, extremes of cold, drought and moisture excluded. Most originate from hot climates and thrive in well-drained, infertile sandy soils. In the wild, herbs are not constantly harvested, so fertile soil is not necessary, and the aromatic oils produced in their leaves and stems help prevent excessive loss of water.

In the garden, you may have to offer the plants a little extra help to ensure they perform well. In cold areas, winter shelter from chilly, drying winds is necessary to prevent evergreens such as bay turning brown. In summer, the plants will benefit from the shelter and shade provided by herb hedges and wooden fencing.

If the soil is infertile, work in well-rotted, home-made compost or a bagged, proprietary compost in autumn or spring. The added compost gives the plants extra nutrients so they keep producing new shoots throughout the growing season. The addition of compost will also help water retention in dry soils. Heavy clay soils need similar additions of compost to open them up and prevent water-logging. Clay soils also need gravel or coarse material such as sand worked in to make them free draining.

Choosing the site

For best results, choose a site in full sun, protected from cold or drying winds and with soil that is well manured, well dug and drains efficiently. Naturally, in exceptionally dry seasons you will have to water the plants. Remember that herbs in containers may need watering at least once a day, especially in sunny sites during dry, warm spells.

For you, easy access to the herb garden is essential. If you plan to grow herbs solely for kitchen use and have limited space, choose a site near the back door. That way, you can harvest fresh herbs in all weathers, just a step outside the kitchen.

Making a plan

Before you begin to mark out the site or prepare the soil, draw a plan on paper. Measure the chosen area of the garden. Scale down the actual measurements so that you can fit them on to sketch paper or squared graph paper. 1 metre can be represented by 4cm (1m = 4cm). The sides of the original plan shown measured 12 × 12cm, representing 3 × 3m. If you use imperial measure, scale the measurements down so that the actual measurement of 10 × 10ft is represented by a square with sides 5 × 5in (ie 2ft = 1in).

Shape is an important consideration. You may want a square herb garden with equal sides, or prefer a rectangle to take into account an existing site with irregular sides. Circular herb gardens are attractive and suit a small garden. In a large herb garden you could combine squares, rectangles, triangles and circles (see diagram).

Once the plan is on paper, indicate the points of the compass to give it a directional reference – knowing where the sun casts shadow or is at its strongest helps you position plants correctly. You can then avoid planting tall herbs where they block out light for less vigorous or low-growing plants.

Paths and other features

Whatever the size and shape of your herb bed, you need to be able to work the soil from all angles without treading on it and flattening it with your feet. Similarly, you need to be able to maintain the plants without damaging them, and may need to create access paths. These allow a circulation of air in and around the herb beds, thereby reducing the likelihood of disease. Sensibly planned paths also divide a large herb garden into manageable units and form the framework for herb hedges (see p112).

Mark any proposed paths on the plan. At this stage you may decide on a central feature such as a sundial or an old chimney pot, statuary or a bird bath, which can also be shown on the plan.

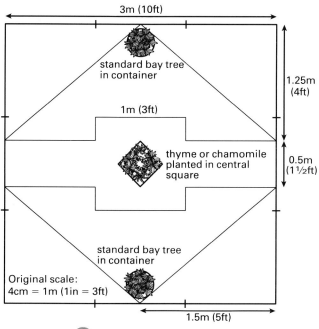

3m (10ft)

standard bay tree
in container

1m (3ft)

1.25m
(4ft)

thyme or chamomile
planted in central
square

0.5m
(1½ft)

standard bay tree
in container

Original scale:
4cm = 1m (1in = 3ft)

1.5m (5ft)

SELECTING HERBS

Now you are ready to make the most important decision of all: which herbs to grow. If your space is limited, grow only the basic herbs that you enjoy and know you will use often.

Chives, parsley, sage, thyme, rosemary, mint, tarragon and bay are eight favourites that provide year-round flavour in fresh, frozen or dried form. Chives, a perennial plant that dies down in winter, can be potted up in autumn to grow indoors. Parsley normally survives outdoors but for convenience can be grown indoors in winter. Sage, thyme and rosemary are evergreen perennials that will survive most winters unprotected in mild climates. Bay plants in containers and those in cold areas need protection from wintry winds in exposed sites. Mint and tarragon, also perennials, die back in winter, but you can persuade them to keep growing by providing a little gentle heat, or 'forcing' them. Pot up rooted pieces of mint, grow them on a warm windowsill or in a greenhouse and keep them well watered. Tarragon

can be treated similarly, but if you leave it growing outdoors in winter, protect its roots with a straw cover or mulch.

ORDERING SEED

Herb seed specialists provide a wide range of herb and wildflower seeds, while general seed merchants stock the most popular and basic culinary herbs. Most herbs are easily grown from seed, but some require special conditions of heat or cold to get best results. Seed

catalogues generally describe ideal sowing conditions, eventual size and harvest time for the individual herbs.

Perennials

Perennial herbs produce new growth and flowers each year and survive for many seasons. It is best to buy them as young plants or raise them from cuttings or by division, as it may take a while to establish them from seedlings, or they may not grow well from seed. On the other hand it may be worth considering growing from seed those that will, if you need large numbers of plants.

Annuals and biennials

The easiest herbs to grow from seed are annuals. They germinate quickly and develop in one growing season into plants that produce flowers and set seed. Annuals can be hardy (grow outdoors in all weathers), half-hardy (need a little protection while they are young) or tender (need very warm weather to grow outdoors).

Herbs that take two seasons to reach maturity and set seed are called biennials. These can be sown in spring and used through the first year, but once they have flowered in the second year they will set seed and die. You are likely to have many new plants from their seed, as they self sow abundantly.

ORDER EARLY
Order seeds early so that you can be ready to sow tender, half-hardy and hardy annuals indoors, in the greenhouse or into their growing positions in early spring.

SEED TO ORDER

ANNUALS
Basil • Borage • Chervil• Coriander • Dill • Nasturtium • Orach • Perilla • Pot marigold • Salad rocket • Summer savory

BIENNIALS
Angelica • Caraway • Evening primrose • Mullein • Parsley

PLANTS TO BUY
Bay • Box • Chives • Curry plant • Fennel • French tarragon • Lavender • Lemon verbena • Lovage • *Rose • Sage • Salad burnet • Southernwood • Thyme • Wall germander

*Plant out bare-root roses direct into their growing sites.

PLANTING A CULINARY SQUARE

On graph paper, divide the rectangle into quarters. Number them 1, 2, 3, 4 and then write in your planting plan for each quarter. Use chives and parsley to make the herb hedges that line the paths. There are several different types of thyme, rosemary and sage which offer attractive foliage and shape, as well as aromatic leaves and fragrant flowers.

■ *Mint should be kept in a bed of its own, otherwise it will rampage through the whole herb garden. Once again, there are several types that you can group together to make an attractive and aromatic mint collection.*

Plant each sort in separate containers to stop them overwhelming each other, and then sink the containers into the ground. Make sure the containers have drainage holes.

■ *Plant tarragon at the back of one of the north-facing quarters. It grows to 60cm (2ft) and will otherwise cast a large shadow on the other herbs.*

■ *In the round area at the centre of the four quarters, place a bay tree in a container. In cold areas, move it into a frost-free greenhouse when severe weather threatens.*

practical project

MAKING A HERB DRYING FRAME

From spring until autumn one of the main tasks of a herb gardener is managing the harvest of leaves, flowers and seeds. They can all be preserved to keep their flavour, colour and fragrance, ready for you to use in cooking or to make scented presents.

In midwinter most of the basic culinary and cosmetic herbs are dormant or still in their seed packets. Evergreen herbs, such as thyme and bay, and those that you have potted up to overwinter on your kitchen windowsill, are best used fresh. Don't bother to cut and dry them now. Leave the main harvest and drying time until late spring and summer.

Many herbs dry well when tied into bunches and hung from shelves or hangers in a dry, dark and well-ventilated shed or loft. However, if you plan to dry large quantities for your own use, to sell or to give as presents, you will need a suitable drying frame to hold the herbs while they dry.

The free-standing frame shown here provides six shelves, but can be adapted to suit individual needs. Give it added height by standing it on a table, for easier access to the lower shelves.

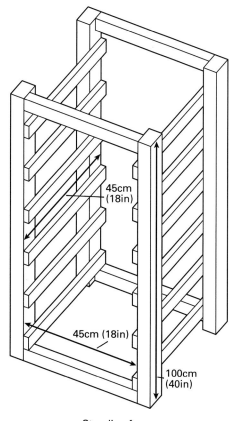

45cm (18in)

45cm (18in)

100cm (40in)

Standing frame

YOU WILL NEED

bradawl
screwdriver
set square
electric or hand drill
hammer
sandpaper
pencil and ruler or tape measure

MATERIALS

For the standing frame:

4 pieces untreated 5 × 5cm (2 × 2in) softwood cut to 100cm (40in)

16 pieces 5 × 2.5cm (2 × 1in) cut to 45cm (18in)

8 × 7.5cm (3in) flat-headed wood screws

48 × 4cm (1¹/₂in) nails

For the shelves:

24 pieces softwood 2.5 × 2.5cm (1× 1in) cut to 44cm (17¹/₂in)

24 × 4cm (1¹/₂in) nails

6 pieces muslin or cheesecloth cut to 50 × 50cm (20 × 20in)

Approximately 30 drawing pins per shelf

NOTE

■ *Before you begin, sand down any rough edges.* ■

CONSTRUCTING THE STANDING FRAME

■ With a pencil, mark each upright at the top and bottom, 2.5cm (1in) from the edge and centred. Turn the point of a bradawl in the wood where marked. This will ease the wood and prevent the drill bit slipping. Use a hand or electric drill to make eight holes right through each pencil mark on the four uprights.

■ Lay the uprights down on your work surface so that each has the drill holes facing upwards. With the pencil and tape measure, mark the position of the shelf runners. Measure from the top of the upright and make marks at 15cm (6in) intervals along it. These marks indicate the position of the lower side of each shelf runner.

■ Pair the uprights and lay them down 35cm (14in) apart. Align the lower edge of the first shelf runner with a pencil mark. Use a set square to check that the wood edges align to make right angles. Fix the runner in place with two nails at each end. Next put the lowest shelf runner in place. This ensures that the two uprights are parallel. Continue until all the shelf runners are fixed in place.

- Use the four remaining battens to join together the four uprights, front and back, top and bottom. You will need someone to hold the frame steady as you do this. Fix the uprights together using 7.5cm (3in) screws turned into the pre-drilled holes.

TO MAKE THE SHELVES

- To make a shelf, use four pieces of wood. Nail the side pieces so that they fit snugly just inside the front and back pieces. To-

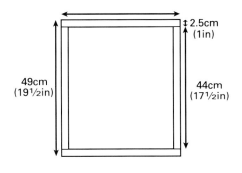

49cm (19½in)

44cm (17½in)

2.5cm (1in)

*T*HE SIMPLEST METHOD

Stretch a piece of garden wire across the shed or loft, fixing it at each end onto cuphooks or brackets in the walls. Peg wire coat-hangers onto the wire and tie herb bunches to the hangers.

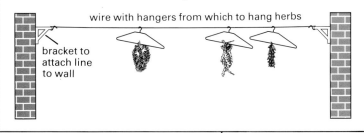

wire with hangers from which to hang herbs

bracket to attach line to wall

gether the four pieces of wood form a rectangle. Repeat this to make the rest of the shelves. Give the frame and shelves a protective coat of varnish, if you wish.

- Cover each shelf with a piece of muslin. Fold the muslin over at each edge to neaten it off and tack it in place along the top edge of each shelf, spacing the drawing pins evenly.

- Now you can slide the shelves into position and wait for the burst of harvest activity that begins soon after spring. In the meantime, keep the herb drying frame dust-free with a sheet of clean plastic or a dust sheet. Each time you use it check the shelves for stains and tears, and replace them when worn.

Later on, in spring, summer and autumn, you can dry herb leaves and flowers in various ways.

HERBS TO DRY IN BUNCHES:
Anise hyssop flowers
Lady's mantle flowers
Lavender flowers
Lemon balm
Mint
Rosemary
Sage
Sage flowers
Thyme

HERBS TO DRY FLAT:
Bay leaves
Bergamot flowers
Chamomile flowers
Hop flowers (individually)
Lady's mantle leaves
Lemon verbena leaves
Marigold flowers
Mint leaves
Rose blooms
Sage leaves

HERBS TO DRY ON WIRE RACK:
Chive flowers
Helichrysum flowers

ALTERNATIVE FRAMES

To dry herbs and flowers in bunches you need suitable hanging space. Use garden canes to construct a tent-like frame. Use two pairs of canes to make the end supports.

Rest a cane along the top and then wire as many canes as you need across the framework. The end result looks rather like an old-fashioned clothes dryer.

JANUARY

plants
OF THE
month

Bay

BAY
(*Laurus nobilis* – Lauraceae)

Bay, a shrubby tree, offers evergreen and aromatic foliage that can be clipped into decorative topiary shapes to provide year-round ornament in the garden.

type	Evergreen shrub or tree
flowers	Small, creamy white, early summer (in hot climates only)
leaves	Oval-shaped, smooth green leaves
height	Depending on situation and climate, in time up to 12m (40ft). Slow-growing and suits containers. Can be clipped as a cone or standard to 1–1.2m (3–4ft).
spread	Up to 9m (30ft)
planting	Plant in autumn or spring
position	Sunny and sheltered
soil	Any, but best in light, well-drained soil. Container-grown bay needs a well-aerated, loam compost
care	In cold areas and in the first year of growth, protect with hessian windbreaks. Overwinter container-grown bay in frost-free conditions. From midwinter onwards check branches and undersurfaces of leaves for scale insects
propagation	Heel cuttings in late summer
species and varieties	*Laurus nobilis* 'Aurea' has yellowy-gold leaves and *L.n. angustifolia*, or willow-leaf bay, has narrow leaves. These varieties are best used ornamentally
harvest	Pick leaves throughout the year, but at their peak for drying in spring and early summer
herbal value	Leaves are used to flavour soups, fish stock, stews, marinades and in pickling

CHIVES
(*Allium schoenoprasum* – Liliaceae)

Offering onion flavour without the tears, chives' grassy leaves and mauve flowers provide bold clumps of colour and are ideal as edging.

type	Hardy perennial with onion-like bulbs
flowers	Densely packed heads of pink-to-mauve flowers, early to mid summer
leaves	Hollow, long, upright
height	30cm (12in)
spread	20–30cm (8–12in)

planting	Plant in spring or autumn, sow seed in spring and pot up a clump or two for kitchen use over winter
position	Sun or partial shade
soil	Any, but grows best in moist, rich, loamy soil
care	Cut back in autumn. Lift and divide large clumps in autumn or spring. Water during dry spells and nip out some flower stems to keep leaf flavour strong
propagation	Divide in autumn or spring. Plant into enriched soil and cut leafy shoots to ground level. Sow seeds outdoors in spring or into trays in the greenhouse in winter
species and varieties	Chinese or garlic chives (*Allium tuberosum*) has flat, strappy leaves with a garlic flavour and delicately scented, star-like white flowers
harvest	Use leaves fresh all year. Can be frozen, chopped into ice cube trays or whole. Dry in a cool oven
herbal value	Florets can be used whole or broken into individual flowers in salads and to flavour and colour vinegar. Add chopped leaves to salads, dressings, omelettes, soft cheese dips and herb butters

FRENCH TARRAGON
(*Artemisia dracunculus* – Compositae)

French tarragon's narrow leaves hold its delicately bittersweet, aniseed flavour, prized in cooking. In the garden it makes a shapely block of feathery foliage.

type	Herbaceous perennial, tender in cold areas
flowers	Insignificant, and do not set seed. Best to encourage leaf production by clipping back flowering shoots
leaves	Long and strappy, pale green
height	60cm (24in)
spread	30cm (12in)
planting	Plant in spring and autumn to grow outdoors. To grow indoors in winter, pot up roots in autumn, expose plants to cool conditions (below 4°C/40°F) for three weeks, then grow on a sunny windowsill or in the greenhouse
position	Full sun
soil	Well-drained, light
care	Make sure roots are not waterlogged at any stage, and in winter protect with a straw mulch.

	Divide plants every three years to retain leaf flavour
propagation	Take soft stem cuttings in summer and feed cuttings through the growing season with a liquid fertiliser. Divide clumps in autumn or spring
species and varieties	French tarragon has the best flavour. Russian tarragon *(Artemisia dracunculoides)* is a strong-growing, large plant but is less distinctively flavoured
harvest	Pick leaves to use fresh as you need them, but best flavour in summer. Freeze in water in ice-cube trays, bag up and keep in the freezer until required. Can be air dried, but lose flavour if dried too quickly at high temperatures
herbal value	Use in *fines herbes* (see p65), in salads, dressings, herb butters, to flavour vinegar, classic sauces and fish and poultry dishes

ROSEMARY

(*Rosmarinus officinalis* – Labiatae)

Delicate flowers and strongly aromatic leaves are the ornamental attractions of rosemary, an evergreen shrub long valued in cooking, herbal cosmetics and remedies.

type	Evergreen shrub, hardy except in very cold areas
flowers	Depending on species and variety, small white, blue or pink flowers in spring and early summer, sometimes in autumn
height	Available in dwarf, prostrate and tall-growing forms up to 2.4m (8ft)
spread	Up to 1.5–1.8m (5–6ft)
planting	Plant outdoors in spring or autumn. Select strong-growing cuttings in autumn and pot up for kitchen use in winter
position	Full sun in sheltered site
soil	Well-drained loam
care	Needs winter protection in exposed sites, or grow in containers and bring into a frost-free greenhouse. Prune to keep shape if leggy. Do not overwater
propagation	Take cuttings in spring or summer to plant out the following autumn. Layer stems in summer or sow seed uncovered in spring, but germination is uneven and requires a temperature of 21°C (70°F)

species and varieties	*Rosmarinus officinalis* 'Miss Jessopp's Upright' has white flowers and can be grown as a hedge. *R.o.* 'Majorcan Pink' is half-hardy and has pink flowers. *R.o. lavandulaceus* is tender with thin leaves and blue flowers. *R.o.* 'Sudbury Blue' has delicate deep blue flowers
harvest	Pick leaves through the year as needed. For drying in bulk, pick leaves in late summer. Dry whole stems and sprigs
herbal value	Use rosemary flowers and leaves in salads. Use leaves with meat dishes, especially lamb, and in herb butter, jams, jellies and summer drinks as well as to flavour sugar for desserts

WINTER SAVORY

(*Satureja montana* – Labiatae)

Winter savory provides a spicy, aromatic flavour to salads and cooked dishes. It is often used as an informal edging plant.

type	Hardy, evergreen, shrubby perennial
flowers	Small pink to white flowers in late summer to autumn
leaves	Small, pointed light green leaves
height	Up to 40cm (16in)
spread	Up to 45cm (18in)
planting	Plant out in spring. Grows well in . containers indoors
position	Prefers full sun
soil	Well-drained, slightly alkaline and coarse soil
care	Cut sprawling stems back in spring. Give winter protection if in a damp and shady position
propagation	Sow seed onto soil surface in spring. Take stem tip cuttings, layer stems or divide overgrown plants in spring
species and varieties	Creeping winter savory *(Satureja spicigera)* has aromatic leaves and makes good ground cover
harvest	Harvest young plants in their second year from early summer onwards. Cut flowering tips and leaves from soft stems
herbal value	Mix with other herbs in *bouquet garni* (see p65). Use sparingly on its own as it has a strong flavour. Antiseptic properties are useful in astringent face preparations and to ease insect stings

Chives

Rosemary

French tarragon

FEBRUARY

During the last days of winter, decorative herb flowers such as primrose and cowslip offer delicate shape and colour to brighten the evergreen herbs at this quiet time in the herb garden. Slow though the plants may be at this season, you have a potentially busy time ahead. Activity is centred around preparing the ground for sowing and planting later in spring and planning the framework of non-plant features such as paths, seats and fencing. Weather is the main factor that determines how busy you are able to be. There is no point in attempting to work the soil in cold and frosty weather or after heavy rain. Instead, take advantage of every opportunity that mild weather provides to get out and prepare the ground. It is hard work, but healthy, strong-growing plants are the reward. Good preparation includes weeding, digging and, if necessary, enriching the soil, as well as improving its drainage. Now is also the time to start a compost heap, so that at the end of autumn you will have your own herbal compost ready to add to the soil.

If a new herb site is to be cut out of an area under lawn, wait until after the last snow or frost before you clear the turf and begin preparing the ground. As a general rule, it is more practical to start from scratch in autumn.

Once the ground is prepared, begin to put in place the permanent framework of the herb garden you have planned on paper. Paths, seats, statuary, sundials and fences are known as the hard landscape features. Your choice of these will be governed by the size of the herb garden and the cost of materials. At first these features may look stark, but in a short while the herb plants – the soft landscape features – will soften the edges. If the weather keeps you indoors, remember you can keep company with overwintering aromatic plants such as canary balm, lemon-scented eucalyptus and woolly thyme.

tasks
FOR THE
month

CHECKLIST

☐ Prepare existing and new herb beds
☐ Start a compost heap
☐ Choose permanent herb garden features
☐ Make early seed sowings

PREPARING AN EXISTING HERB BED

If your new herb garden site is part of an existing border or vegetable plot, the initial preparation is relatively easy.

■ Mark out the site carefully.

■ Next, the site will need weeding to remove long-term or perennial weeds such as dock, dandelion and thistle. They have long tap roots and also seed themselves freely each year. Other perennials such as bindweed, couch grass and creeping buttercup with underground stems or runners, are difficult to remove completely, as they regrow from small pieces of root.

■ Loosen individual dock, thistle and dandelion plants with a fork and work at them until you have removed as much as possible of their tap root. Similarly, loosen the soil and dig out weeds with creeping stems.

■ Fork over the soil and check that you have removed all visible pieces of their creeping root systems.

■ Seedlings of short-term annual weeds such as chickweed and hairy bittercress are easier to remove, but they must be tackled before they flower – which begins very early in spring – and self sow. Use a hoe to chop the leaves away from their roots. The leaves and stems can then be forked into the soil, where they will eventually decay and increase its fertility.

■ If the soil has been used regularly to grow vegetables or flowers, it will need enriching with well-rotted home-made or proprietary compost to replenish lost goodness. Dig this in, then fork the area over to break the newly-exposed soil down into a crumblier texture.

■ Once the site is weed free, you will be able to transplant herbs that are overcrowded or whose position you wish to alter.

CUTTING A NEW HERB GARDEN FROM A TURFED AREA

If the new site is to be cut out of the lawn, mark out its shape, but wait until after the last snow or frost before clearing the turf and preparing the ground.

■ Use garden twine and wooden pegs to mark out the first side of a rectangular bed.

■ Then measure the second, third and fourth sides, using a set square or builder's square to make perfect right angles where each side meets.

■ Lay a straight-edged batten on the ground to act as a cutting guide. If you have an alternative use for the turf, use an edging tool to mark it into even sections to a depth of 5cm (2in).

■ Then use a spade to lift each section and remove it carefully. Store in shade and re-lay it into a new site within 24 hours, before it dries out.
   If you don't wish to re-use the turf elsewhere, you can incorporate it into the new herb site. Before you begin, remove any perennial weeds such as dock, thistle and dandelion.

Double digging
■ Make a trench to one spade's depth at one end of the marked out herb bed.

■ Put the soil and turf from this first trench into a wheelbarrow and keep it aside to add to the last trench you dig.

■ Fork over the trench to another spade's depth, add manure and work it into the soil.

■ Work across the site, moving backwards. Remove turf and

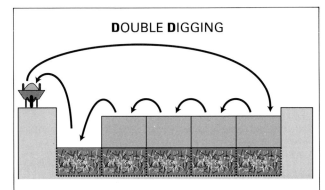

DOUBLE DIGGING

Double digging improves drainage, exposes deeply embedded weeds and eases incorporation of compost

soil, turning turf over so that the grass is face downwards, and replace it in the first trench.

■ Continue in this way, replacing soil and turf in the last trench dug, until you have a trench left at the other end. Then add the turf and soil from the wheelbarrow.

Enriching the soil

Although herbs generally do well in poor soils, if your herbs are likely to be cut frequently for use it is well worth adding fertiliser or compost to ground that is earmarked for spring sowing and planting. Lightly fork it in and let the ground settle before you finally rake it to make a level surface.

Start a herb compost heap, so that by autumn you will be able to use your own home-grown organic matter to enrich the soil and improve its structure and drainage.

STARTING A COMPOST HEAP

■ Fence off an area 60 × 60cm (24 × 24in) in a sheltered part of the garden, using four posts and fine-mesh wire netting.

■ Construct it so that the front piece of netting can be opened like a door.

■ Dig out the topsoil of the enclosed area and keep it to one side. Line the base with twigs or branches to allow circulation of air underneath your heap.

■ During the year, add layers of disease-free garden and kitchen vegetable waste to the heap.

■ Build the heap up in layers about 15cm (6in) deep. Between each layer add a thin layer of the topsoil you removed from the base.

■ Cover the heap with a piece of old carpet to keep it dry, raise the temperature and increase the rate of decomposition.

■ Every few weeks, make several holes vertically through the heap using a strong stick. This aerates the mound and prevents any slushiness in the middle.

■ When the top of the fence is reached and the heap is full, start a second one. The compost from the first heap will be ready to use by the autumn, when you will begin preparing new beds or maintaining older parts of the herb garden.

CHOOSING PERMANENT FEATURES

■ *Paths* Important for many reasons, as discussed on page 22. It is also very pleasant to walk into the herb garden along an even path edged with fragrant flowers and aromatic foliage.

■ *Seats* Offer similar pleasures. From a well-located bench you can enjoy the decorative shapes, as well as the delightful aromas and perfumes, of your flourishing herb plants.

■ *Sundials and statues* Might be considered unnecessary follies, but in a herb garden they provide fitting focal points and add height. Many herbs are low-growing, and a statue can lift your eye and create interest at a different level. Statues or large containers are particularly attractive when they mark the meeting of several paths. All-weather stone or terracotta urns can be used as permanent features to house tender herbs such as lemon verbena during the summer.

■ *Arches and arbours* Similar dual-purpose roles to play. They again lift your eye, and also offer support to climbing plants for the scented herb garden. Honeysuckle, jasmine and roses provide fragrant cover, but will need to be tied in to the support system.

SOWING SEED EARLY

Many herbs germinate quite easily, but some require special conditions to ensure a high success rate, and early sowing to give them the long growing season they need.

Parsley, perilla and basil all need warmth to germinate, and basil and perilla also need warmth as seedlings and for growing outdoors.

If you can provide a temperature of 18–23°C (65–75°F), basil and perilla will germinate in about a week. If you do not have the space and cannot provide them with constant heat before transplanting into the sunniest part of the garden in midsummer, there are two solutions. Sow basil and perilla later and you won't have to give them house room for so long. Or, you can treat the basil seeds as a sprouting crop and make several sowings indoors on kitchen tissue. You must use seed that has not been treated with fungicide.

■ Place the tissue on a plate, wet it well, sow basil seed on the surface and enclose the plate and tissue in a loosely tied polythene bag.

■ After about a week the seeds will sprout and you can cut the stems and seedling leaves off to use in salads. Keep the tissue moist and the basil sprouts will keep you supplied for up to several weeks, depending on the quantity sown.

■ Parsley needs more warmth for germination. Provide temperatures of 21–27°C (70–80°F) and, once the seedlings have germinated, lower the temperature to 15–18°C (60–65°F) and grow on in a cool greenhouse.

■ Transplant when the seedlings are well established, but avoid handling and disturbing the roots, as the stress will cause the plants to flower and set seed prematurely.

COMPOST MATERIALS

Use leaves of annual weeds *(before they flower and set seed)*

Lawn clippings, wood ash and any soft-stemmed herbal material from the herb garden

Comfrey can be used as a special compost crop: cut it and add to the heap several times a year.

From the kitchen, use fruit and vegetable peelings, egg shells, tea leaves and coffee grounds.

THINGS TO DO

Sow seed
Indoors or greenhouse: basil, canary balm, cowslip, eucalyptus, evening primrose, French marigold, parsley, perilla, safflower, thyme, wild strawberry, woad
Outdoors: chervil (can also be sown into pots for kitchen use), German chamomile

Plant out
Bare-root roses, clary sage, sweet violets

Propagate
Take cuttings: chicory, sea holly
Divide: chives, costmary, ginger, sorrel

Harvest
Flowers: sweet violet
Leaves: winter purslane

Routine maintenance
■ Divide herbs such as chives and hyssop – which begin to lose vigour when they form large, congested clumps – into small, healthy sections. Cut back stems by about one-third to one-half and replant. Firm the new plants in and water well

practical project

PATHS THROUGH THE HERB GARDEN

Herringbone

YOU WILL NEED

builder's square
brick-laying trowel
spirit level
lump hammer
lines (strings and sticks)

At the most basic level, a path is for access and to ensure that as little of the growing area as possible is damaged by people walking over it.

In a small herb patch a path may not be necessary: you may be able to reach the centre easily and weed, plant, water, mulch and harvest without having to step onto the soil at any point. If you cannot work the herb garden in this way, then you need to lay a path of some sort. The simplest pathway is made by placing stepping stones across a square-shaped bed to divide it into quarters. In a circular bed, arrange the stepping stones as an inner circle a convenient distance in from the edge.

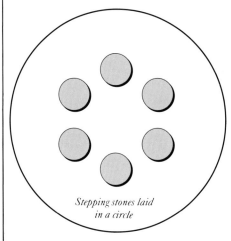

Stepping stones laid in a circle

In a large herb garden, the path may provide the main route from kitchen to compost heap, and must therefore be suited to heavier use. Such paths become integral features of the herb garden as they weather and plants grow to soften the hard edges.

PATH TYPES

There are many different materials which can be used for paths and the choice will depend on your budget and taste. If you are cutting a bed from a grassed area, it is simple to leave strips of lawn in place to form the paths. Make sure that the width is adequate to allow your lawn mower through or you will have a problem keeping the paths mown.

Gravel or washed pea-shingle are relatively low-cost materials that look effective in a hot, Mediterranean-style herb garden. Lay black polythene over the base to suppress weeds. Cover this with a layer of pea-shingle 3cm (1¼in) deep: any deeper and it

will be difficult to walk on. Edge the path with narrow battens of treated wood, so that the gravel does not spread into the herb beds.

Brick looks very attractive laid in patterns and is the most traditional material for herb garden paths. It is more expensive than gravel, but is very hardwearing. If you live in a cold climate, make sure that the bricks you use are frostproof.

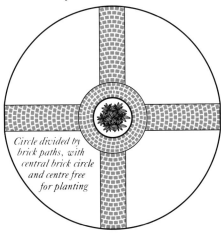

Circle divided by brick paths, with central brick circle and centre free for planting

Other materials include setts and cobbles, reconstituted and natural stone pavers, log rounds, woodchips and bark. The paths in the project are made from reconstituted stone pavers and divide the herb garden into four. The central area can be left empty to allow for a plant or a container, sundial or piece of garden statuary.

MATERIALS

16 or 17 paving slabs 45 × 45cm (18 × 18in)

hardcore, hogging or ballast

plastic sheet on which to mix concrete

mortar mix 1 : 6 (1 part cement to 6 of sand and shingle mix)

water

NOTE

■ *If the weather is very cold or frost is forecast you may still be able to do the ground work for the path, but don't mix or use the mortar until conditions are more favourable.* ■

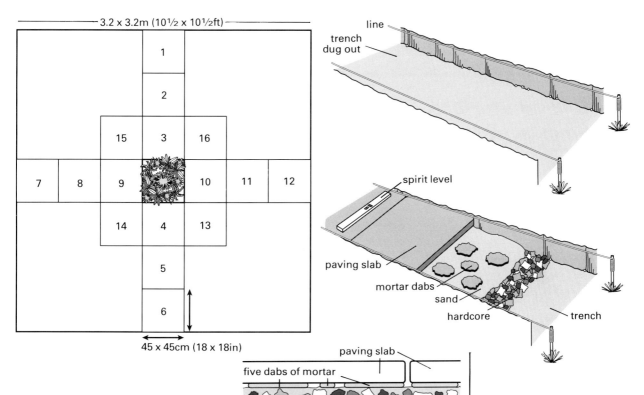

3.2 x 3.2m (10½ x 10½ft)

| 1 |
| 2 |

| 15 | 3 | 16 |

| 7 | 8 | 9 | | 10 | 11 | 12 |

| 14 | 4 | 13 |

| 5 |
| 6 |

45 x 45cm (18 x 18in)

line
trench dug out

spirit level

paving slab

mortar dabs
sand
hardcore
trench

paving slab
five dabs of mortar

hardcore and sand base

LAYING THE PATH

■ Mark out the site, using the builder's square to ensure straight edges, and sticks and strings as guides for the excavation.

■ Where the path is to be laid, dig out the soil deep enough to allow for a layer of hardcore, the dabs of mortar mix and the thickness of the path material. In this case allow 10cm (4in) for hardcore, 3cm (1¼in) for sand, 2.5cm (1in) for mortar dabs and 5cm (2in) for paver – a total of 20.5cm (8¼in).

■ Compact the base of the trench either by walking back and forth along it, or rolling it with a lawn roller.

■ Put a layer of hardcore into the base of the trench and tamp it down.

■ Cover with a layer of sand 3cm (1¼in) thick.

■ Mix up some mortar. Prepare it in batches as you use it. Mortar stays workable for up to two hours, depending on temperature. Always use clean water to be sure of a soft and easy-to-apply mix.

■ Place five dabs of mortar where the paving slab is to sit.

■ Lay the slab against the string, with the smooth side down (rough surface is non-slip) and use the spirit level to check that it is level.

■ Carry on laying the rest of the slabs in the same manner.

■ Mix up a fresh dry batch of mortar but don't add water to it. Brush it in between the paving slabs and water in using a watering can.

■ Allow the mortar to set before using the path. Mortar takes up to 36 hours to dry depending on temperature and humidity. It is best to leave the path 3–5 days before using it.

■ If you have left the central square (where the four paths meet) unpaved, add compost and plant it up with thymes or lavender. If you prefer to pave it, use a decorative container of herbs to make a focal point.

Basketweave

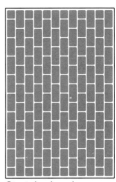

Stretcherbond

plants
OF THE
month

Chervil

Parsley

CANARY BALM
(*Cedronella canariensis* – Labiatae)

Aromatic leaves and dome-shaped heads of small pink flowers are the attractions of canary balm. It grows well indoors and in sunny sheltered sites outdoors.

type	Half-hardy shrub
flowers	Pink to mauve heads of small tubular flowers from late summer through to early autumn
leaves	Musk and citrus-scented matt-green leaves are divided into three oval-shaped, pointed leaflets with toothed edges which grow along square stems
height	1m (3ft)
spread	1.2m (4ft)
planting	Sow seed in spring or grow from rooted cuttings. Protect plants by growing in pots and overwintering indoors in cold areas
position	Full sun
soil	Well-drained loam
care	Plants grown in pots may need support in their first year. In their second year stems become strong and woody. Water plants in containers frequently. Bring container-grown plants indoors in winter or protect with mulch and hessian netting cover
propagation	Sow seed in spring or take stem cuttings in autumn
species and varieties	Canary balm is sometimes sold as False Balm of Gilead or Balm of Gilead (*Cedronella tryphylla*)
harvest	Pick leaves before flowers appear and dry to use in pot-pourri. Harvest flowers as they open from summer to autumn
herbal value	Crush dried leaves to use in pot-pourri. Use fresh leaves to make an aromatic hand- or facewash. Add whole dried flowers to pot-pourri. The whole plant is useful as a decorative and fragrant indoor or conservatory plant

CHERVIL
(*Anthriscus cerefolium* – Umbelliferae)

In shady and moist conditions chervil produces abundant feathery, fern-like leaves with a spicy aniseed-flavour useful in salads, sauces and soups.

type	Hardy annual
flowers	Creamy flowers in midsummer
leaves	Bright green, downy and finely cut foliage that changes to pinky-mauve during summer
height	30–50cm (12–20in)
spread	22cm (9in)
planting	Sow seed into the growing site every five to six weeks from early to late spring and again through the autumn. Barely cover the seed with soil and thin seedlings to 23cm (9in) apart
position	Spring-sown chervil does well in partial shade, while autumn sowings do best in full sun during the winter months. In full sun, spring-sown chervil may flower and seed too quickly to be of use
soil	Moist but well drained
care	Water well in dry conditions or the plant will flower and produce seed too quickly. Cut leaves back to produce an extra flush of growth from the base. Keep weed free
propagation	Chervil does not transplant well, so increase by a series of regular sowings through spring and autumn. Allow some plants to self sow at the end of each growing season
harvest	Pick fresh leaves as you need them through the year. Chervil leaves can be dried but it is better to freeze sprigs between sheets of freezer plastic
herbal value	Use leaves in soups, salads and fish dishes. Chervil is a classic ingredient of *fines herbes* (see p65). Use it generously in uncooked dishes and add it towards the end of the preparation of cooked dishes to preserve its flavour

PARSLEY
(*Petroselinum crispum* – Umbelliferae)

Parsley's aromatic and vitamin-rich leaves have long been used to add a distinctive, mildly spicy flavour to salads and cooked food. Grow it indoors in containers; outdoors as a herb hedge.

type	Hardy biennial
flowers	Greenish-yellow flowers in summer of second year. Remove flower stems to promote leaf production
leaves	Mid-green, flat and deeply cut or tightly curled and mossy

height	30cm (12in) before flowering, with flowering stalk to 60cm (24in)
spread	20cm (8in)
planting	Sow indoors in early spring in seed trays or pots. Seeds need a temperature of 21–27°C (70–80°F) for up to three weeks before germination will take place. Transplant to a spacing of 20cm (8in). Sow into the growing site early autumn or late spring when the soil is warm and thin out as the seedlings grow
position	Warm with some shade
soil	Moist, enriched with compost or well-rotted manure
care	Water in dry conditions, keep weed free, and in severe winters cover with cloches to keep leaf flavour. Nip out any flowering stems in the second year to prevent seed production and continue leaf harvest
propagation	From seed only. Allow some plants to produce seed and self sow. Sow several times a year to ensure a good supply of flavoursome fresh leaves
species and varieties	*Petroselinum crispum* 'Neapolitanum', also called French or Italian parsley, has flat leaves and a strong flavour. *P.c.* 'Tuberosum' or Hamburg parsley has good leaf flavour but is grown mainly for its roots
harvest	Pick leaves all through the year as they are needed, but they are at their peak in summer of the first year. Best used fresh or frozen. Freeze chopped into water in ice-cube trays or whole, sealed in freezer bags. Can be dried, but needs to be dried quickly in a cool oven to keep a flavour and colour
herbal value	Leaves are used to flavour soups, sauces and salads. Classic ingredient of *bouquet garni* (see p65). Used as a garnish and to make herbal tea. Hamburg parsley roots are used in stews and have similar flavour to the root vegetable celeriac. Mix 25g (1oz) crushed, fresh parsley with 15g (½oz) clear honey to make a face mask. Wash your face, pat it dry and then apply the sticky paste. Leave in place for 15-20 minutes then rinse off using warm water

SAGE

(*Salvia officinalis* – Labiatae)

Sage leaves bring delicious flavours to cold and cooked food. Grow sage for its range of leaf colour, flowers and aroma.

type	Hardy evergreen sub-shrub
flowers	Usually small pink to mauve flowers, though in some forms white or red. Late spring to summer
leaves	Depending on species or variety, silvery-green to pink and purple, textured and aromatic
height	60cm (24in)
spread	45cm (18in)
planting	Plant in spring or autumn. Grow in containers indoors in winter
position	Full sun, good air circulation
soil	Prefers a light, dry, well-drained alkaline soil
care	If growing for leaves, cut out flower stems. After flowering, cut back spent flower stems. Trim regularly to keep compact and encourage new shoots. Mulch in winter and protect plants in heavy, damp soil. Replace with new plants after five years
propagation	Take cuttings spring to mid-autumn and root in a heated propagator. Sow seed indoors in spring. Alternatively, layer sage branches by pinning down side shoots and covering with soil. They take about eight weeks to root.
species and varieties	Purple or red sage (*Salvia o.* 'Purpurascens') has dark purple leaves. *S.o.* 'Tricolor' is variegated purple with light pinky-white splashes. Golden variegated sage (*S.o.* 'Icterina') has yellow and green leaves and a mild flavour. Spanish sage (*S. lavandulifolia*) has a balsamic flavour. Pineapple sage (*S. elegans*) has pineapple-flavoured leaves
harvest	Broad-leaved sages are at their best before flowering or in summer. To keep colour well the leaves need a long, slow drying period. Freeze sage leaves in plastic bags in small quantities
herbal value	Astringent qualities are good in steamy baths. Sage leaves are often used in stuffings, cooked meat dishes, salads and for flavouring vinegars

Sage

MARCH

If your herb garden preparation was delayed by cold weather and impenetrable soil last month, this one will be busy. If the weather is still against you, concentrate on the many indoor activities that must be started now. Get indoor seed sowing into full swing. Starting seed off indoors results in earlier harvests, as you can plant sturdy seedlings into the soil when it begins to warm up in late spring.

If you have neither the space nor the inclination to grow your herbs from seed, buy young plants from specialist herb nurseries and garden centres. Check that the plants are healthy, with no dead or damaged stems, and are not root-bound in their pots.

Now is the ideal time to set out established and pot-grown plants in the herb garden. Always plant into well-prepared soil that has been enriched with well-rotted compost or fertiliser. Water the plants in thoroughly and let them get settled before you begin harvesting leaves.

Early spring is also a good time to begin planning and planting outdoor herb containers. If you don't have space for a herb garden, this is an ideal way of growing at least the herbs you use frequently. Herbs grown in containers need regular watering (at least once a day during warm, dry spells), and staking if they grow too tall. Attractive containers and decorative herbs make striking features on patios, balconies and in the herb garden itself.

By training and pruning certain herbs, such as rosemary and lavender, you can create unusual shapes that make attractive focal points. It takes time and patience, but the results are fun and worth the effort. If you use bought plants, choose them with their future, trained shape in mind. For example, upright-growing rosemary suits a formal shape, while prostrate rosemary trained onto a circular wire shape becomes a living wreath.

tasks

FOR THE

month

AVOID OVERSOWING
Nature ensures the survival of
most flowering plants by providing
innumerable tiny seeds. Not all
will survive the prevailing
conditions if they self sow, but
where you can control conditions
in the greenhouse or on the
windowsill, you could end up
with more than enough seedlings.
So the first rule about sowing
your own seed is don't overdo it
– unless you have a large herb
garden with plenty of empty
space to fill!

CUTTING BACK
In an established herb garden,
now is the time to begin cutting
back and clearing the stems and
foliage of herbaceous perennials,
such as fennel and salad burnet.

A CLEAN START
Hygiene is most important in a
closed environment such as a
greenhouse. Always use clean
seed trays or pots, and a good
sterilised seed compost.

CHECKLIST

- Continue soil preparation
- Clean containers
- Continue indoor seed sowing and check daily for signs of germination
- Pot seedlings on and harden off
- Cut back winter-damaged stems
- Divide large clumps of herb plants
- Buy and plant out hardy herbs
- Plan and plant up container herb gardens
- Begin training herb topiaries
- Plant roses

GROWING HERBS FROM SEED

Growing plants from seed is a
magical and rewarding task.
The transformation of powdery
or oddly shaped seeds into
plants is something that
nature can do without the
gardener's help, but once
involved in sowing your own
herb plants you will find
yourself hooked to an
enjoyable and seasonal cycle.

Growing from seed is an
inexpensive way of providing a
large stock of plants. If your
herb garden is small and you
only need one or two plants of
each herb, then you should
buy these direct from herb
nurseries.

Indoor sowing gives you
strong seedlings to plant out
as soon as the weather
permits. It gives you a longer
growing season, and therefore
more material to use and
preserve. Once the soil is
warm, sow seeds outdoors
into the growing site and in
succession, to ensure a steady
supply of good leafy material.
You can sow annuals and
biennials indoors, but chervil,
parsley, cumin, coriander and
dill don't always transplant
well. These plants suffer
setbacks in growth when their
roots are disturbed, and this
speeds them into flowering
and setting seed, instead of
producing foliage. If you do

start them off indoors, handle
very gently when transplanting
and water well to get the
plants established.
Alternatively, sow a few seeds
into trays of formed soil blocks.
When you transplant them,
the block is easier to handle
than a small seedling and can
be placed straight into the
planting hole.

SOWING SEED AND GROWING ON

■ Fill the seed trays with
compost until they are three-
quarters full.

■ Tamp down the surface
lightly with a flat board, then
water the compost using a
watering can fitted with a fine
rose, or stand the trays in a
bath of water. Allow the water
to drain off before sowing. If
you wish, mix the water with
a fungicide to help prevent
damping off and subsequent
failure of the seedlings.

■ When the compost is moist,
sow fine seed thinly onto its
surface. Large seeds, should
be well spaced out and covered
with a thin layer of soil, just to
the depth of the seed itself.

■ After sowing, cover the seed
tray with a piece of glass or
clear plastic. This ensures that
the compost does not dry out.

■ Place the tray in a dark or
shady part of the greenhouse
or on the kitchen windowsill,
or cover with a piece of folded
newspaper.

■ Most seeds need warmth to
germinate: a heated
propagator where you can
provide an even temperature
of 15°C (60°F) is ideal.
However, parsley (see p24)
needs higher temperatures of
21–27°C (70–80°F) and
lavender germinates at
temperatures lower than 10°C
(50°F).

A cold start
Some seeds need a period of
cold before they germinate.
This dormancy mechanism
prevents them from
germinating too early and
being killed by cold weather.
In natural conditions, the seed
falls to the ground or is blown
to its growing site. There it
stays until after the cold
periods of autumn and winter.
Once the soil warms up again,
the seed germinates.
Stratification can be done
artificially (see p88 for
details).

Check seeds daily
Seeds must be checked every
day and if the compost begins
to dry out, water with a
watering can fitted with a fine
rose. As soon as germination
takes place and white shoots
are visible on the surface,
remove the newspaper and
move the seed tray into a
lighter but cooler situation.
Water the seedlings from the
base of their pots or with a
fine rose.

Potting on
Once the seedlings are large
enough to handle, transplant
them into individual pots to
allow strong root structures to
develop.

Hardening off
Before you plant seedlings out
into their growing positions,
they need to be acclimatised
to outdoor conditions. This is
called 'hardening off'. Move
the seedlings out of the
greenhouse or kitchen to a

sheltered, shaded site during the day and bring them in again at night. After about seven days you can transplant them. Plant half-hardy annuals out into their growing positions when all danger of frost is over.

BUYING AND PLANTING HERBS

Most garden centres stock a range of popular culinary and decorative herbs. If space is limited and your herb needs are basic, then buying well-established plants will be efficient and cost effective. There are also numerous specialist herb nurseries that sell plants direct from their premises or through mail order.

If you buy direct, choose healthy looking, well-established plants. Avoid any that are dried out in their pots or are competing with weeds for survival. A thriving potted herb plant should have a good root system — if the plant is pot-bound, you will see matted roots coming out of the drainage holes. The best sign of good health is the compact growth of fresh new shoots.

▪ When you get your plants home, water them and place in a warm, sheltered site until you are ready to plant them out. Always get plants into the ground as soon as possible after purchase, but avoid planting in hot conditions during the middle of the day.

▪ Dig a hole in well-prepared, enriched and weed-free soil. The hole should be large enough to accommodate the plant's roots without cramping them.

▪ Remove the plant from its pot, set it in the hole and replace some of the soil around the plant.

▪ Firm the soil in, backfill with the rest of the soil and firm in again.

▪ Water the plant in thoroughly, and then daily in dry conditions until it is growing strongly.

PLANTING FOR A ROSY FUTURE

Plant roses in spring for summer perfume in the herb garden or autumn for the following year's enjoyment. At these times of year the soil is warm and the plants can establish well before colder weather sets in. Bare-rooted rose plants that have been lifted from the growing fields with no soil around their roots, should be planted soon after purchase or delivery from specialist nurseries. If this is not possible, due to lack of time or frosty weather, you will need to give them interim care.

▪ Keep them in a frost-free place, with roots moistened in a sand- or peat-filled box or tub.

▪ If you have no space in a shed or garage, give the roses a temporary home by digging a shallow trench in the ground and covering the roots. This is called 'heeling in .

▪ When the time comes to plant the roses, ensure the soil has been well dug and manured.

▪ Dig a planting hole large enough to allow the roots to be spread out.

▪ Place the plant in the hole and check that the graft or union mark (where the rose stems are grafted onto the rootstock) is just below soil level.

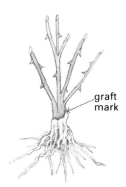

graft mark

▪ Backfill the hole and tread the soil in firmly so the rose does not rock.

▪ Sprinkle rose fertiliser over the surface and lightly fork it in.

▪ Water the plant in well.

HERBS FOR A COLD START

ANGELICA
DYER'S GREENWEED
JUNIPER
NEW JERSEY TEA
PLANT
SOAPWORT
SWEET CICELY
SWEET VIOLET
SWEET WOODRUFF

THINGS TO DO

Sow seed

Indoors: agrimony, aniseed, anise hyssop, artemisia, bergamot, bistort, borage, canary balm, caraway, chives, coreopsis, coriander, cumin, dyer's greenweed, echinacea, elecampane, evening primrose, fenugreek, feverfew, flax, Good King Henry, heartsease, herb bennet, hyssop, lady's mantle (self seeds), lemon verbena, marjoram, mullein, mustard, nasturtium, orach, pinks, poppy, pot marigold, salad burnet, scented pelargonium, sea holly, smallage, sorrel, spruce, strawberry, summer savory, sunflower, sweet woodruff, tansy (self seeds), teasel, traveller's joy, vervain, weld, winter savory, yarrow

Thin

Coreopsis sown in autumn

Plant out

Box, catmint, chives, costmary, jasmine, juniper, lady's mantle, liquorice, marsh mallow, pennyroyal, peony, pink, rosemary, sage, sorrel, spearmint, spruce, strawberry, sweet cicely, tarragon, wall germander, welsh onion, winter savory, witch hazel

Propagate

Take cuttings: dyer's chamomile (basal), rosemary and thyme (heel), winter savory (stem tip), witch hazel (semi-ripe)
Layer: winter savory
Divide: anise hyssop, artemisia, chicory, chives, costmary, dyer's chamomile, echinacea, elecampane, herb bennet, hyssop, lady's mantle, liquorice, rue, salad burnet, soapwort, sorrel, spearmint, strawberry, sweet violet, sweet woodruff, tansy, wall germander, winter savory, yarrow

Pot up

New honeysuckle plants from stems layered in autumn

practical
project

GROWING HERBS IN
CONTAINERS

Terracotta or glazed pots, stone urns, wooden tubs and old sinks are attractive and convenient containers for herb growing in limited garden space. They can also be used to make eye-catching features in a large herb garden.

TYPES OF CONTAINER

Old stone containers are expensive but indestructible, elegant and, because of their weight, permanent. Reconstituted stone containers look almost as authentic and are considerably cheaper. Moulded concrete urns and pots are cheaper still, but for the first few growing seasons look a little new and raw. Once they have aged and a little moss or algae is growing on them, however, they will blend into the garden. You can hasten the process by painting the new containers with milk or yoghurt to encourage the growth of algae.

Terracotta containers have a warm, sunny feel to them, but be sure only to buy frostproof pots if you intend to leave them outdoors through the winter. Plastic containers are, of course, the cheapest and last a long time. Once they are planted up with attractive herbs, they can look just as elegant and showy as more expensive containers.

SOIL

For herbs in containers you must use the best potting medium possible. Garden soil is not suitable in such a confined space as it may well be lacking in sufficient nutrients, and at the same time could be harbouring a concentrated number of soil pests. Instead use bagged, and therefore clean or sterilised, potting compost. If the container is large and permanently sited, this should be soil based; it will be heavy once watered, so make sure you position the tub *before* you fill it with compost and plants.

To provide the free-draining medium that most herbs prefer, add several handfuls of grit to the compost and line the base of the container with pieces of broken terracotta, stones or a layer of gravel before filling with compost.

HERBS TO CHOOSE

Decide on a colour, fragrant or culinary theme for your container herb garden, but combine plants that have similar growth habits and enjoy similar conditions. Avoid growing thuggish plants like mint with delicate, slower-growing herbs such as prostrate rosemary. Grow shade- and moisture-loving herbs such as mints and sweet cicely together, and combine sun-lovers like lavender and thyme in a warm position.

*Pots of herbs used
as eye-catching
features*

Pot of silver

A POT OF SILVER HERBS

Site this cool-looking pot of silver foliage herbs on a sun-drenched patio. The leaves of purple sage add a touch of drama and accentuate the silver leaves of the other plants. Cheddar pink and lavender combine the silver theme with a long flowering season for the container.

MATERIALS

Terracotta pot 40cm (16in) wide and 35cm (14in) deep
25 litres compost
Gravel, broken pottery or grit
Lavandula angustifolia 'Hidcote'
1 Thymus × citriodorus 'Variegatus'
1 Dianthus gratianopolitanus (pink)
1 Stachys byzantina (lamb's ears)
1 Salvia officinalis 'Purpurascens' (purple sage)

PLANTING UP THE POT

▪ Begin by putting the broken pottery or gravel at the base of the pot to make a drainage layer.

▪ Fill the container two-thirds full with the compost.

Pot of gold

▪ Remove the plants from their individual containers. Uncurl any pot-bound roots by teasing them out gently.

▪ Arrange the plants in the terracotta pot. Place the lavender and sage towards the back of the pot, with the furry-leaved lamb's ears in the centre. Position the pink and thyme at the edges of the pot, to the right and left of the centre.

▪ Fill the gaps between the plants with the remaining compost and water in thoroughly. Mulch the visible soil surface with grit to prevent rain splashes muddying the foliage.

POTS WITH POUCHES

Terracotta 'parsley' pots and plastic columns with planting pouches are space-saving homes for your herb collection.

For both types of container, make sure there is a good drainage layer. To make watering easier, insert a piece of perforated tube *(Continued on page 34.)*

PLANTS TO USE FOR A POT OF GOLD

Golden-leaved sage (*Salvia officinalis* 'Icterina')
Golden bay (*Laurus nobilis* 'Aurea')
Golden marjoram (*Oreganum vulgare* 'Aurea')
Golden thyme (*Thymus vulgaris aureus*)
Golden lamb's ears (*Stachys byzantina* 'Primrose Heron'). This form of lamb's ears is more prostrate than the silver one, so place it at the front of the pot.

Terracotta containers are available in many shapes and sizes

plants
OF THE
month

Borage

ANISE HYSSOP
(*Agastache foeniculum* – Labiatae)

Anise hyssop leaves make an excellent herb tea, while the aniseed-flavoured foliage provides an interesting addition to a salad. The plant is attractive to bees.

type	Hardy herbaceous perennial
flowers	From midsummer to early autumn with spikes of mauve-purple flowers
leaves	Short-stalked, oval to triangular in shape, light green and anise-scented
height	Branched stems grow up to 60–120cm (24–48in)
spread	60cm (24in)
planting	Plant out in spring
position	Sheltered and sunny site
soil	Well drained average
care	Spray with fungicide if affected by mildew in hot dry summers. If the plants are badly infected, cut off the foliage leaving the stems 7.5cm (3in) tall
propagation	Sow seed in spring under glass. Divide older clumps in spring. Take soft or semi-ripe cuttings from mature plants in summer
harvest	Pick the leaves during the growing season. Pick flowers to dry just as they begin to open
herbal value	The leaves make an excellent tea and may also be used in salads as a seasoning. Flowers keep their colour well in dried arrangements

BORAGE
(*Borago officinalis* – Boraginaceae)

Once associated with courage and happiness, today borage is appreciated for its profuse clusters of azure blue, starry flowers and its cucumber-flavoured leaves.

type	Hardy annual
flowers	Mid-blue, occasionally pink or white, star-like flowers appear in spring and summer
leaves	Grey-green, oval with pointed ends and wrinkled, bristly texture
height	75cm (30in)
spread	30–45cm (12–18in)
planting	Plant in spring
position	Open, sunny
soil	Light, dry, stony
care	Prune after flowering, to keep tidy
propagation	Sow seed in autumn for spring flowers, or in spring for summer flowers. Borage self seeds freely
harvest	Use the flowers and young foliage as needed. Borage leaves lose their colour and flavour if dried. Freeze the flowers into ice cubes
herbal value	Add the fresh flowers to summer salads or crystallise for cake decoration. Add shredded young leaves to wine cups, summer aperitifs or fresh lemonade, and to salads or cream cheese sandwiches

NASTURTIUM
(*Tropaeolum majus* – Tropaeolaceae)

Nasturtium is a cottage-garden plant, grown for its spurred, showy blooms produced non-stop from late spring until the first frost.

type	Hardy annual
flowers	Flowers range from creamy white to yellow, orange, scarlet, apricot and crimson and appear from late spring until autumn
leaves	Round, grey-green and distinctly veined, with a central stalk
height	From 15cm (6in) for dwarf forms to 3m (10ft) or more for trailing forms
spread	15–30cm (6–12in)
planting	Transplant container-grown seedlings in late spring
position	Full sun
soil	Average or poor, dry. The poorer the soil, the better the flowers
care	Keep well watered and weeded until established. Provide support for tall-growing forms. Deadhead regularly and pinch out any blackfly-infested growing tips
propagation	Sow seed in mid-spring, indoors or into the growing site
species and varieties	Attractive forms include 'Alaska', with mixed flower colours and white-splashed foliage; the dwarf 'Empress of India', with crimson flowers; 'Peach Melba', semi-dwarf, with pale yellow, scarlet-blotched blooms; and 'Gleam Series', with double flowers
harvest	Pick flowers and leaves as needed, use unripe seeds for pickling
herbal value	Add the flowers and peppery fresh leaves, rich in vitamin C, to salads. Fill the flowers with soft cream cheese for unusual canapés. The fiercely peppery pickled seeds are substitutes for capers or, chopped, for horseradish

PENNYROYAL
(*Mentha pulegium* – Labiatae)

Creeping pennyroyal is a compact mint, ideal for growing between paving slabs. When trodden on, it releases a heady scent.

type	Hardy herbaceous perennial
flowers	Tiny heads of purple flowers in summer
leaves	Tiny, bright green, round
height	15cm (6in)
spread	Wide spreading
planting	Plant in spring or autumn, 15cm (6in) apart
position	Sun or light shade
soil	Damp
care	Trim in autumn. To renew, lift and divide every four or five years
propagation	The floppy stems root where they touch the soil, and can be detached and planted elsewhere
species and varieties	Upright pennyroyal (*Mentha pulegium* 'Upright') grows to 30cm (12in). Its small, narrow leaves are peppermint scented
harvest	Harvest sprigs of pennyroyal as you need them to use for moth sachets
herbal value	Pennyroyal's flavour is pungent and enjoyable in a scented path. Use the fresh leaves, crushed, to make insect-repellent bouquets for doorways and windows, and dried leaves, crumbled, in moth sachets for drawers

SORREL
(*Rumex acetosa* – Polygonaceae)

Sorrel's sharply acidic, fresh lemony taste has long been partnered with rich food. In the garden, sorrel is a weedy, coarse-looking plant, best confined to an out-of-the-way spot.

type	Hardy herbaceous perennial
flowers	Spikes of tiny, densely packed greenish-red flowers in mid-summer and early autumn
leaves	Arrow-shaped, dull green, tinged crimson, in a large, basal clump
height	60cm (24in)
spread	45cm (18in)
planting	Plant in spring or autumn and grow under plastic cloches in winter
position	Sun or light shade, shelter
soil	Average or rich, well drained
care	Protect from slugs, snails and rabbits. Pinch out flower stalks as soon as they appear. Lift and divide plants every four or five years
propagation	Sow seed into the growing site in spring and thin to 30cm (12in) apart. Lift and divide established plants in spring or autumn
species and varieties	French or buckler-leaved sorrel *(Rumex scutatus)* is smaller growing 15–45cm (6–18in), with broader, shield-shaped leaves and a less sharply acidic flavour
harvest	Young leaves have the best flavour. Sorrel loses its flavour when dried, but can be frozen
herbal value	Use in salads, soups and omelettes, or to make classic sorrel soup or sorrel sauce for rich meats, poultry or fish. The young leaves can be cooked as spinach. Sorrel has a high oxalic acid content, and should not be eaten in large quantities

Sorrel

VERVAIN
(*Verbena officinalis* – Verbenaceae)

Vervain's long-held medicinal reputation is for purification and cleansing. Its leaves make soothing teas and cosmetic hair rinses.

type	Hardy herbaceous perennial
flowers	Numerous delicate mauve trumpets on tall stems from midsummer to mid-autumn
leaves	Softly textured, dark green with deeply cut edges
height	60–90cm (24–36in)
spread	30cm (12in)
planting	Sow in spring in pots or trays in a greenhouse with the temperature at 18–21°C (65–70°F). Germination is often slow and patchy. Plant out in groups 30cm (12in) spacing apart
position	Full sun or partial shade. Indoors, grow vervain in a deep container on a sunny windowsill
soil	Prefers slightly chalky or alkaline, well-drained but fertile soil
care	Plant in groups so that the flowers make a strong show. May need staking in an exposed site
propagation	Grow from seed and divide mature plants in spring or autumn
harvest	Cut leaves in summer before and during flowering
herbal value	Use fresh leaves to make cosmetic rinses and dry leaves in teas

Pennyroyal

Vervain

PLANTS FOR A TOWER OR 'PARSLEY' POT

Chives ● Sage ● Common thyme
Silver thyme ● Gold thyme
Marjoram ● Parsley ● Basil
Bay ● Chervil ● Lemon Verbena
Rosemary ● Summer savory
Winter savory

All grow well in these containers.

(Continued from page 31)

drainpipe, or hosepipe into the centre of the pot. Fill the bottom few centimetres (inches) of the pipe with small stones to weight it down and aid waterflow to the roots. Then fill the container with compost to the level of the first pouch or planting window. Set the plant in place and continue filling with compost and planting in the same way until each pocket is planted up and the container filled with compost. Water with a long-spouted watering can. Insert the spout into the top of the perforated tubing and allow the water to trickle into the soil.

A POT FOR SUN

Place lavender in the centre of an urn with creeping thymes planted around the edge. As they grow, the thyme plants will tumble over the rim.

A POT FOR SHADE

Plant sweet cicely at the centre of the container to give the design height. Next to it plant variegated apple-scented mint, which has an upright habit. Around the rim plant one or two wild strawberries, creeping mint and a variegated trailing ivy.

A FORMAL HERB TUB

For a formal herb design in a small space, plant chives at each corner of a wooden 'Versailles' tub and thyme between the chives. Set a wooden trellis obelisk in the tub and plant the small, pink-flowered ground-covering rose 'Grouse' in the centre. As it grows it will spill out of its obelisk frame, and the vigorous stems can be tied in to cover the trellis.

Alternatively, grow nasturtium to trail over the edge of the tub and sweet peas to climb up and through the obelisk.

A TROUGH FOR TEA

Place rosemary, upright thyme and bergamot – all tall-growing plants – at the back of the trough. In the front plant creeping thyme, peppermint, hyssop, sage, chamomile and lemon balm.

A STONE VASE OF KITCHEN HERBS

Plant chives and parsley in the centre with sage, prostrate rosemary and winter savory around the edges of the pot.

AFTERCARE

Small, shallow containers must be watered frequently. Check large, deep containers every few days to see if they need water. In very hot weather, water them every day. During the spring and summer, while the herbs are growing vigorously, provide a high potassium liquid fertiliser once a week when you water. Reduce the liquid feed as autumn approaches, and when the plants are dormant don't feed them at all.

If the herbs grow too large for the container, or become pot-bound, you will need to remove and divide them. Do this in early spring. Discard plants that are weak, diseased or badly damaged. Trim those you intend to grow on, reducing each plant's roots and top growth by about one-third. Then replant in fresh compost.

practical
project
2

MAKING HERB
TOPIARY

**HERBS TO CHOOSE
FOR TOPIARY**

Bay ● Box ● Cotton lavender
Curry plant ● Lavender
Lemon verbena ● Myrtle
Rosemary ● Roses ● Sage
Scented pelargonium
Winter savory

Shaping a standard

A good deal of gardening is about gardeners imposing a particular order on the way plants grow. Usually the order provides the grower with better crops, or flowers held more attractively in view. In the herb garden, the most formal order is imposed when herbs are clipped and pruned into unnatural shapes purely for ornamental interest. This type of training is called topiary.

The herbs that respond to this treatment are often slow-growing and it may take time and patience to achieve the shape you desire. Bay, for instance, takes several years to reach 1.2m (4ft). Woody perennials such as rosemary, lavender, bay and box, as well as soft-stemmed perennials such as cotton lavender and scented pelargoniums, can be trained into formal standards and conical shapes. Some, such as rosemary and bay, can be grown into hoops, using wire to train the plant in a particular direction.

Herb topiaries make attractive and aromatic focal points for patios, front-door areas and indoor decoration, as well as outdoors in the herb garden. Here, they are useful for creating taller features at the centre of formal beds of herbs.

SHAPING A STANDARD

■ Start your topiary off by taking softwood cuttings in spring. Choose a straight, strong-looking stem, cut it from the parent plant, remove the lower leaves, dip the cut end in hormone rooting powder and pot it up in a 7.5cm (3in) pot of compost mixed with grit or perlite.

■ Keep the cutting in a warm and well-lit site. Mist it daily and water if compost dries out.

■ After a few weeks, when the cutting has rooted, move it on into the next size pot. Use loam-based compost.

■ Water with a liquid fertiliser and, before the roots have spread, insert a thin bamboo cane into the compost. Tie the whippy cutting to it with pieces of raffia.

■ When the cutting has reached a minimum height of 37.5cm (15in), remove all leaves and any side shoots that grow below the 30cm (12in) mark.

■ Once the remaining leaf growth takes up about 15cm (6in) of the length, nip out the growing point. The spindly head of leaves will, in time, bush out to form a substantial mophead standard shape. As the plant becomes sturdier, pot it on into larger containers.

■ Trim the young standard every four weeks in the growing season, as new side shoots develop. When the topiary is mature, allow it to flower (if it is a flowering plant such as lavender or scented pelargonium). To ensure this, avoid pruning it too heavily in spring.

Alternatively, if you are impatient and want to cut the growing time by a season, buy an attractively branched young plant about 25cm (10in) tall and trim off any stems or leaves that don't fit into the shape you are creating.

Choose plants with two strong-growing lower stems for training around a hoop into circular or heart-shaped forms.

Training around a hoop

AFTERCARE

Once you have achieved a tall enough standard shape with a mophead, trim the plant every four weeks in the growing season. Always remove dead and diseased leaves as they occur and water frequently in the growing season. Apply a liquid feed every week in early spring to ensure good leafy growth.

SHAPING A CONE

Choose a rosemary or bay that has a strong main stem and plenty of side shoots throughout its height, especially at the base. In spring and at the end of the growing season, cut back the side shoots so that they taper into a conical shape. Leave the growing point or top bud intact until the shape has reached the desired height, then snip it out to prevent any further vertical growth.

plants
OF THE
month

Sunflower

SPEARMINT
(*Mentha spicata* – Labiatae)

Of all the fresh-flavoured mints, spearmint, with its bright green, pointed leaves, is the most popular. Grow it where it can spread without overwhelming other plants.

type	Hardy herbaceous perennial
flowers	Round or pointed spikes of pale lavender flowers in summer and early autumn
leaves	Toothed, bright green, oblong or lance-shaped
height	60cm (24ft)
spread	Wide spreading
planting	Plant in autumn or spring. To control mint's invasive roots, grow it in a bottomless bucket or surround it with corrugated plastic or metal sheeting buried vertically in the soil. It is ideal in containers. For winter crops, cloche or pot up and bring indoors in autumn
position	Sun or light shade, with shade at the roots
soil	Light, moisture retentive but well drained
care	Cut back to ground level in autumn. Lift, divide and replant every four or five years, to renew vigour and prevent rust infection. If rust appears, dig up and burn infected plants, and replant elsewhere
propagation	Lift and divide established clumps in spring or autumn. Stem cuttings root easily in a glass of water
species and varieties	Handsome variegated forms include ginger mint (*Mentha × gentilis* 'Variegata'), with yellow-splashed leaves; and apple mint (*M. suaveolens* 'Variegata'), with white-edged and splashed foliage. Other attractive forms include the woolly-leaved apple mint (*M. × rotundifolia*), lemon-scented *eau de cologne* mint (*M. × piperita citrata*), with purple-tinged leaves, and curly mint (*M. spicata* 'Crispa') with frilly, bright green leaves. Bowles' mint (*M. × villosa alopecuroides*) is a tall-growing form, up to 90cm (36in) high. Mints hybridise freely, and if several forms are grown, seedlings of mixed value may appear
harvest	Pick fresh leaves as needed in the growing season. Mint can be dried or frozen
herbal value	Mint sauce and jelly are traditional accompaniments to lamb, and fresh mint enhances the flavour of young peas or new potatoes. The leaves are added to fresh fruit salads and summer drinks or are used to make mint tea, said to soothe anxiety, sleeplessness and stomach upsets. Use crystallised leaves to decorate cakes or puddings. Peppermint oil flavours toothpaste, liqueurs and confectionary

SUMMER SAVORY
(*Satureja hortensis* – Labiatae)

Once used as an aphrodisiac and an aid to digestion, today summer savory is mainly valued as a highly aromatic culinary herb with a thyme-like peppery taste.

type	Hardy annual
flowers	Clusters of tiny white, lilac or purple flowers appear in mid- and late summer
leaves	Small, narrow, dark green and strongly aromatic
height	15–45cm (6–18in)
spread	10–30cm (4–12in)
planting	Plant outdoors in spring, or indoors in pots
position	Sunny, sheltered
soil	Light, well drained
care	Thin seedlings to 20cm (8in) apart. Keep well watered and weeded until established
propagation	Sow in spring
harvest	Pick fresh leaves as needed. Harvest leaves just before flowering to dry, and flowering tops in late summer
herbal value	Cook with beans for improved flavour. Make savory jelly with apples. Add to salads, sausages, egg and meat dishes, and to fish or poultry stuffings. Apply crushed leaves to wasp or bee stings

SUNFLOWER
(*Helianthus annuus* – Compositae)

Easy to grow and eye-catching as tall focal plants in the herb garden, the sunflower's huge daisy-like flower heads produce edible seeds attractive to birds and humans alike.

type	Hardy annual, grown as a half-hardy annual
flowers	Bright yellow flowers appear in mid- to late summer

leaves	Mid-green, large and oval, with pointed ends, toothed edges and hairy surface
height	Up to 3m (10ft). Short and dwarf-growing hybrids are available
spread	Up to 30cm (12in) flowerhead
planting	Transplant container-grown seedlings in early summer
position	Sunny, sheltered
soil	Well drained
care	Stake as necessary
propagation	Sow seeds indoors in mid-spring
species and varieties	Compact garden forms include 'Italian White', 1.2m (4ft) high, with black-centred white blooms; 'Teddy Bear', 60cm (24in) high, with double, rich yellow blooms; 'Taiyo', 30–45cm (12–18in) high, with yellow flowers; and 'Sunburst', 1.2m (4ft) high, with flowers in shades of yellow, bronze and maroon
harvest	When the flower heads droop, cut them off and hang until thoroughly dry. Place paper or a small-mesh wire sieve underneath the flower heads to catch the seeds that fall out when fully dry
herbal value	The raw or roasted seeds are nutritious snacks and useful additions to salads, as are the flower buds, lightly boiled

SWEET CICELY
(*Myrrhis odorata* – Umbelliferae)

Sweet cicely, or myrrh, offers graceful, ferny leaves, cow parsley-like flowers and a rich, woodland scent. In the kitchen, its seeds, roots and leaves are equally welcome.

type	Hardy herbaceous perennial
flowers	Flat white flower heads appear in late spring and early summer
leaves	The ferny leaves appear early in spring and remain green well into autumn. They turn a rich purple before dying back
height	90cm (36in)
spread	60cm (24in)
planting	Plant in spring or autumn
position	Sun or light shade
soil	Average, well drained
care	Pinch out flower heads to retain the fresh flavour of the leaves
propagation	Sow seed in autumn, they need low temperatures in order to germinate (see page 88)
harvest	Begin picking leaves in early spring

as you need to use them, and continue until they die down in autumn. The leaves dry well. Pick unripe seeds when green, ripe when browny black. Dig up the roots of one or two plants in late autumn to candy

herbal value	Add the leaves to soups, stews or salads. The leaves and seeds can also be added to tart rhubarb or gooseberry fruit dishes, as a natural sweetener. Boil the roots and serve hot as a vegetable or cooled, chopped and added to salads. The roots can also be candied, and used in the same way as candied angelica

Spearmint

SWEET VIOLET
(*Viola odorata* – Violaceae)

Rooting where its runners touch the soil, sweet violet makes attractive, sweetly scented, weed-proof ground cover in the fragrant herb garden.

type	Hardy herbaceous perennial
flowers	Violet, rose-pink or white flowers appear from early to mid-spring
leaves	Mid- to dark green leaves are heart-shaped, slightly hairy and evergreen
height	10–15cm (4–6in)
spread	30–40cm (12–16in)
planting	Plant in early spring
position	Cool, open, semi-shade
soil	Rich, moist, well drained
care	Keep weed free. Cut back long shoots in midsummer to encourage a second crop of flowers. Mulch in spring
propagation	Sow seed in autumn or spring, with cold treatment (see page 88). Lift and plant rooted runners in spring. Keep the runners well watered until established
species and varieties	Popular, old-fashioned named hybrids, or florists' violets, with larger flowers include the pink 'Coeur d'Alsace', the blue-violet 'Princess of Wales' and the double-flowered mauve Parma violet, 'Duchesse de Parme'
harvest	Pick young flowers and leaves as needed. Air dry the leaves and flowers in shade
herbal value	Crystallise the petals to decorate cakes and confectionary, or add raw to spring salads. Add the dried flowers to pot-pourri

Sweet cicely

Sweet violet

APRIL

This month, evergreens and other perennial herbs begin to produce soft new shoots with fresh green leaves. Let them grow a little before you swoop on them eagerly for the first harvest of the season. Check that these plants, the permanent framework of the herb garden, are in good health after the winter. Cut out any frost-damaged or dead stems, see that the plants are firm in the ground and mulch the soil at their base with a dressing of well-rotted compost. Some plants that have grown into large clumps, such as lemon balm, fennel and lady's mantle, will need to be divided.

Mid-spring is the time when regular outdoor activity begins in the herb garden. By now the weather should be more settled and you can start to prepare the soil for outdoor sowing. If it is still too cold and damp, warm and dry it artificially. By covering the soil with a 'blanket' made from specially spun material, plastic tunnels, a sheet of black plastic or an old window frame and glass, you can increase the soil temperature and keep it dry. When you sow herb seeds, use sufficient for a decorative herb garden, with plenty to cut to use fresh or dry later in the year. In mid-spring, lightly prune herb plants as they begin to grow. This keeps their shape bushy and promotes leafy development instead of flower production. Be sure to do this on warm days when all danger of frost has passed — frost damages fresh new shoots and is stressful for the plant.

Herb garden projects, such as creating a scented path or lawn, provide you with attractive and fragrant features to enjoy at the peak of summer. Similarly, an archway for fragrant climbing plants makes a focal point and provides height in the herb garden. You could combine the two projects by constructing the arch over a central herb lawn. As you walk through the archway you will be beguiled by the fragrance both underfoot and overhead.

tasks

FOR THE

month

C H E C K L I S T

☐ Prepare the ground for sowing by covering, weeding and raking

☐ Sow seeds of hardy plants direct into the soil and protect with cloches or fleece

☐ Check daily for signs of germination

☐ Put down slug pellets or crushed egg shells to deter slugs

☐ Make new plants by dividing clumps

OUTDOOR SOWING

Now, at last, you can really begin to work outdoors in the herb garden, sowing seeds and dividing herbs to produce a stock of new plants to fill the garden.

■ In a warm and dry spring, make an early start on preparing the ground for sowing herbs direct.

■ For best results the soil must be warm and the surface raked to a dry, fine and crumbly texture.

■ If the ground is wet and cold, then warm the soil by covering it in a 'blanket' to alter the conditions. Fleecy spun material from garden centres, black plastic, old windows or plastic tunnels or cloches are all effective in warming the soil so that it can be worked into what gardeners call a 'fine tilth'. This crumbly or friable soil is perfect for sowing.

■ After a week or two under cover the temperature will be higher and the soil dry enough to rake. The soil should still retain moisture, but the drying effect of the covering will have reduced any waterlogging.

■ Lift the cover and fork the bed over lightly.

■ Remove any remaining perennial weeds and hoe off annual weed seedlings.

■ Break down any large clumps of earth, and keep raking until the soil particles are fine and crumbly and you have achieved the desired fine tilth.

Sowing seed
■ If you are sowing herbs as you would a vegetable crop, in straight lines, then simply make a furrow or drill in the soil using the edge of a hoe.

■ If you are mixing herbs in a more ornamental and decorative way, mark the bed out into semi-circles. Use a cane to draw the shapes in the soil.

■ Then, with a cane or hoe edge, mark out short drills within the semi-circles.

■ Before you sow, water the drill using a watering can or hose fitted with a fine rose.

Germination
■ If it is very dry, once again cover the area with the fleecy material or clear plastic after watering to keep the surface moist.

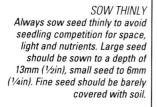

SOW THINLY
Always sow seed thinly to avoid seedling competition for space, light and nutrients. Large seed should be sown to a depth of 13mm (½in), small seed to 6mm (¼in). Fine seed should be barely covered with soil.

■ Remove the plastic once the seedlings germinate. The fleecy material can be left in place as it is porous, provides shade and at the same time adequate light. It will also act as a windbreak, and a rabbit and bird deterrent.

■ Check under the cover daily for slug damage.

■ Remove the cover once the herb seedlings are well established.

Thinning out

If germination has been successful, you may find that you have sown too closely. Remove the excess seedlings, so that the remainder have a chance to grow well and are not stressed through competition. Depending on variety, if you leave the seedlings in place until they have grown a few leaves and shoots, you can use the thinnings as an early seedling crop to sprinkle on salads and in soups.

For successive seedling crops, sow herbs such as coriander, rocket and dill in blocks or rows direct in the herb garden every few days in the early summer. As each patch gets to about 7.5cm (3in) high, snip it off and use fresh. Leave the last block sown to flower and set seed.

MAKING NEW PLANTS: DIVISION

Many herb plants increase in size by spreading roots or developing into large clumps. In time, the clumps may become too dense and the vigour of the plant will be affected. Also, you may wish to limit the plant's spread or fill a gap elsewhere in the herb garden. Take advantage of the plants' natural tendency to spread and you will have extra plants at no cost. This type of plant increase is called division. You can also increase plant numbers by taking root, soft and semi-ripe cuttings (see p76).

Now, and in autumn, you can combine tidying the herb garden with increasing plants. Spring and autumn are the best times to do this, as the plants are either still dormant or just about to come to the end of the growing season. What you do now will not harm or disturb their structure. Chives, hyssop, soapwort, lady's mantle and wall germander are among the many plants you can divide.

■ The best way to do this is to use a fork to lift the plant out of the ground.

■ Then use two forks back-to-back to prise the plant gently in two.

■ If the plant has grown to form a huge clump, divide it into more than two sections.

■ Remove the middle, older part of the plant and replant healthy roots and stems where you need the extra plants.

■ Water them in well and cut back by half to a third all stems above ground. This prevents stress to the plant caused by excess loss of moisture through the leaves.

NOTE

■ *Some plants such as mint, comfrey, chamomile, tarragon, costmary and lovage have small, rooted plantlets growing next to the parent plant. These are called offsets, and they can be separated from the main plant and will grow into healthy plants in their new positions.* ■

THINGS TO DO

Sow seed
Outdoors: bistort, chervil, chicory, dill, evening primrose, feverfew (unless already self sown), German chamomile, hyssop, lemon balm, marjoram, marsh mallow (in a seedbed for later transplanting), mullein, mustard, nasturtium, orach, parsley, pot marigold, sea holly, smallage, summer purslane, traveller's joy

Plant out
Lawn chamomile (as new paths or lawns, or as offsets into gaps in an established chamomile lawn), nasturtium, New Jersey tea plant (into pots for a sunny patio or as a feature in the centre of a herb bed), woad

Thin
Poppy seedlings

Propagate
Take cuttings (stem): catmint, curry plant, lavender
Divide: anise hyssop, chives, comfrey, fennel, hyssop, Joe Pye weed, lady's mantle, lemon balm, lovage, soapwort, wall germander

Harvest
Flowers: sweet woodruff
Leaves: alexanders, bay, wild strawberry
Shoots: alexanders

Routine maintenance
Check evergreens such as bay, hyssop, lavender, rosemary, sage for winter damage to stems
Firm plants into ground
Lightly prune new growth to encourage bushy shape and leafy development

practical project

MAKING AND PLANTING A SCENTED ARCHWAY

Arches, pergolas and covered arbours are a space-saving way of adding extra height, plant colour and fragrance to your herb garden. An arch or small pergola can also be used to soften an opening in a fence or hedge that divides the garden into sections.

An archway makes an excellent support for climbing plants and itself acts as a focal point. It can also be used as a frame to lead your eye further on, to a second focal point in the herb garden.

TYPES OF ARCH

There are many styles and materials available from which to choose, and your decision will depend on the style of your garden and the budget available. There are many ready-made arches available in plastic-coated metal, wood or metal, but if you prefer to make your own, you can design it to fit your garden perfectly. If your house is modern, keep the arch as simple as possible, using clear, straight lines. Avoid fussy and ornate embellishments. For a traditional country cottage garden, use rustic wooden poles or split logs. For a town house, choose the geometric and formal shapes of a trellis-clad arch.

A SIMPLE WOODEN ARCHWAY

The dimensions of the archway shown here can be altered to suit your requirements, but the timber used is the minimum size for an arch. For a large, sturdy construction use 15 × 15cm (6 × 6in) timbers. Always use treated timber as this will have a longer life than untreated wood.

MATERIALS

For the uprights:

4 pieces treated timber 10 × 10cm × 2.7m (4 × 4in × 9ft)

For the horizontals:

2 pieces treated timber 10 × 10cm × 1.8m (4 × 4in × 6ft)

4 coach bolts at least 23cm (9in) long, and nuts to fit them

15cm (6in) galvanised nails

ready-mixed bagged concrete, water

MINIMUM HEIGHT
The minimum practical above-ground height for an arch is 2.1m (7ft). You need to bury 60cm (2ft) and still be able to walk comfortably under the archway, while giving plants enough space to hang down.

YOU WILL NEED

hammer
electric drill and bit with same diameter as the coach bolts
2 spanners to tighten the coach bolts
spirit level
tape measure and pencil
spade
wooden pegs
hardcore or hoggin
an assistant

■ First measure the area that you wish to be covered by the arch. Hammer pegs into the ground to mark the position of the uprights. Make sure that the pegs are correctly spaced or the arch will not be straight. To do this use a piece of string to check that the distance between peg A and peg D is the same as between peg B and peg C.

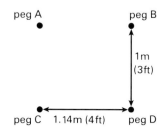

■ Dig a hole at each point marked by the pegs. The holes should be approximately 30cm (12in) across and 60cm (24in) deep to give a good, solid foundation for the arch.

■ Use the tape measure and pencil to make a mark 5cm (2in) from the end of each of the uprights. Drill a hole right through each upright at the point marked.

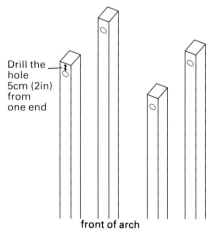

■ You now need help from your assistant. Place an upright into each hole and wedge it with the hardcore. Make sure the drilled holes are all at the top of the timber and facing the same way. Check that the tops of the uprights are level with each other. Rest one of the horizontals across two uprights and check the level with the spirit level. If one is too high remove it from the hole, dig the hole a bit deeper and replace the upright. Keep doing this until you are sure that all the uprights are level. They must also be absolutely vertical.

■ Add water to the bagged, mixed concrete and pour some into each of the holes around the posts to just below ground level. Check again that they are perfectly vertical. If not, tap them gently with the hammer until they are. When you are satisfied that they are level, leave the concrete to set for 48 hours.

■ Face the arch and, with your assistant's help, hold one of the horizontals up to the top of a pair of uprights. Make sure it extends an equal amount past the edge of each upright. Ask your helper to walk round to the inside of the arch and stick a pencil through the holes at the top of the uprights to make a mark on the horizontal. Repeat this with the other horizontal, then drill through the horizontals at the four marked points.

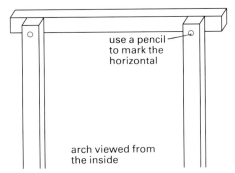

use a pencil to mark the horizontal

arch viewed from the inside

■ Use the coach bolts to secure the horizontals to the uprights. Screw the nuts on as tightly as possible, using one of the spanners, hold the head of the bolt still with the other.

■ Finally, place the two remaining horizontal pieces on the top of the arch at right angles to the previous two horizontals, making sure they extend equal amounts beyond each upright. Nail them down to the horizontals already in place, using galvanised nails.

■ If necessary, you can support climbing plants with trellis or rustic timber nailed to the uprights. Garden wire is just as effective and less expensive.

(*Continued on page 46*)

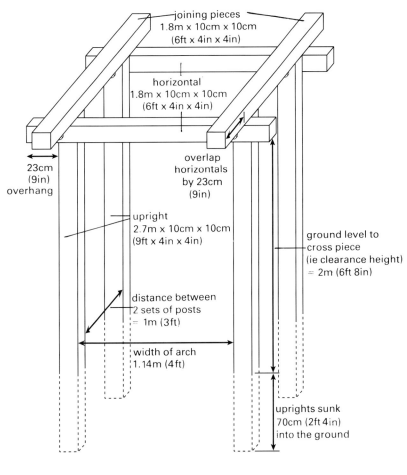

joining pieces
1.8m x 10cm x 10cm
(6ft x 4in x 4in)

horizontal
1.8m x 10cm x 10cm
(6ft x 4in x 4in)

23cm
(9in)
overhang

overlap
horizontals
by 23cm
(9in)

upright
2.7m x 10cm x 10cm
(9ft x 4in x 4in)

ground level to
cross piece
(ie clearance height)
= 2m (6ft 8in)

distance between
2 sets of posts
= 1m (3ft)

width of arch
1.14m (4ft)

uprights sunk
70cm (2ft 4in)
into the ground

VARIATIONS

side view

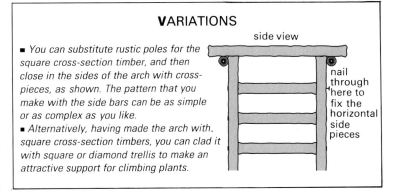

■ *You can substitute rustic poles for the square cross-section timber, and then close in the sides of the arch with cross-pieces, as shown. The pattern that you make with the side bars can be as simple or as complex as you like.*

■ *Alternatively, having made the arch with square cross-section timbers, you can clad it with square or diamond trellis to make an attractive support for climbing plants.*

nail through here to fix the horizontal side pieces

plants
OF THE
month

Bergamot

BERGAMOT or BEE BALM
(*Monarda didyma* – Labiatae)

Native to North America, bergamot is an attractive tall plant for a focal point in a herb garden. Its flowers and leaves make a soothing tea.

type	Hardy herbaceous perennial
flowers	Velvety red flowers are carried above the leaves from late summer through to autumn. Also available in pink, white and mauve forms
leaves	Leaves are oval with pointed ends and toothed edges. The young leaves have the strongest fragrance
height	45–90cm (18–36in)
spread	60cm (24in). In a small herb garden bergamot can become invasive
planting	Plant 45cm (18in) apart, using three or five plants to make a good show
position	Sun or partial shade
soil	Moist, well drained, enriched in spring with a compost mulch
care	Stake plants in exposed sites. Cut down after flowering and harvesting. Apply a systemic fungicide in summer if powdery mildew appears on the leaves. Divide plants in autumn every few years and discard the older, central rootstock
propagation	Propagate from stem tip cuttings in summer and root divisions in autumn. Sow seed in spring into trays in a cold frame or greenhouse. Transplant into the flowering position when the seedlings are well established
species and varieties	Wild bergamot *(Monarda fistulosa)* has violet-coloured flowers. Lemon bergamot *(M. citriodora)* has greenish-white flower bracts that darken to mauve, and lemon-scented leaves. Bergamot is also called oswego tea plant and bee balm
harvesting	Gather leaves before flowers appear. Harvest flowers as they open. Dry leaves and flowers or use fresh
herbal value	Use leaves fresh or dry in teas. Add young leaves and flowers to salads and wine cups. Use both dried leaves and flowers in pot-pourri

BISTORT
(*Persicaria bistorta* – Polygonaceae)

Pretty spikes of pink flowers and mounds of fresh green leaves make bistort an attractive herb for an ornamental corner of the herb garden. May also be sold as *Polygonum bistorta*.

type	Hardy herbaceous perennial
flowers	Small pink flowers clustered at the top of long flowering stems from midsummer through to autumn
leaves	Light green, lance-shaped leaves wrapped round the flowering stem at their base
height	In flower 75cm (30in)
spread	Creeping rootstock. Can be invasive
planting	Plant in spring and divide plants in autumn
position	Enjoys partial shade
soil	Moist
care	Water in drought conditions
propagation	Divide plants in autumn or spring
harvest	Harvest leaves before flowering in spring to make a traditional north of England pudding
herbal value	Eat young leaves in salads or cooked, as spinach. Mix with nettle tops, young dandelion and lady's mantle leaves, boil and strain to make the traditional herb pudding known as Easter Ledges. Serve it as a vegetable accompaniment to meat

DILL
(*Anethum graveolens* – Umbelliferae)

Finely cut leaves, tiny yellow flowers and seeds are the aromatic delights of dill – a tall-growing plant for the centre of a herb bed.

type	Hardy annual
flowers	Masses of tiny yellow flowers carried on umbrella-like flower stalks from midsummer through to mid-autumn
leaves	Fresh green, feathery, deeply divided leaves
height	Up to 1.5m (5ft)
spread	30cm (12in)
planting	Sow in succession from mid-spring in rows, and thin to 30cm (12in)
position	Full sun in a sheltered site
soil	Well drained, average
care	Water newly sown seed frequently using a watering can or hose with a fine rose or nozzle. Make frequent sowings through the

spring and summer to enjoy a long harvest of leaves, as dill flowers and goes to seed quickly in hot weather

propagation	Sow seed by pressing it into the soil and leaving uncovered
harvest	Harvest young leaves to use fresh and to dry. Collect flower heads just as seeds begin to form, and harvest seed when flower heads darken to brown. Use dill fresh, frozen or dried
herbal value	Crumble frozen leaves into soups, stews, sauces and fish dishes. Use fresh in salads, herb butters and herb vinegar. Use flower heads for pickling. Use seed as a digestive at the end of a meal, as practised in many parts of India

FEVERFEW

(Tanacetum parthenium – Compositae)

Feverfew's simple daisy flowers provide attractive colour in the herb garden, while the ferny leaves are said to relieve migraine.

type	Hardy herbaceous perennial
flowers	White petals with yellow central cushion of stamens. Several flowers per stem and can be double or single. Blooms through summer into autumn
leaves	Fern-like leaves, with soft texture and strong aroma
height	45cm (18in)
spread	30cm (12in)
planting	Sow in autumn or spring and remove excessive self-sown seedlings or leggy older plants
position	Full sun
soil	Well drained, average
care	Cut back after flowering to prevent self seeding and to produce a second flush of flowers. Cut back after later flowering
propagation	Sow seed in spring or autumn. Feverfew will self sow abundantly if not cut back
species and varieties	There are double and single-flowered forms. Also golden feverfew (*Tanacetum parthenium* 'Aureum')
harvest	Harvest young leaves to dry or use fresh. Dry flowers
herbal value	Use dried or fresh leaves to make a bedtime tea. Flowers are useful in pot-pourri and infusions. Also used in drawers to repel moths

Heartsease

HEARTSEASE

(Viola tricolor – Violaceae)

The wild pansy, heartsease, provides dainty flowers on ground-covering plants. Use them to provide colour at border edges.

type	Hardy short-lived perennial or annual
flowers	Tri-coloured – usually purple, yellow and white, but there are many variations. Abundant flowers produced from late spring to late summer, with a delicate perfume
leaves	Oval with serrated edges
height	15cm (6in) but it also grows through other plants and uses them as support
spread	30cm (12in)
planting	Use it in the front of a herb border or as a colourful infill between box hedges in a knot garden
position	Prefers full sun
soil	Any well-drained, loamy soil
care	Nip off spent flowers to avoid self seeding
propagation	Sow seed into the growing site in spring or into seed trays in late winter to transplant in spring. Once established, heartsease self seeds, but for a particular colour take cuttings in summer
species and varieties	There are many garden hybrids, but the tri-coloured heartsease is traditional for herb gardens
harvest	Pick flowers in spring and summer to use fresh or dry
herbal value	Add fresh flowers to salads and summer drinks. Freeze them into ice cubes to use in drinks. Can be dried and added to pot-pourri for colour and scent. Dry the flowers to decorate stationery, bookmarks and small pictures

Feverfew

Bistort

(*Continued from page 43*)

●
PLANTS TO USE

These plants offer fragrance, colour and cover for an archway, and are traditionally associated with herb gardens.

■*Honeysuckle* combines scented flowers with attractive foliage. *Lonicera japonica* 'Halliana' and *L.j.* 'Aureo-reticulata' are both evergreen and the latter has decorative gold-variegated leaves.

■ *Clematis*, depending on species, provides perfume, attractive seed heads and good cover. The wild clematis or traveller's joy *(Clematis vitalba)* has pretty white flowers, followed by whirly seed heads that dry well to use for decorative wreaths for festive occasions. *Clematis flammula*, the 'fragrant virgin's bower', has richly scented, small white flowers in late summer and autumn. In frost-free areas evergreen, scented *Clematis armandii* flowers in early spring.

■ *Climbing, rambling and pillar roses*, such as the late-flowering rambler 'Félicité Perpétué' with evergreen foliage and clusters of scented pink to white flowers, are excellent for clothing archways. 'Zéphirine Drouhin' is a thornless Bourbon climber that flowers over a long period in summer with heavily scented blooms. 'American Pillar' has clusters of single pink flowers with white centres.

■ *Hops* Use either the plain green or golden-leaved form. The plant dies back at the end of autumn. Use hop flowers in sleep pillows and twining stems for festive wreaths.

■ *Jasmine* For scent in the garden and to dry and use in pot-pourri, jasmine is a delightful solution. *Jasminum officinale* and *J.o.* 'Grandiflora' both provide scented, tubular white flowers and are strong climbers.

■ *Passionflower* In warm climates, passionflower's unusual flowers and edible fruits add a semi-tropical look to an archway.

●
PLANTING UP THE ARCH

Once the arch is in place and secure, dig trenches in the soil at its base, add well-rotted compost and water well. Set the plants into the ground so that they grow near the timber uprights, or spread them along the width of the arch. As they grow, train them with wires or add trellis to the archway. Keep the plants well watered and mulch in spring. Feed roses in spring and prune clematis and roses as normal.

practical project 2

PLANTING AN AROMATIC LAWN

YOU WILL NEED

garden fork
trowel
15cm (6in) measuring stick

PLANTS FOR A HERB LAWN

CHAMOMILE
Traditional plant used for a herb lawn, path or seat

Chamaemelum nobilis 'Treneague'
Non-flowering. Gives the most uniform and easily maintained result. Mow or clip lightly during summer to encourage sideshoots to root as they grow. This helps to create a dense mat which weeds find hard to penetrate

C. n. 'Flore Pleno'
Double-flowered. Makes a pretty edging plant for the herb border next to or on either side of the path

A herb lawn planted with a ground-hugging plant such as lawn chamomile or creeping thyme offers an alternative and more interesting texture than grass and, when you walk on it, releases a delicious fragrance.

On a large scale, a herb lawn is not a realistic substitute for grass, nor is it easy to maintain. Keep your herb lawn small – a metre or yard square is big enough.

Apart from grass, few plants tolerate constant tramping, so avoid a site that is heavily used. If you have to choose a busy site for the herb lawn, place a few stepping stones across it to prevent the plants becoming worn down. A herb lawn will thrive if the site is well prepared and in a sunny position.

●
MATERIALS

horticultural grit, bonemeal

40 chamomile plants per sq m
(36 plants per sq yd)

●
PLANTING THE LAWN

■ In spring, autumn or winter dig over the soil and remove roots of perennial weeds, annual weed seedlings or plants, stones and any other rubbish. If possible, leave the site for a week or two in spring before planting, then weed again. During the time lapse, another crop of weeds may grow. Hoe them off or dig them out to minimise competition with your herb plants.

■ If your soil is heavy, fork in horticultural grit to improve the drainage. A bucketful per square metre (square yard), dug into the top 15cm (6in) of the soil, is sufficient.

■ Choose plants of the same size and quality to achieve an even look to the lawn. Stand all the plants in position to check that you have enough for the site. Space the plants 15cm (6in) apart in staggered rows which are also 15cm (6in) apart.

■ Work systematically across and down the site, using a trowel to make the planting holes. Mix a sprinkling of bonemeal with the soil at the base of each planting hole before you set the plant into place.

■ Water the plants in, and continue to water

regularly until you are certain that they are growing well. Within three months the herb lawn will have thickened to form a fragrant carpet.

ALTERNATIVE HERB CARPETS

Your herb lawn can be combined with a path through the herb garden and, by raising it, you can transform it into a scented garden seat.

A herb path
By setting stepping stones into a herb lawn, you can change it into a herb path. Use herb pathways to divide a formal herb garden into neat compartments. A herb path is also attractive under an arch or pergola at the centre of a herb garden. Prepare the path as you would a herb lawn. Before planting, set the stepping stones into the path. Bed them directly into the soil, then plant as you would a herb lawn.

A herb seat
The simplest way to create a herb seat is to build a rectangular raised bed against an existing wall. Use brick, or old railway sleepers bolted together. Build up the sides to create 'arm rests' and make it more of a seat than a raised bed. Fill the bottom of the bed with rubble and the top 15cm (6in) with a light loam or potting compost. Plant the herbs in the same way as at ground level.

Low-maintenance herb lawn
Herb lawns are time-consuming to establish and maintain – regular hand weeding is essential to keep the texture even. If your time and labour is limited, plant stepping stones of chamomile or thyme in blocks across the conventional lawn. Use six plants to a block. Maintain the lawn as you would a normal grass sward. This approach eliminates hand weeding, but still provides you with an aromatic waft of scent as you walk over or mow the lawn. You won't need to mow the herb blocks as flat as the normal lawn, but you may need to replace the herb plants each year if they die back and become straggly. If you use thyme, avoid mowing it flat while it is in flower, using a high cut to keep it in order.

Table-top lawn
Even if you have no garden, you can still enjoy the fragrant delights of a miniature herb lawn in a pot. Admittedly you will not be able to walk through it, but on a balcony you can use it as a foot rest or simply run your hands through it to release the perfume.

HERB LAWN CARE

- *Deadhead flowers of thyme by shearing over with clippers*
- *Trim off straggly stems*
- *Mow occasionally with blades set high; otherwise, walk over the herb lawn or give it a good roll several times in the growing season*
- *Remove weed seedlings as they appear – never use a lawn weedkiller*
- *Topdress the lawn with sieved soil and sand (50:50) in autumn*
- *Apply a general fertiliser in spring*
- *Water during dry weather*

MINT
Two species of mint are useful to make a short-lived herb lawn

Spanish mint *(Mentha requienii)*
Also known as Corsican or *Crème de menthe* mint, is the most successful. It grows 2.5cm (1in) high and has dark green, small and rounded leaves, with pale mauve flowers in summer. It may need replanting each spring

Creeping pennyroyal (*M. pulegium*)
Prettier plant with bright green shiny leaves, but it makes less dense growth

Both these prostrate mints prefer light shade and moist soil conditions, but they may die out in a cold, damp winter

Creeping thyme *(Thymus serpyllum)*
Easier to maintain as a lawn than chamomile and it has the bonus of pink, white or crimson flowers (depending on variety) in spring

As an alternative, choose the golden-leaved form *T.s.* 'Aureum', or use *T. herba-barona*, which is caraway-scented and grows to 7.5cm (3in), with pale lilac flowers in summer.

Bees are attracted to thyme flowers, so take care not to get stung as you relax on the thyme herb seat!

Herb stepping 'stones' across the lawn will produce an effective aroma but are not such hard work

plants
OF THE
month

Hyssop

Lemon balm

HYSSOP
(*Hyssopus officinalis* – Labiatae)

Grow hyssop as an informal hedge at the front of a herb border, and use its flowers and young leaves in salads and with meat and vegetables.

type	Semi-evergreen sub-shrub
flowers	Small clusters of blue, pink or white flowers from late summer through to early autumn
leaves	Long, thin, pointed
height	60cm (24in)
spread	30cm (12in)
planting	Sow in spring and thin to 20cm (8in) for hedging and 30cm (12in) in borders
position	Full sun in a sheltered site
soil	Well drained, light
care	Cut back in spring to encourage compact, bushy growth. Cut back after flowering in mild climates where frost damage is unlikely
propagation	Take stem cuttings in spring and summer, or sow seed in rows into the growing site
species and varieties	Rock hyssop (*Hyssopus officinalis* ssp *aristatus*) has deep blue flowers and a compact shape
harvesting	Harvest leaves before the plants flower, and dry in a shady site. Pick flowers for salads as they open
herbal value	Use leaves and flowers sparingly to flavour food. Flower tops can be used to make a soothing tea for coughs. Add flowers to pot-pourri

LAWN CHAMOMILE
(*Chamaemelum nobile* – Compositae)

Use lawn chamomile to make a fragrant pathway or a scented area. Its apple-scented leaves relax and soothe.

type	Hardy evergreen perennial
flowers	Upright chamomile has white daisy-like flowers in summer, if allowed to bloom but lawn chamomile is non-flowering
leaves	Mossy, finely cut, scented leaves
height	Upright chamomile grows to 20cm (8in), the creeping form grows to 7.5–10cm (3–4in)
spread	30cm (12in)
position	Full sun
soil	Moist but well-drained loam
care	Cut plants with shears to flatten and encourage ground-level spread. Cut off any flower heads

on tall or upright chamomile if forming a lawn. Hand weed

propagation	Take side shoots in summer and divide plants in autumn
species and varieties	The best form for lawns is *Chamaemelum nobile* 'Treneague'
harvest	Harvest flowers of upright chamomile as they appear and dry in a frame or a cool oven. Pick leaves to dry before flowers appear
herbal value	Add leaves and flowers to pot-pourri. Use flowers in hair rinses and facial steam baths. Add to a bath to soothe. Use flowers to make a relaxing tea

LEMON BALM
(*Melissa offinalis* – Labiatae)

Lemon balm forms dense aromatic mounds of deep green foliage. Use the citrus-scented leaves for pot-pourri, teas and in baths.

type	Hardy herbaceous perennial
flowers	Flowers change colour as they age from yellow to white and blue. Blooms from summer to autumn
leaves	Coarse, hairy leaves with serrated edges. Deep green when young but fade after flowering.
height	90cm (36in)
spread	60cm (24in)
planting	If space is limited it is best to buy one plant, as it spreads rapidly and self seeds abundantly
position	Shade from strong sun. Gold-leaved form scorches in full sun
soil	Moist, well drained, enriched with well-rotted compost or fertiliser
care	Water well in drought conditions. Cut back after flowering to prevent seed spread, if necessary. May need mulching with straw in winter in very cold areas
propagation	Sow seed in spring in seed trays in a heated propagator. Barely cover the seed with compost and transplant seedlings into the growing site. Divide mature clumps in autumn or take cuttings in summer. Take cuttings or divide variegated form
species and varieties	Gold-splashed, lemon-scented form 'Aurea' and golden form 'All Gold' need partial shade for good colouring
harvest	Cut in midsummer to autumn. Leaf flavour is best as flowers open.

When picking to dry, handle leaves as little as possible and dry in a dark but well-ventilated room. When dry, only keep leaves that have retained their colour. Lemon flavour is quickly lost, so dry a fresh batch every year

herbal value Use to make a soothing tea. Add to soups and stews, salads and fruit salads, fish and poultry. Use as a substitute for lemon grass for teas and salads. Add to herb pillows, pot-pourri, cosmetic waters and hot baths

LOVAGE

(*Levisticum officinale* – Umbelliferae)

Large in flavour and size, just one lovage plant is sufficient to provide leaves and seeds for cooking, as well as ornament and height in the herb garden.

type	Hardy herbaceous perennial
flowers	Large heads of closely clustered small yellow flowers from mid- to late summer
leaves	Celery-like, divided and toothed fresh green leaves with a strong savoury aroma
height	In flower, up to 1.8m (6ft)
spread	60cm (24in)
planting	Plant out seedlings and bought plants in spring or autumn
position	Sun or partial shade
soil	Moist, well dug and fertile
care	In severe winters mulch roots with straw to protect from frost damage. In summer, water well to ensure abundant and flavoursome foliage
propagation	Lovage will self sow or you can collect fresh seed to sow in late summer. Also take root cuttings in autumn or spring
harvest	Pick leaves as needed, but keep the central growing point intact. Leaves are more flavoursome before flowers appear. Nip off flower stems to prevent seed production. This also allows the root to develop well. Use leaves fresh or dry or freeze. Dry leaves in a cool oven or airing cupboard, store away from sunlight in air-tight jars.
herbal value	Use fresh, dried or frozen in soups, stews, and stocks. Fresh leaves add spice to salads and to

stuffings for poultry and pork. Use seeds to flavour bread and biscuits. Roots can be washed and peeled and used fresh or cooked as you would celeriac

MARJORAM

(*Origanum species* – Labiatae)

Aromatic green or golden leaves and dainty pink or white flowers are the culinary and decorative offerings of the various majorams.

type	Hardy perennials except for sweet or knotted marjoram (*Origanum marjorana*), a tender perennial best treated as a half-hardy annual
flowers	White, pink or purplish-pink flowers from late summer through to autumn
leaves	Small, oval leaves in fresh green or golden yellow
height	Up to 60cm (24in) depending on species
height	Up to 60cm (24in)
spread	Up to 60cm (24in)
planting	Divide older plants in spring or autumn. Sow sweet marjoram in seed trays under glass in mid-spring to plant out in late spring
position	Full sun in an open position
soil	Well drained, fertile
care	Protect sweet marjoram with cloches or pot up to bring indoors in winter. Water well in dry seasons. Cut back to promote new leafy growth after flowering
propagation	Sow seed of sweet marjoram in spring. Perennials self seed readily. Divide in spring or autumn. Take cuttings of wild marjoram in spring and summer
species and varieties	Wild marjoram (*Origanum vulgare*) is also known as oregano and has deep purplish flowers. *O.v.* 'Variegata' has gold-splashed leaves and *O.v.* 'Aureum' has gold leaves. Pot marjoram (*O. onites*) has white or pink flowers
harvest	Use fresh leaves all year but harvest for drying in late summer. Pick leaves and non-woody shoots after dew has dried. Dry in shade. Dry flower heads
herbal value	Aromatic leaves are used with meat dishes, in stuffings, soups and salads and can also be added to pot-pourri and used in sachets. Use to add aroma to barbecued dishes and in vinegars

Lovage

Marjoram

MAY

Late spring is full of outdoor activity. Successional outdoor sowing continues and, while it tails off gradually, the work goes on transplanting seedlings into their growing positions or into larger pots. In this later and warmest part of the spring, plant out nursery-bought herbs or well-established home-grown cuttings of perennials such as bay, rosemary or lavender.

It is a lovely time to watch the herb garden grow. It seems that if you blink you will miss a sudden spurt of growth. Plants begin to grow taller and leafy plants make full, but fairly neat, mounds of beautifully textured leaves. Herbs like borage seem suddenly too big for their places and may spill into neighbouring plants.

Even though every plant seems to be growing rapidly, the herb garden still has a long, low look. Statuary, arches and centrally-placed containers help to increase the height and alter the low-level pattern of the herb garden. It is more satisfying, though, to alter the levels with plants. Some are just statuesque in their height and, if grown in large clumps, make an impressive show. Others offer height because you can train them into tall shapes such as standards.

Then there are the climbing plants that clothe arches and trelliswork to provide good ornament at different levels. You can also introduce an element of height by growing herbs in hanging baskets, perhaps suspended from a central 'maypole'. Herbs in hanging baskets are successful on balconies and just outside the kitchen window, especially if your space is limited.

Throughout the herb-garden year there are flowers that you can use to candy or eat fresh in salads, as a garnish or add to drinks. If you wish, design your herb garden around an edible theme.

tasks

FOR THE

month

RAISING EYE LEVEL WITH TALL PLANTS
Some herb plants, such as fennel, lovage, angelica and Joe Pye weed, grow so large and tall that they provide the necessary height to alter the herb-garden eye level without any help from you, the gardener. Such plants look good if they are grown in blocks of several together. This provides a strong show of colour and the plants give each other mutual support. However, in exposed sites and windy seasons, you may need to provide additional support with garden twine wound round a few strategically placed tall canes.

CHECKLIST

◻ Prune or cut back herbs
◻ Train herbs for height
◻ Provide plant supports
◻ Control pests and diseases
◻ Make herbal fertiliser
◻ Pick spruce tops to make spruce beer
◻ This is the last chance to sow fennel
◻ Lay down madder stems to promote root formation for dyes
◻ Add material to the compost heap

CLIPPING HERBS

As the spring sun gets warmer and the soil temperature rises, growth in the herb garden is clearly visible. To make sure the plants grow into the shape you want and produce good leafy material for immediate kitchen use and later harvest, there is maintenance work to be done.

Clip back young specimens of shrubby herbs with woody stems, such as sage, lavender, some artemisias and santolina. Cut back to 15cm (6in) artemisias such as mugwort, southernwood and wormwood. Cut back old leggy growth of sage, lavender and santolina and cut out damaged wood of rosemary, but only clip other shoots if you are maintaining a particular shape. Thyme plants benefit from a good shearing over to remove leggy and damaged shoots.

Avoid pruning older, well-established woody herb plants severely, as they might suffer die-back.

TRAINING HERBS FOR HEIGHT

Height is an important element in making the herb garden more visually interesting as the plants themselves are generally low growing. You can provide height by manipulating plants into shapes or buying plants already grown as standards. Rose standards offer scent, colour and shape, as well as change in height. Climbing plants such as traveller's joy (wild clematis), hops and honeysuckle will also oblige by growing up and across large supports, including arches and trelliswork.

Create your own standards from gooseberry bushes or by using climbers such as honeysuckle.

■ For a honeysuckle standard, make a support from a pole or piece of timber 1m (3ft) or more, high with an upturned wire basket (chains removed) attached to the top.

■ Sink the pole securely into the ground and make a planting hole near its base.

■ Cut back the honeysuckle so that there are just two or three stems. Tie them in to the support and watch them wind their way up to the wire basket: fast-growing honeysuckles such as *Lonicera periclymenum* 'Belgica', 'Serotina' and 'Graham Thomas' will send shoots through the wire basket in several weeks.

■ Push the stems through the basket's framework to cover it.

■ When the basket is covered sufficiently, cut back the honeysuckle stems to keep the rounded shape of the standard.

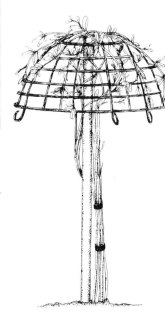

Creating a hop wigwam
Use the naturally vigorous growth habit of hops to provide a luxuriant, leafy high point in the herb garden.

■ Sink three or four 3m (10ft) bamboo canes into the ground to make a wigwam framework.

■ Make planting holes at the base of each cane and plant a hop into each hole.

■ Water in well and continue to water regularly, especially in dry periods. The hop plants will wind up the cane framework, making abundant leafy stems, and by midsummer the canes will be hidden.

■ Once the hops reach the top of the framework their tendrils wave and curl freely, adding extra shape and height.

SUPPORTS FOR HERB PLANTS

Some herbs, such as borage, tend to sprawl and push into their neighbours' growing space. Keep them within bounds by supporting them with multi-stemmed twiggy branches. Old-fashioned shrub roses that send out long arching stems weighed down with buds are best supported with round, iron frames or plastic-coated wire stakes. The more natural the supports look, the better for the overall character of the herb garden. If possible, use other plants as supports for climbers – but make sure they are compatible in colour and growth habit.

KEEPING HERBS HEALTHY

Spring is not just a time of new beginnings for your plants: it is also the time when insect pests and fungal diseases begin their activity. Generally, herbs are not troubled by pests and diseases, unless they are growing under stress. Then, if they are overcrowded in containers, or conditions are too moist or too dry, they may be susceptible to pests and disease.

Companion planting
Herbs such as chives and tagetes are useful as pest deterrents, and are grown for this purpose as companion plants in traditional vegetable gardens.

Tagetes roots act on soil to deter certain soil pests. They are also used in the greenhouse and outdoor cultivation of tomatoes as a whitefly deterrent. Chives and other members of the onion family keep aphids away from roses and seem to reduce levels of black spot infection on roses. Summer savory, delicious cooked with broad beans, is used as a blackfly deterrent and companion plant to the beans.

Aromatic herbs such as thyme, savory, hyssop and sage act in a different way. They attract many beneficial insects, including bees and butterflies for pollination, and hoverflies that eat aphids.

Some herbs such as borage and nasturtium seem to increase the strength and vigour of neighbouring plants. But beware of the overpowering strength of rue and wormwood. Both these plants have reputations as insect repellents when used fresh or dried in the home. As they grow, their leaf and root secretions are powerful deterrents on soil insects, but the plants often swamp nearby young or weak plants.

Hygiene
The simplest way to keep pests and disease out of the herb garden is to practise good hygiene. First, keep the herb garden as weed free as possible. Weeds are the nursery ground and winter home for many pests and diseases. Once you have weeded or pruned, remove material from the site, since the shady moisture and shelter of debris is attractive to slugs.

Act early
Early action is the best policy if pests do attack your plants. As soon as you see a pest, such as the mullein caterpillar, remove it by hand or it will soon have the mullein leaves and buds chewed up. Similarly, if you see the winding tunnels of leaf miners on sorrel or lovage leaves, remove the affected leaves before the insect spreads too far. Crushed egg shells, 'slug-pubs' filled with a little beer, or gravel mulches are some of the favourite organic deterrents for slugs.

Last resorts
If you feel you have to use more severe methods to deter insects or clean up infected plants, it is best to use organic insecticides and fungicides. These will not harm the insects that are useful predators and the herbs will be safe for you to use and handle. There are many proprietary brands available at garden centres.

Over the years gardeners have experimented with making effective liquid pesticide from herbal material. Thyme, elder, rhubarb and basil leaves are suitable, as are garlic cloves.

Other herbs that have been used in this way include tansy, wormwood and feverfew.

Mint and lemon balm are susceptible to fungal attacks called rusts. The spores of this fungus can survive in the soil over winter. Cut away affected parts of the plants and burn. If infection is severe, you will have to dig up and destroy the plants. Scorching the soil in autumn to destroy the spores is the most effective method of dealing with mint rust.

HERBAL FERTILISER

Although nasty-smelling in the making, a brew made from comfrey and nettle leaves and stems is one of the most effective liquid herb fertilisers. Use an old dustbin with a lid as the container. Half-fill it with chopped leaves and stems. Fill the bin with water and leave for up to six weeks, depending on the weather. The brew is ready when the leaves have decomposed and the awful smell they produce is reduced.

THINGS TO DO

Sow seed
Outdoors: aniseed and basil (if frosts are over), chervil (successional sowings), dill, fennel, heartsease, hop, Joe Pye weed, lemon balm, orach (successional sowings), pot marigold, traveller's joy

Plant out
Cumin, eucalyptus (if frosts are over), French marigold, perilla (harden off), sunflower

Propagate
Take cuttings: hop and lavender (stem tip), marsh mallow (softwood)
Layer: madder, sage, thyme

Harvest
Leaves: bay, fennel, lemon balm, lemon grass, sage, wild strawberry, winter savory
Flowers: heartsease, rosebuds

Routine maintenance
■ Cut comfrey to add to the compost heap

MAKING SPRUCE BEER

Harvest young, fresh green shoots of Norway spruce now to make spruce beer for summer and end-of-year festive drinking.
■ *Pick about 40-45 shoots, wash them well and boil in 4½ litre (1 gal) water for 30 minutes. Strain off spruce tips and pour liquid into a fermenting bucket.*
■ *Mix in 350g (12oz) sugar and 100g (4oz) dark treacle. Add a yeast solution to the mixture when it is cool.*
■ *Cover and leave to ferment for a week, then siphon into bottles, taking care not to bottle any of the foamy scum on top of the fermented mixture. Cork the bottles and check them each day – if too fizzy, the pressure will push the cork out of the bottle.*
■ *Drink the beer after a week. Continue to make it until midsummer – and save some for the end of the year!*

practical project

CREATING A
HANGING BASKET
HERB GARDEN

PLANTS FOR A CULINARY BASKET

1 moss-leaved parsley (1)
1 flat-leaved parsley (2)
1 salad burnet (3)
1 chive (4)
2 marjoram (5)
4 common thyme (6)
3 purple basil (7)
1 French tarragon (8)
(Choose small specimens as they are easier to handle)

WATCH THIS SPACE
If you are planting up your basket before basil plants are available, simply keep a space free and add them later. Put three empty pots into the compost where the basils are to go. Later in the season, remove the pots and plant the basils into the spaces.

Many herbs grow successfully in hanging baskets, so even if garden space is limited you can still grow a good range. Use hanging baskets on patios, balconies, just outside the kitchen door or even on a sturdy maypole-like structure in the main garden – herb hanging baskets are another effective means of raising eye level and providing height in a herb garden.

Like all container-grown plants, herbs in hanging baskets need extra attention. You need to provide water and a good supply of nutrients throughout the growing season, so that the plants look decorative and offer you a succession of leaves, flowers and seeds to use.

MATERIALS

1 × 35cm (14in) diameter wire basket with chains

1 bag moss

1 × 30cm (12in) diameter circle of black polythene, with holes for drainage

15L peat or coir compost
fertiliser sticks
or resin-coated slow-release fertiliser
water-absorbent granules

PLANTING A HANGING BASKET

■ Rest the basket on top of a large flower pot to stop it rolling about while you work. Place the flower pot on a table or greenhouse bench so that you are working at a comfortable height.

■ Line the basket with moss to form a layer 7.5cm (3in) deep that covers the base and comes about half-way up the sides of the basket.

■ Place the polythene on top of the moss inside the base of the basket. The polythene acts as a 'reservoir', holding enough water to prevent the compost drying out too quickly.

■ Mix the water-absorbent granules and fertiliser sticks or granules into the compost. Fill the basket with the compost to the level of the moss lining at the sides.

■ Now begin to add the plants. Start with the thymes and marjorams. Remove the plants

from their pots and place them on the compost at the edge of the pot. Carefully feed the foliage through the wire at the front of the basket from the inside. If the plant is too large to handle easily, simply wrap a small sheet of paper round the foliage to form a tube and push this through the basket wire.

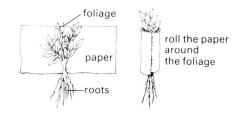

foliage
paper
roots
roll the paper around the foliage

■ Position the plants so that there are a pair of thyme plants on each side of the basket, with the marjoram as a counter-balance (*illus A*).

■ Continue lining the upper half of the basket with moss and add a little more compost.

■ Remove the other plants from their pots and plant as follows: place the salad burnet and chives side by side, about 7.5cm (3in) apart at the back of the basket. Set the parsley further forward, one on each side, and the French tarragon in the middle. Finally, plant the basil at the front (*illus B*).

■ To finish, fill all the gaps with compost and place a thin layer of moss on the surface between the plants. This keeps the compost in place and acts as a mulch to help retain moisture. Water the basket thoroughly, allow it to drain, then hang it up in position (*illus C*).

AFTERCARE

Watering
In hot weather you will need to water the basket at least twice a day. If it is fixed in place, use a pump-action sprayer with tubing long enough to reach the basket comfortably. If the basket can be lowered, water it with a long-spouted watering can. Avoid flushing surface compost off each time you water.

Feeding
If you haven't used fertiliser sticks or granules, add a soluble fertiliser to the water every seven days.

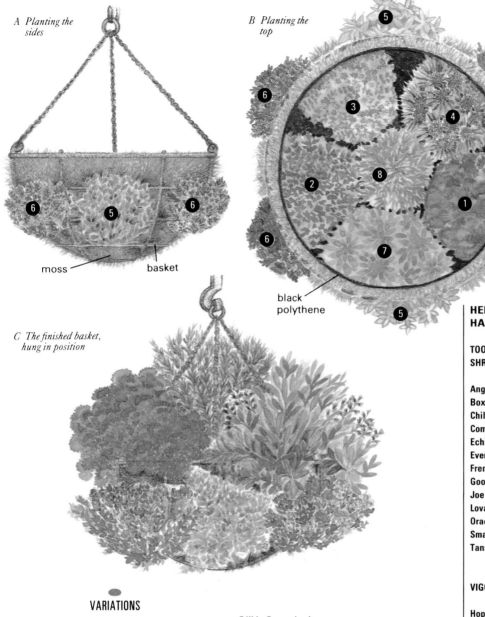

*A Planting the
   sides*

moss   basket

*B Planting the
   top*

black
polythene

*C The finished basket,
   hung in position*

VARIATIONS

Basket for shade

If you intend to hang the basket in a shady
site, use wild strawberries in place of the
thyme plants and sweet violet instead of marjoram. The chives and parsley will grow
fairly well in shade, but substitute variegated
applemint for the salad burnet and use creeping pennyroyal to edge the basket.

Summer basket

For a summer basket of scented foliage,
combine scented pelargonium, curry plant
and various basils.

Edible flower basket

Use thymes to edge the basket and to line
the sides. In the top, grow pot marigold and
borage (they will need staking). Let nasturtium plants tumble over the edge and place
one or two chive plants (use white-flowered
garlic chives as an alternative) between the
nasturtiums around the edge of the basket.

Winter basket

Grow sage, parsley, thyme and rosemary in a
basket placed in a sunny, sheltered position
near the kitchen door to provide you with
herbs for use in cooking over winter.

HERBS UNSUITABLE FOR HANGING BASKETS

TOO TALL AND TOP HEAVY OR SHRUBBY

Angelica • Artemisia •
Box • Bay • Bergamot •
Chilli pepper • Clary sage•
Comfrey • Cumin •
Echinacea • Elecampane •
Evening primrose • Fennel •
French tarragon • Foxglove •
Good King Henry • Hyssop •
Joe Pye weed • Lemon balm •
Lovage • Marsh mallow •
Orach • Perilla • Poppy •
Smallage • Soapwort •
Tansy • Yarrow

VIGOROUS CLIMBERS

Hops • Traveller's joy

M A Y

plants
OF THE
month

Fennel

ANGELICA

(*Angelica archangelica* – Umbelliferae)

Tall and stately, with huge leaves and starbursts of flowering heads, angelica makes a dramatic central display in the herb garden.

type	Hardy biennial or, if flowering stems removed, short-lived perennial
flowers	Several large, yellow-green clusters of small flowers from late summer through to autumn in the second year of growth
leaves	Aromatic, large and deeply divided, with toothed edges and light green colour
height	1–2.4m (3–8ft)
spread	1m (3ft)
planting	Angelica will self sow profusely or you can collect seed and sow in autumn, or stratify it and sow in early spring
position	Best in partial shade
soil	Fertile, moist
care	To encourage leaf growth, nip out flower buds
propagation	From seed. Germination is better if seed is fresh and stratified over winter (see p88). Thin plants to 1m (3ft) apart
harvest	Cut young stems in early summer of their second year and harvest seed in early autumn. If you plan to harvest roots to use as fixative for pot-pourri, lift and dry them in autumn
herbal value	Candy stems to use on desserts and cakes. Young leaves boiled with rhubarb reduce its acidity

FENNEL

(*Foeniculum vulgare* – Umbelliferae)

Feathery leaves, stems and seeds that are edible and aromatic make up the kitchen offerings of fennel. In the herb garden its height provides a strong accent.

type	Hardy herbaceous perennial
flowers	Small yellow flowers in clusters from midsummer to autumn
leaves	Wispy, thread-like leaves in blue-green or bronze
height	2m (6ft)
spread	30cm (12in)
planting	Plant fennel at the back of a border or use it to make a central feature in a bed. Keep fennel, dill and coriander separate or they will be cross-pollinated and the resulting seed will not produce exact replicas of the parent plant
position	Full sun
soil	Well-drained, fertile loam
care	Pinch out flower stems to increase leaf production, if you are not interested in seed. Stake plants. Keep well weeded
propagation	For the long season necessary to ripen seed, sow indoors in early spring. Or sow in late spring outdoors in shallow drills 35cm (14in) apart and thin seedlings to 30cm (12in). Transplant fennel when it is young, and early in the growing season, as it dislikes root disturbance. Divide established plants in spring or autumn
species and varieties	Apart from the green and bronze-coloured leaf forms, there is also Florence fennel (*Foeniculum vulgare* var. *dulce*), grown for its aniseed-flavoured stem bases
harvest	Pick fennel leaves fresh, as you need them, through spring and summer. Freeze leaves to use later. Pick seed before it is fully ripe and still green. Discard any that become mouldy
herbal value	Use leaves fresh and raw in salads, in marinades and to flavour cooked fish dishes. Young stems can be cut into salads and used to flavour soups and stews. Sprinkle seed into bread mixes and onto cakes and savoury biscuits. Seeds are also useful in roast meat dishes and in stews. Use flower heads in pickle mixtures, and fresh leaves to flavour vinegars and oils

GOOD KING HENRY

(*Chenopodium bonus-henricus* – Chenopodiaceae)

One of the oldest salad herbs known to gardeners, Good King Henry or wild spinach grows well in rows and can be used decoratively as a tall back-of-the-border plant.

type	Hardy herbaceous perennial
flowers	Spikes of tiny green bobble-like blooms in early summer
leaves	Arrow-shaped and bright green in colour
height	60cm (24in)
spread	30cm (12in)

planting	Plant or thin seedlings to 30cm (12in) apart in rows
position	Full sun or partial shade
soil	Well prepared, enriched and well drained
care	Allow plants to establish in their first growing season before harvesting on a regular basis. Lift and divide in autumn
propagation	Sow seed in spring and barely cover with soil. Divide large clumps in autumn
species and varieties	Mexican tea or wormseed *(Chenopodium ambrosioides)* is a taller plant with larger leaves and flowers that turn red in high summer. Its leaves add flavour to South American cuisine – but don't let it self sow! Fat hen *(C. album)*, usually seen as a garden weed, can be used in soups, salads and cooked dishes
harvest	Pick leaves as needed. Harvest flowering spikes as they open
herbal value	Leaves can be used raw in salads. Cook them as spinach and use in soups and stews. Flowers can be boiled or steamed and eaten as a green vegetable

HONEYSUCKLE

(*Lonicera periclymenum* – Caprifoliaceae)

Honeysuckle's fragrant flowers have long been associated with herb gardens. Enjoy it for the height, colour and perfume that it provides.

type	Hardy deciduous climber
flowers	Clusters of red and creamy yellow-white tubular flowers carried in spring and early summer
leaves	Dark green oval leaves
height	1.8–9m (6–30ft)
spread	As above
planting	Plant deciduous species in autumn or spring and mulch with well-rotted manure
position	Sun or partial shade, with roots in light shade
soil	Average, well drained, but enriched with well-rotted manure or fertiliser
care	If soil is too rich, honeysuckle will make leafy growth at the expense of flower production. If necessary, thin out old wood after flowering. Train as a fragrant archway or standard
propagation	Take softwood cuttings from non-flowering shoots in summer, hardwood cuttings in late autumn or winter, or layer shoots in autumn
species and varieties	There are numerous species and varieties with a range of flower colours. They are available as shrubs that can be clipped into a hedge and as evergreens
harvest	Pick flowers just as they open to dry
herbal value	Honeysuckle flowers can be dried to add shape, texture and fragrance to pot-pourri. In the garden the intense perfume is more potent at night

HOP

(*Humulus lupulus* – Cannabidaceae)

Twisting and twining stems, attractively shaped leaves and ornamental flowers are the attractions of the hop, famous for its use in English beer.

type	Hardy deciduous climber
flowers	Papery green flowers from late summer for several weeks. Male and female flowers are carried on different plants
leaves	Rough-textured, toothed, palmate leaves in fresh green or gold
height	Depending on support, 6m (20ft)
spread	As above
planting	Grow into larger shrubs, trees, across trellis or pergolas, or up a tripod support to make a feature
position	Full sun
soil	Well dug, well drained
care	Cut back in autumn. Spray against aphids in spring and summer
propagation	Take tip cuttings in early summer or divide clumps in spring or autumn. Take cuttings from female plants as their flowers are the most ornamental and useful
species and varieties	The ordinary hop has bright green leaves, but *Humulus lupulus* 'Aureus' has buttery gold leaves
harvest	Pick tips in spring to use fresh or to freeze. Pick female flowers in late summer to autumn to dry. Pick trailing vines to dry for decoration
herbal value	Use hop tops in salads, soups and omelettes or cooked as a vegetable with cream sauce. Traditionally, hop flowers are used dried in sleep pillows, and they are used in brewing to preserve beer. Flowers can also be infused in a hot bath

Honeysuckle

Hop

practical project 2

USING HERB FLOWERS

Stepping stones make it easier to sow, plant and harvest the flowers

The flowers of many garden herbs have just as great a part to play in flavouring and decorating food as the leaves. Both sweet and savoury dishes can be made more interesting by adding herb flowers.

Flowers are added fresh to salads, soups, sauces and sorbets. They can be preserved by crystallising and then used to decorate cakes and desserts. Flower colour and flavour is preserved in jams and jellies, sugars and butters. Frozen into ice cubes, herb flowers make floating decorations for wine cups and summer drinks. Never experiment with flowers that you aren't sure of, but within the list of flowers that are edible you can experiment to create the combinations that appeal to you.

As you walk around your herb garden, gather the flowers you wish to use. First smell them: smell and taste are closely related. Nibble at the edges of a petal or two to get a better idea of the flavour, but only those you know to be edible. Some herb flowers, such as rosemary, taste very similar to the leaves, but are slightly milder in flavour. Others, such as the bright red blooms of pineapple sage and the deep blue flowers of borage, are best used for the vivacity of their colours. You can mix and match colours and flavours to enjoy in food and drink, as well as in the garden as they grow.

CREATING AN EDIBLE HERB FLOWER GARDEN

The size and scope of your edible herb flower garden depends on the space available, but you can also incorporate edible flowers into your existing borders, into a vegetable garden or into a container garden on a patio or roof.

For best results, choose a sunny site. Except for mint, sweet woodruff and primroses, which enjoy shade, most herbs produce their aromatic oils best in sun. Sow annuals for the edible flower garden each year and grow them in well-drained, fertile soil. In spring, avoid nitrogen-rich fertilisers that encourage leaf production. Keep the edible herb flower garden well watered and weed free, and remove spent flowers.

HARVEST TIME

Only eat flowers that you can identify positively. Cut the flowers on the day you intend to use them. Pick them early in the day, once the dew has dried, but before the sun is too strong. Don't use wilted or damaged blooms. Handle roses and nasturtiums gently or they will bruise. Cut lavender, sage and marjoram with long stems, then snip or pinch out the individual flowers just before use.

'cool' colours – blues/whites   'hot' colours – reds/oranges/yellows

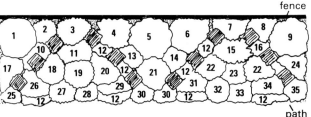

fence

path

a =annual
the annuals in the two front triangles, taller plants at the back of the garden

1 rose	9 rose	17 chives	27 oregano
(Rosa gallica)	(Rosa gallica	18 rocket (a)	28 chervil
2 mint	versicolor)	19 cornflower (a)	29 sweet basil
3 rosemary	10 cowslip	20 coriander (a)	30 pinks
4 mullein	11 borage (a)	21 lavender	31 opal basil (a)
5 rose	12 thyme	22 nasturtium	32 pot marigold (a)
(Rosa 'Ispahan')	13 marjoram	23 dill	33 salad burnet
6 fennel	14 musk mallow	24 garlic chives	34 tagetes
7 anise hyssop	15 golden sage	25 sweet violet	35 heartsease
8 sweet woodruff	16 primrose	26 summer savory (a)	

PREPARING THE BLOOMS

Rinse the flowers in cool water to remove insects. Gently shake or pat the flowers dry between sheets of absorbent paper. Trim off the white parts of rose or pink petals before using them as it gives a bitter flavour. Until you are ready to use them, store individual flowers between pieces of damp absorbent paper in the refrigerator. Stand long-stemmed flowers in cold water out of direct sun.

USING FRESH FLOWERS

The simplest use is for decoration. Toss prepared flowers into salads, use them to garnish food or chop over cooked vegetables. Float them in wine cups or use them to ornament fruit desserts. Sweet woodruff flowers go well with strawberries and rhubarb, while lavender suits blackberries and raspberries.

For eating, basil, salad burnet, chive, dill, marigold, rocket and thyme flowers combine well with green salad leaves. Nasturtium flower petals can be added individually, or the whole flower stuffed with cream cheese or egg mayonnaise. For a tangy tomato and onion salad add basil leaves, basil and rosemary flowers and dress with walnut oil and wine vinegar.

USING PRESERVED FLOWERS

Preserved flowers can be used throughout the year to flavour and colour chutney, jelly, vinegar and oil, sugar and butter. They can also be dried to make tea, and crystallised for cake and biscuit decoration.

CRYSTALLISED FLOWERS

For decorating cakes and sweets, crystallise or candy the petals of roses, primroses, pansies, lilac, violets, borage and scented pelargonium.

■ Rinse and dry the flowers. If using roses and pansies, separate the petals and remove the white parts of roses. Use other flowers whole.

■ Hold the flower or petal in one hand, dip a small pastry brush into egg white and paint the flowers. Make sure you cover all sides of the petal or flower.

■ Sprinkle gently with fine-grain sugar to coat. Leave the flowers or petals on waxed paper to dry overnight. If you need to speed the process, place the petals in a cool oven for several hours.

Flower sugar
Adding flowers to ordinary white sugar transforms it into a highly flavoured sweetener for fruit and cream. Anise hyssop, lavender, lilac, rose, scented pelargonium and violet flowers add their own individual scents and flavours to sugar.

■ In a jar with a tightly fitting lid, make alternate layers of sugar and flowers. Keep adding layers until the jar is almost full – about 1cm (½in) below the lid.

■ Seal the jar and shake it well. Store it out of the light for about three weeks before using. The longer you leave it, the stronger the flavour. Herb sugars keep for up to a year.

Flower butter
Use basil, chive, coriander, dill, fennel, marigold and rosemary flowers to make savoury butters to use on bread, and with pasta, fish, meat and vegetable dishes.

■ Soften as much butter as you wish to use. Wash, dry and chop the flowers into small pieces and mix with the butter. Add salt and pepper as necessary.

■ Pack the mixture into a small ramekin and keep in the refrigerator until you are ready to use it. You can freeze the butter but, once thawed, it should be used within a week.

Flower vinegars
Use basil, chive, dill, fennel, marigold, marjoram, nasturtium and rosemary flowers to add colour and flavour to vinegar. The choice of vinegar is important: try not to use one that will overwhelm the flower flavours. Distilled vinegar can be too acidic. White wine and apple vinegar are best, as they complement the flower flavours. Their pale colour is useful too, to take on the colour of the petals.

■ Rinse the flowers and place them in a clean and sterilised jar. Heat the vinegar until just hot, then pour over the flowers.

■ Seal the jar and leave it in a warm, dark place for two weeks. Strain through muslin or cheesecloth into a sterilised bottle and store out of direct sunlight.

For more ideas and information on making floral and herbal vinegars, see page 91.

EDIBLE HERB FLOWERS

Latin names are included in these lists as correct identification is essential

SPRING TO SUMMER FLOWERING

Chives *(Allium schoenoprasum)*
Cowslip *(Primula veris)*
Heartsease *(Viola tricolor)*
Primrose *(Primula vulgaris)*
Rosemary *(Rosmarinus officinalis)*
Sweet rocket *(Hesperis matronalis)*
Sweet violet *(Viola odorata)*
Sweet woodruff *(Galium odoratum)*

SUMMER FLOWERING

Anise hyssop
  (Agastache foeniculum)
Bergamot *(Monarda didyma)*
Borage *(Borago officinalis)*
Chicory *(Cichorium intybus)*
Chives, garlic *(Allium tuberosum)*
Coriander *(Coriandrum sativum)*
Dill *(Anethum graveolens)*
Fennel *(Foeniculum vulgare)*
Hollyhock *(Alcea rosea)*
Lavender *(Lavandula angustifolia)*
Lemon balm *(Melissa officinalis)*
Lovage *(Levisticum officinalis)*
Marjoram *(Origanum vulgare)*
Mint *(Mentha spp)*
Mullein *(Verbascum thapsus)*
Musk mallow *(Malva moschata)*
Nasturtium *(Tropaeolum majus)*
Pineapple sage *(Salvia elegans)*
Pink *(Dianthus caryophyllus)*
Pot marigold *(Calendula officinalis)*
Rose *(Rosa spp)*
Sage *(Salvia officinalis)*
Salad burnet *(Sanguisorba minor)*
Summer savory *(Satureja hortensis)*
Thyme *(Thymus vulgaris)*
Winter savory *(Satureja montana)*

FLOWERS TO AVOID

Do not eat the following flowers:

Buttercup *(Ranunculus ficaria)*
Delphinium *(Delphinium elatum)*
Foxglove *(Digitalis purpurea)*
Iris *(Iris florentina)*
Lupin *(Lupinus polyphyllus)*
Monkshood *(Aconitum napellus)*
Narcissus
  (Narcissus pseudonarcissus)
Oleander *(Nerium oleander)*
Periwinkle *(Vinca major)*
Wisteria *(Wisteria sinensis)*

plants
OF THE
month

Pot marigold

JOE PYE WEED

(*Eupatorium purpureum* – Compositae)

Use the stately Joe Pye weed for a tall stand of rose-coloured flowers for late summer. Leaves and stems offer a strong aroma as you brush against them.

type	Hardy herbaceous perennial
flowers	Clusters of pink flower buds that open to a pinkish-cream in summer
leaves	Large, oval aromatic leaves arranged around the stems in groups of four. Green with purplish markings on veins
height	1.2–1.8m (4–6ft)
spread	1m (3ft)
planting	Plant in autumn or spring
position	Sun or partial shade
soil	Moist but well drained
care	Cut back after flowering and divide large clumps in autumn
propagation	Split large clumps in autumn or grow from fresh sowings in spring
species and varieties	Hemp agrimony (*Eupatorium cannibinum*) has pink-mauve flowers
harvest	Pick ripe seed to produce a dye. Harvest leaves of hemp agrimony all through the year for use as a fly repellent
herbal value	Also known as gravelroot, Joe Pye weed's root was dried and used as a medicinal infusion. In the herb garden today, it is best grown for its decorative value

ORACH

(*Atriplex hortensis* – Chenopodiaceae)

Orach, a useful salad herb, offers colour and height in the herb garden. Grow it in clumps with support to make blocks of colour, or in formal rows as hedging.

type	Hardy annual
flowers	Small green-gold or red bobble-like flowers in summer followed by attractive papery seed heads
leaves	Arrow-shaped leaves in ruby red or greenish gold
height	1.2m (4ft)
spread	30cm (12in)
plant	Sow in succession if you plan to harvest it as a salad or vegetable crop. Best grown in clumps for good colour effects. Thin seedlings to 30cm (12in)

position	Prefers full sun, but will tolerate partial shade
soil	Any, but for good height and leaf growth prefers fertile, well drained
care	Water well, especially in dry conditions, to prevent it going to seed too quickly. Plants may need staking for support in an exposed situation
propagation	Sow seed direct into the growing site in early spring. Cover the seed with 1cm (½in) of soil. Sow every few weeks to keep a succession of salad material. Orach will self seed, so in future years simply hoe off any unwanted seedlings
species and varieties	Gold orach (*Atriplex hortensis*) grows to the same height as red orach (*A. h. 'Rubra'*)
harvest	Pick leaves as you need them before flowering, if you have successive crops growing. Pick seed heads on fairly long stalks before seeds are ripe, to use in dried arrangements
herbal value	Use young leaves fresh for a mild flavour and good colour in salads; use older leaves cooked in place of spinach, or to flavour soups

POT MARIGOLD

(*Calendula officinalis* – Compositae)

Bright and bold splashes of flower colour in the herb garden and in summer salads are the gifts of pot marigold. Petals can also be dried for pot-pourri.

type	Hardy annual
flowers	Large orange to yellow daisy flowers from late spring to autumn
leaves	Large spoon-shaped leaves form a basal mound with light green, strappy leaves growing up flowering stems
height	30–60cm (12–24in)
spread	30–45cm (12–18in)
planting	Once you have grown marigold you will always have it, as it is a prolific self sower. Remove spent flower heads to prevent it spreading and remove unwanted seedlings in spring
position	Any, but best in sun
soil	Will grow in poor soil, but well-drained, fertile soil is best. Will not do well in waterlogged conditions

care Deadhead for prolonged flowering. Thin out seedlings so plants have space to grow well

propagation Sow seed in spring into the growing site. Cover with 1cm (½in) of soil. Can also be sown in autumn for earlier flowering in spring. May need to cover seedlings with a cloche in cold areas. Sow single seed into pots for indoor growing and window boxes

species and varieties Available in double and single forms in many named varieties

harvest Harvest flowers just as they open from late spring through to autumn. Use fresh, dry or freeze whole flower heads. Can also be preserved in or used to flavour olive oil

herbal value Use petals fresh in salads or dried in pot-pourri. Can also be used to make face cream and in bath bags

SUMMER PURSLANE
(*Portulaca oleracea* – Portulacaceae)

Purslane's mildly flavoured leaves and stems add a crunchy taste to salads. In the herb garden it makes a decorative ground cover around taller-growing herbs.

type Half-hardy annual

flowers Small yellow flowers from late summer through to autumn, but best to nip them out

leaves Oval-shaped succulent green or gold leaves

height 15cm (6in)

spread 30cm (12in)

planting Sow into seed trays in mid-spring or direct into the ground in early summer, barely covering the seed with compost or soil

position Sheltered in full sun

soil Tolerates most soil conditions, but best on light and well-drained soil

care Remove flower buds to keep leaf production going. Protect young plants from slugs. Keep well watered and it will be ready to harvest six weeks from sowing

propagation Sow seed in rows and thin out to 15cm (6in) apart. Keep sowing through the summer for a succession of fresh leaves

species and varieties Summer purslane comes in upright, creeping and golden-leaved forms

harvest Cut leaves throughout the summer, to use fresh. Can be preserved with vinegar and pickling spice to use with meat. If the plant is allowed to flower, the leaves will not be so flavoursome

herbal value Use fresh leaves and stems in salads, vinaigrettes and mixed with soft cheese to make a sandwich filling. Use with fish, meat or egg dishes, but add just before serving. Use with sorrel in sorrel soup

SWEET ROCKET
(*Hesperis matronalis* – Cruciferae)

Height and sweet fragrance are the dual offerings of sweet rocket, an old-fashioned cottage garden plant.

type Short-lived herbaceous perennial, usually treated as a biennial

flowers Long flower spikes with many small flowers in white, mauve or purple from summer through to early autumn. Scent is more pronounced in the early evening

leaves Small, dark green, lance-shaped

height 60–90cm (24–36in)

spread 45cm (18in)

planting Thin or transplant to a distance of 45cm (18in) in autumn. Plant in clumps for good colour effect

position Best in full sun, but will tolerate partial shade

soil Prefers a rich, moist but well-drained soil

care Cut off flowering spikes once flowers are over. New flower stems will grow, though shorter than the first stems. In exposed sites plants may need staking

propagation Sow in mid-spring in an outdoor seed bed. Thin or transplant to the growing site in autumn. Sow into the growing site in autumn for early spring flowering

species and varieties *Hesperis matronalis* 'Nana Candidissima', grows to 45cm (18in). For deep purple flowers grow *H.m.* 'Purpurea'

harvest Pick young leaves before flowering to use fresh. Pick flowers to use fresh or to dry for later use

herbal value A few young leaves add a spicy bite to salads. Use flowers to flavour and decorate salads. Add dried flowers to pot-pourri

Sweet rocket

Summer purslane

M A Y

J U N E

As the warmth of early summer settles in, the herb garden becomes
a fast-growing, jungle-like centre of activity. Many herb plants
are just ready to burst into flower. Lemon verbena, pot marigold,
elder, sweet cicely and cumin are among the season's flowers.
Now, just before flowers open, is a good time to harvest herb
leaves. Their aromatic oils, always potent in full sun, are at their
best before flowering. Start harvesting flowers as well for drying to
use in pot-pourri, scented sachets or bath preparations.
Despite the need to harvest, dry, and later store the first bounty
from your herb garden, you will also discover quieter pleasures to
savour in the midsummer herb scene. It is a time to enjoy the shape
and spread of the plants themselves. Many that started as neat
and compact mounds will now be soft and lax in their growth.
In the kitchen, the herb-centred activity continues with the creation
of classic culinary sauces to use fresh or to freeze for later use.
Most herb leaves are sublime used fresh, but turned into splendid
sauces and frozen, you can later bring back the tastes and flavours
of the summer's best offerings.
From the rose garden, scented rose petals, rosebuds and full-
blown flowers offer plentiful fragrant kitchen and cosmetic
delights. Use the petals fresh to flavour sugar that will add
summer's fragrance to desserts and cakes later in the year. Dried
petals will add the same perfume to pot-pourri to bring summer
indoors in autumn and winter.
It is time to think ahead to another season and make sowings of
landcress, winter purslane and parsley so that you have salad
herbs to come. If you want to increase your stock of herbs such as
tarragon, lemon verbena and myrtle, take softwood cuttings now.
Although it is a busy season of harvesting and preserving, make
sure that you leave the plants looking balanced and attractive, so
that you can continue to enjoy them as they grow in the garden.

tasks
FOR THE
month

CHECKLIST

- Start harvesting and preserving herb leaves
- Sow seed outdoors for winter salad herbs
- Take softwood cuttings
- Divide thyme, pennyroyal and lawn chamomile
- Move tender herbs in pots outdoors
- Pinch out flowering shoots to encourage leafy growth
- Harvest flowers for pot-pourri and for use in salads

THE HERB HARVEST

Although evergreen herbs such as thyme and bay will provide you with fresh leaves for cooking throughout the year, and herbaceous perennials such as fennel and marjoram offer leaves from spring to autumn, there is something special about harvesting and preserving your own herbs. You can dry, freeze or preserve them in vinegar or oil for your own use or for gifts.

Start harvesting your herbs as soon as they show signs of good leafy growth. Let annuals and herbaceous perennials grow into a good shape before you begin cutting. If you want to cut a large quantity, take material from each plant in an even-handed way, so that the plants look balanced. Avoid overcutting, or the plant may look lopsided and may not recover well enough to grow new shoots for later use.

When to pick
For the most flavoursome leaves, pick before the plants come into flower – then the aromatic oils in leaves and stems will be at their most potent. Pick leafy herb shoots on dry sunny days. Cut them early in the day, after the sun has dried off the morning dew, but before it gets too hot.

Only cut as much material as you can handle easily in one drying or preserving session. Use flat wooden boxes, a garden trug or ordinary kitchen trays to collect the herbs as you cut them. Don't heap them in the trays as they will damage easily.

Pick herb flowers either in bud or when they are just open. Be gentle with them as you pick so that they do not get damaged or bruised. If you are drying them to use in winter arrangements, keep their stems long.

DRYING HERBS

Warmth, good air circulation and shade are the basic requirements for herb drying. Speed and gentle handling are also essential. If you intend drying small quantities only, place them on several layers of kitchen towel on a baking sheet and dry them in a cool oven, warming drawer or airing cupboard. For a more serious herb harvest, use your herb drying frame in a warm room or shed (see p14).

Work in the shade in a cool site as you prepare the herbs. Cut individual leaves off stems and place them on the drying rack. Only dry material that is in good condition. Discard any weather- or insect-damaged leaves or flowers. If herbs have dust or soil on them, wash it off and allow plant to dry before picking leaves.

Drying takes place gradually over a number of days. At first provide a high temperature of 32°C (90°F), then for the rest of the drying time 24°C (76°F). With constant heat, good ventilation and shade, most herbs will dry well in about a week. If you cannot provide constant temperatures the herbs will take up to a fortnight to dry and may lose flavour.

Herbs can also be dried in bunches. Some people use them in a decorative way in the kitchen. This, however, is not the best place to dry herbs. It has a moist, light atmosphere and the herbs are likely to be swamped by other culinary smells.

Tie woody-stemmed herbs such as rosemary, sage and bay into bundles of ten and hang them upside down from hooks or pegged to wire coat-hangers in your drying shed or room. It is best to dry individual types in single bunches, as the drying time for different herbs varies. Never cram too many herbs into one bunch, as the stems in the middle may become mouldy.

(Herbs can also be preserved by freezing or microwaving. For instructions on these methods, see p101).

NOTE

● *Herbs contain up to 70 per cent water and start losing their moisture content as soon as they are picked. Make sure you get the drying process started quickly to retain colour, flavour and the herb's essential oils.* ■

STORING DRIED HERBS

When crisp to the touch, crumble the leaves and store in airtight jars in a cool place. Either store in dark containers (glass or plastic) or in a dark place, as they deteriorate in strong sunlight. If well dried they keep their flavour for up to 18 months.

USING ROSES

Apart from enjoying their fragrant and decorative blooms in the garden, you can use rosebuds, petals, leaves and even the rose fruits – rose hips – to make herbal gifts and culinary products.

Always pick flowers early in the day, when the dew has dried but before the sun draws out the essential oils.

Petals
- crystallise to decorate cakes
- dry to use in pot-pourri
- use fresh to flavour sugar
- use as an edible garnish or addition to salads

Buds
- use dried whole in pot-pourri
- use dried in place of cloves in foam-based pomanders

Fruits *(rose hips, harvested in autumn)*
- use to make jellies, sauces and wines

Leaves
- use as base for chocolate leaves to decorate cakes

Crystallised rose petals
Separate the petals from the flower head, discard any blemished petals, then dip each one into a bowl of beaten egg white and dust with caster sugar. Leave the petals on a wire rack to dry in a warm place for several hours or overnight. Once dry, store in layers between sheets of greaseproof paper in an airtight tin or box.

Rose water
Make rose water for a scented face- or handwash by infusing 25g (1oz) of fresh fragrant red rose petals in 600ml (1pt) boiling water. Leave the petals to soak and cool for two hours, then strain through muslin. Pour the liquid into individual bowls for fingerbowls or into a decorative china bowl for a guest bedroom. Float one or two fresh petals in the rose water.

Rose vinegar
Use the darkest red, heaviest-scented roses to make a highly flavoured vinegar. Use all the petals from about four large flowers. Separate the petals and remove the whitish base of each petal, as this may impart a bitter flavour.
Place the prepared petals in a china bowl. Add 1.2L (2pt) wine vinegar. Use a wooden spoon to stir and bruise the rose petals to allow their flavour to escape into the vinegar. Leave to soak in a dark place for up to seven days. Strain through muslin and pour into clean and sterilised bottles. Seal with cork or non-metallic stoppers. Store away from light.

Rose sugar
To make rose-flavoured sugar use 60g (2oz) rose petals to 450g (1lb) caster sugar. Place the sugar and rose petals into a jar in alternate layers. Shake the jar vigorously once a day for two weeks. Keep it sealed, away from light and in a warm place. After fourteen days, sieve the rose petals out and dry the sugar in a cool oven. Store it in an airtight container in a cool, dry and dark store cupboard. Use it in baking and for desserts.

Dried rose-petal powder
Spread rose petals on a large wire sieve or muslin-covered herb-drying rack. Leave them in a warm, dry but well-ventilated place to dry. When they crumble to the touch, place them in a bowl and pound into rose powder with a pestle or wooden meat tenderiser. Store in tightly-stoppered bottles or jars in a dark place. Use the powder to refresh pot-pourri or to fill fragrant drawer sachets.

A rose bag
Use dried petals and rosebuds to fill muslin or cotton squares. Fill the centre of the fabric with the rose petals, dried cloves and dried eau-de-cologne mint leaves. Hold the four corners of the fabric together and secure the neck of the bag with a ribbon.

USING HERBS IN THE KITCHEN

Everything you prepare in the kitchen benefits from a handful of herbs fresh from the garden. Certain herbs are always used with particular dishes, such as rosemary with lamb and dill with fish. There are also some classic combinations that have produced famous sauces and flavourings. But apart from these uses, the fun of herb growing lies in experimenting and finding the taste and flavour that you enjoy most.

Herb butter
Use chives, parsley, chervil, thyme, marjoram and basil to make aromatic butters to serve with cooked meat, vegetables or to spread on fresh bread. Chop the herbs finely, mix them into softened butter, then shape the butter into rounds or sausage shapes. Wrap and store in the refrigerator or freeze.

Flavouring desserts
Use rose- or lemon-scented pelargonium leaves to flavour sorbets and ice creams, and add them to cake mixtures to decorate and flavour. Rosemary adds a spicy flavour to baked rice puddings, while angelica and sweet cicely leaves lessen acidity in cooked gooseberry and rhubarb puddings.

Herb sugars
Rosemary, lavender, scented pelargonium and lemon balm leaves can be used to flavour sugar. Use the flavoured sugar to make cakes, biscuits, to flavour cream and in desserts (see rose sugar).

Herb salts
For extra flavour in table salt and to use in cooking, add herbs such as sage, basil, rosemary, thyme, bay and marjoram to sea or ordinary cooking salt. Put the mix in airtight glass containers and shake every day for ten days. Spread the salt over baking sheets to dry in a cool oven and store in airtight containers.

CLASSIC HERB MIXTURES

BOUQUET GARNI
A bundle or bouquet of fresh or dried herb sprigs tied together with string or wrapped in muslin bags. Parsley, thyme and bay are the traditional *bouquet garni* herbs. The herb bundle is added to soups and casseroles, or any dish that involves lengthy cooking in liquid, and removed at the end of the cooking time.

FINES HERBES
Parsley, chervil, chives and tarragon are chopped, in equal parts and used to make a classic *fines herbes* mixture. They are either used in dishes that require a short cooking time or added near the end of the cooking time. They are not removed, and their subtle aromas enhance the delicate flavour of fish and egg dishes such as omelettes and soufflés.

STRONGLY AROMATIC HERBS

Basil – Used chopped to make basil butter, pesto sauce, in tomato and mozarella cheese salad.

Bay – Always used in *bouquet garni* and with poached fish or poultry.

Caraway – Leaves used in spicy salads, soups and stews.

Coriander – Leaves used in North and South American, Indian, Thai and Middle Eastern cuisines. Strong spicy flavour raw or cooked.

Marjoram – Much used in Italian and Greek cooking.

Mint – Used to make a sauce with vinegar, or a jelly, always associated with lamb. It is also used to flavour sorbets, ice cream and fruit salads. Delicious with cucumbers and new peas, and leaves can be crystallised to use for decoration.

Sage – Usually used with pork and sausages. Used to make onion and apple stuffings for poultry or pork.

Thyme – Used with poultry and in salads.

practical project

CREATING A HERBAL ROSE GARDEN

Old roses with soft colours, informal flower shapes and deep fragrance are traditionally associated with herb gardens. Part of their charm is that they need little maintenance, other than light pruning in spring to keep their shape. They grow into shrubby plants with a flush of flowers that are delightful visually, as well as aromatically. Their flowering season is relatively short compared to modern roses, but you can continue to enjoy their colour and fragrance in many edible and scented ways. Some old roses have been bred over the years to flower continuously and are called 'repeat-flowering'.

The full and blowsy flowers of all old roses suit the soft edges of informal, circular plantings. The stylised rose-flower design here offers several possibilities. You can plant a different rose in each section or plan for just three species – one in the inner circle and the other two alternating in the six outer circles. Choose fragrant herbs and other garden plants to grow at the base of the roses.

- To mark the central circle, place the marker cane where you wish the centre of the rose garden to be. Tie a piece of string 45cm (18in) long to it. Hold the string tightly and insert canes into the ground at intervals to mark the edge of the circle.

- Repeat the process using a piece of string 1.8m (6ft) long to mark the edge of the outer circle.

- To divide the circle into six segments, peg a piece of string across the centre of the circle (A–A). Lay a 1.8m (6ft) stick from A and mark the point (B) where it touches the edge of the circle. Peg a string across B–B and repeat the process (C–C). Leave the pegs and strings in place.

- To measure and mark the scalloped edges of the rose bed, find the mid-point of the outer edge of each segment. Use the 1.8m (6ft) straight stick with the centre point Y

YOU WILL NEED

central marker cane
24 canes
string
silver sand

PLANTS FOR THE ROSE GARDEN

UNDERPLANTING SCHEME FOR CENTRAL BED

Rosa alba 'Madame Plantier'
1.8 × 3m (6 × 10ft) almost thornless pure white, scented pom-pom flowers (suitable for pot-pourri)
greyish-green foliage
Grow against an iron or wooden rose tripod

CENTRAL BED

For a spring display, combine:
lily-of-the-valley (Convallaria majalis)
white grape hyacinths (Muscari botryoides 'Album')
blue grape hyacinths (Muscari armeniacum)

For a show throughout the year:
Lamium maculatum 'White Nancy' ground-covering

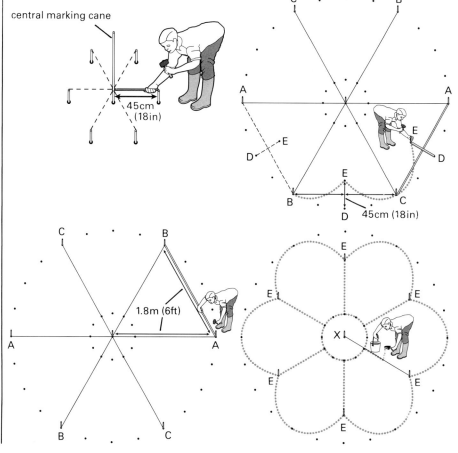

central marking cane

45cm (18in)

1.8m (6ft)

45cm (18in)

marked on it. Lay a ruler at right angles to this touching the edge of the circle at point D. Measure 45cm (18in) and mark point E with a cane or peg. Repeat this process six times to mark the inner points of the scalloped edges.

■ Finally, mark out the rose-shaped bed so that you can plant it up. Use silver sand to mark out the curves that form the petals of the design. Use a string attached to the central marker cane X to each point E as a guideline for the final divisions.

■ Now you are ready to plant up the six outer sections and the inner circle with old roses and attractive herb and garden plants.

ALTERNATIVE ROSE CHOICE

Gallica roses ■ *Rosa gallica officinalis* or Apothecary's rose
Damask roses
■ 'Madame Hardy', ■ 'Ispahan',
Alba roses ■ 'Königin von Dänemark'
■ 'Maiden's Blush'
Moss roses
■ 'Old Pink Moss' ■ 'William Lobb'
Centifolia roses
■ 'Tour de Malakoff'
Repeat-flowering old roses
■ China, Portland and Bourbon.
China roses
■ 'Hermosa', ■ 'Old Blush China'
Portland roses
■ 'Comte de Chambord'
■ 'Rose de Rescht'
Bourbon roses
■ 'Boule de Neige', ■ 'Louise Odier'

PLANTS FOR THE ROSE GARDEN

INNER CIRCLE
Rosa 'Madame Plantier'

AROUND EDGE OF INNER CIRCLE
Combine:
forget-me-nots
chives.
Use either ordinary chives (mauve pom-pom flowers) or garlic chives (starry white flowers)

OUTER SEGMENTS
For a pleasing design, use only two species planted into alternate segments:
1 *Rosa gallica* 'Versicolor' *(Rosa mundi)*
1.2 × 1.2m (4 × 4ft) simple, single flowers with crimson and white markings on petals.
2 *Rosa gallica* 'Charles de Mills'
1.2 × 1.5m (4 × 5ft) full, closely packed crimson petals, deepening to purple as they age

UNDERPLANTING SCHEME FOR OUTER SEGMENTS
Use six different thymes, some upright and some creeping, to form a tapestry of colour at the feet of the roses:
3 *Thymus* 'Doone Valley'
light mauve flowers lemon-scented leaves splashed with gold
4 *T.* 'Pink Chintz'
pink flowers textured leaves and stems
5 *T.* 'Russetings'
pink to purple flowers dark green leaves
6 *T. albus*
white flowers, small green leaves
7 *T. lanuginosus (woolly thyme)*
mauve flowers in late summer, a mat of woolly foliage
8 *T. vulgaris aureus (golden thyme)*
mauve flowers, golden foliage

Alternatively, plant these sections with violas and sweet violets

PATH PLANTS
For path strips between each section and around the inner circle:
9 *silver-edged alchemilla (Alchemilla alpina)*
10 *dwarf lavender (Lavandula angustifolia 'Hidcote Blue')*

Separate plants with stepping stones or group of three bricks

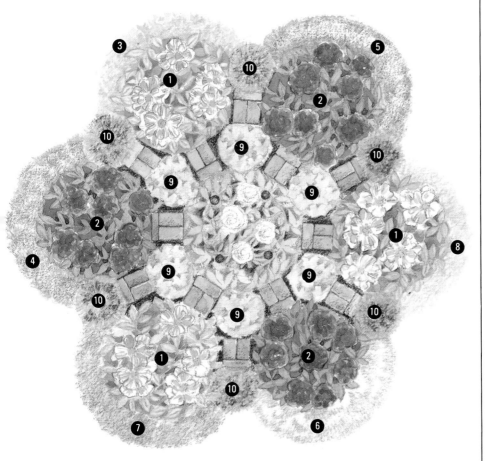

plants
OF THE
month

Basil

BASIL
(*Ocimum basilicum* – Labiatae)

In the kitchen, basil's aromatic leaves bring a spicy flavour to salads and Mediterranean dishes; in the herb garden in high summer its leaves and flowers offer a range of colour and fragrance.

type	Short-lived perennial grown as a half-hardy annual in cold areas
flowers	Several groups of small white, yellow and pink flowers in late summer, arranged in clusters on flowering stems
leaves	Leaves vary in size, but are oval-shaped. Also varieties with curly edges and bright or dark green, purple and green, and purple variegated foliage
height	20–90cm (8–36in) depending on variety
spread	30cm (12in)
planting	Plant outdoors after all danger of frost is over, or grow in pots indoors
position	Sunny, sheltered position, warm windowsill or greenhouse
soil	Light, well drained
care	Water in dry conditions; keep plants in containers well watered, but best to water around midday. Pinch out flowering stems to promote leaf production
propagation	Sow seed in early spring into trays of seed compost and provide a temperature of 13°C (56°F). Prick out at the two-leaf stage into larger seed trays and grow on in warmth. Harden off the seedlings and plant out after all danger of frost is over
species and varieties	Basil is available in a wide range of flower and leaf shape and colour. Choose anise basil with pale pink flowers and anise flavour, purple basil, green ruffles with fringed leaves, lemon-scented basil, Neopolitana basil and cinnamon basil
harvest	Pick and use leaves of outdoor plants fresh from summer to early autumn. Harvest indoor plants until early winter. Dry leaves in a cool oven or in an airing cupboard. Basil leaves freeze well
herbal value	Green ruffles and purple basil are decorative in the garden. Leaves are used fresh and dried in Italian and Asian cookery, especially Thai

cuisine. An infusion of basil leaves is thought to prevent travel sickness. Also useful as an invigorating bath herb. Preserve the flavour of basil in vinegars and oils

CLOVE PINK
(*Dianthus caryophyllus* – Caryophyllaceae)

Fragrant and colourful flowers combined with attractive grey foliage are the garden offerings of clove pink. The flowers are used fresh in the kitchen and can be dried to use in pot-pourri.

type	Evergreen perennial, but may need protection from frost in moist soil
flowers	Pale mauve to pink flowers in summer. Old-fashioned pinks bred from *Dianthus plumarius* flower for longer, in a range of colours including white, pink, red, yellow and bi-coloured
leaves	Long, narrow, pointed greyish-green leaves
height	25–40cm (10–16in)
spread	25–40cm (10–16in)
planting	Plant in spring or autumn 30cm (12in) apart
position	Full sun
soil	Well drained and alkaline
care	Divide crowded clumps in autumn and take cuttings. Pinch out the centre of young plants to ensure growth of side shoots
propagation	Species come true from seed sown from spring to late summer in seed trays in a cold frame or unheated greenhouse. Take cuttings from named cultivars in summer or early autumn. Plants can also be layered in summer
species and varieties	Clove pinks have a distinctive clove fragrance. Old-fashioned pinks include 'Mrs Sinkins' (white), 'Dad's Favourite' (white with crimson edges) and 'Inchmery' with double, pink flowers
harvest	Pick flowers with or without stalks to dry. Also dry petals individually on a drying frame
herbal value	Preserve fresh flowers in vinegar or crystallise them. Use flowers fresh in salads and cooked in fruit dishes. Remove the white base of the petals before using in food, as this gives a bitter flavour. Use dried flowers in pot-pourri

FRENCH MARIGOLD
(*Tagetes patula* – Compositae)

Use French marigold's bright yellow, golden or orange flowers to make the edge of a herb border sparkle. The flowers and leaves add aroma to pot-pourri and the roots deter weeds and soil pests.

type	Half-hardy annual
flowers	Yellow, golden or orange single or double flowers from early summer to late autumn
leaves	Strongly aromatic, finely divided and feathery-looking, dark green
height	30cm (12in)
spread	30cm (12in)
planting	Sow in the greenhouse in early spring to transplant when all threat of frost is over
position	Full sun
soil	Prefers fertile, well-drained soil but will grow in dry and poor conditions
care	Deadhead if not picking flowers for pot-pourri. Keep well watered
propagation	Sow seed in early spring into trays in a greenhouse and transplant to the growing site in late spring
species and varieties	*Tagetes tenuifolia* 'Tangerine Gem' has citrus-scented leaves and flowers. *T. lucida* has an anise fragrance
harvest	Harvest flowers as they open and separate individual petals to dry for pot-pourri. Similarly, harvest and dry individual leaves for pot-pourri
herbal value	Useful companion plants in the herb and vegetable gardens. Secretions from the roots act in the soil to deter pests such as eelworm. They also are thought to have a detrimental effect on weeds such as ground elder, bindweed and couch grass. Flowers and leaves add aroma and colour to pot-pourri

French marigold

LEMON VERBENA
(*Aloysia triphylla* syn. *Lippia citriodora* – Verbenaceae)

Lemon-scented leaves and delicate clusters of small white and purple flowers are the attractions of lemon verbena. Outdoors it needs protection from frost; indoors it grows well in pots.

type	Half-hardy, deciduous shrub
flowers	Pale mauve and whitish flowers arranged in clusters, in late summer and early autumn
leaves	Long, oval leaves with strong vein markings and lemon fragrance
height	Up to 1.5m (5ft). In containers in cold climates it is often smaller. In hot climates it grows to 4.5m (15ft)
spread	Up to 1.2m (4ft)
planting	Sow seed in spring and plant out in pots or into the ground when all danger of frost is over
position	Full sun, in a sheltered position. In cold climates grow it in containers to bring into a heated greenhouse or conservatory in winter
soil	Well drained
care	Cut back outdoor plants and protect crowns with straw in winter. Or lift and repot, and keep in a heated greenhouse over winter. Prune lightly in spring to make small plants bush out
propagation	Sow seed in spring or take softwood cuttings in summer. Pot them up in a sand and peat or peat alternative mix. Keep cuttings under cover and plant out the following spring
harvest	Pick leaves all through the growing season, but fragrance is best before or just as the plant comes into flower. Dry in small bunches or strip leaves off and dry on a frame
herbal value	Use fresh to flavour oil and vinegar and in salads. Dry leaves for tea. Use dried leaves in pot-pourri, and scent bath bags and pillows. Also use fresh in sauces, cakes and fruit desserts

Clove pink

The most practical of herb gardens has a kitchen theme and is packed with as many favourite culinary herbs as possible. Even though it will be constantly harvested, the garden can still be designed to provide both decorative and practical features.

For convenience, choose a sunny site close to the kitchen door. A circle or wheel shape provides attractive form and, depending on size, holds a wide selection of herb plants. Divide the circle into cheese-wedge sections and plant up each segment. You could specialise in a particular herb such as mint, and use the sections to grow as many types as you can find. Try planting a few herbs densely, or numerous herbs in lower concentrations but in an ornamental design.

practical project 2

PLANTING A CIRCLE OF KITCHEN HERBS

MATERIALS

central marker cane, 24 canes, string

silver sand, stepping stones

slates to divide mint sections (optional)

■ Place the marker cane where you wish the centre of the circle to be. Tie a piece of string 1.8m (6ft) long to it. Tie the other end of the string to a second cane. With the string taut, drag the cane through the soil to mark the outer edge of the circle.

■ Mark the circle edge with silver sand.

■ To divide the circle into eight segments, use the silver sand to mark the diameter of the circle in two places, A–A and B–B. Find the mid-point between A and B. Hold the string taut and make sure it passed through point C. Where it reaches point D at the edge of the circle, place a cane.

■ Repeat the process for the other segments, then mark out the edges of each segment with silver sand.

■ If you are growing an invasive plant like mint, keep each type in check by sinking slates on edge into the soil.

■ Put the stepping stones in place before you begin planting. The stones allow you access to the central parts of the herb garden without compacting the soil or damaging the plants.

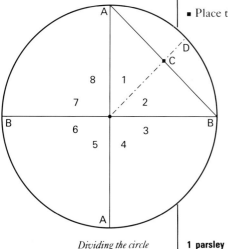

Dividing the circle

1 parsley
2 flat-leaved parsley
3 chives
4 garlic chives
5 salad burnet
6 borage
7 lemon thyme
8 creeping thyme
9 purple sage
10 green sage
11 fennel
12 lovage
13 chervil
14 savory
15 rosemary/bay
16 good King Henry
17 coriander
18 sweet Cicely

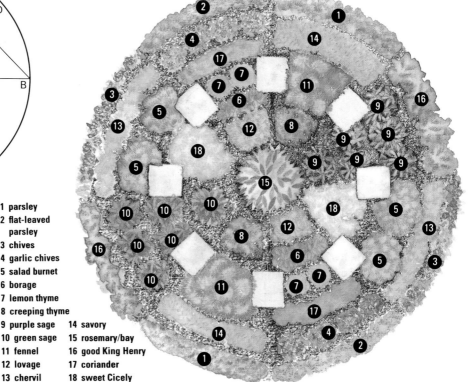

1 garlic
2 dill
3 salad rocket
4 common thyme
5 summer savory
6 chives
7 sweet bay
8 chervil
9 golden marjoram
10 large-leaved basil
11 *Thymus* 'Silver Posy'
12 coriander
13 golden thyme
14 rosemary (prostrate)
15 garlic chives
16 purple basil
17 sweet basil
18 lemon balm
19 tarragon
20 tri-colour sage
21 good King Henry
22 sorrel
23 oregano
24 flat-leaved parsley
25 sweet Cicely
26 Welsh onion
27 moss-leaved parsley
28 winter savory
29 salad burnet
30 tree onion
31 purple sage

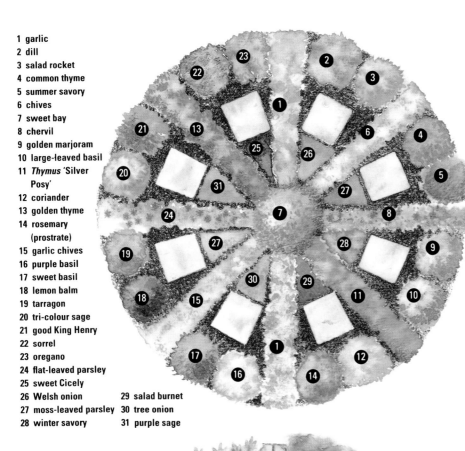

MAINTAINING A CULINARY HERB GARDEN

ANNUALS

Grow from seed each spring. Suitable herbs include basil (sow outdoors in early summer or start in pots in the greenhouse in spring) chervil, coriander, dill, salad rocket and summer savory

BIENNIALS

Sow direct into the ground in spring. Make further sowings through the season to ensure good supplies of flat-leaf and curly parsley and chervil. Plant garlic bulbs in autumn and spring to make sure you have a supply all year round

PERENNIALS

Most perennials need light pruning to keep their shape and encourage leafy growth. To ensure maximum leaf production, cut out flowering stems of sage, marjoram, salad burnet, chives, lemon balm and thyme. Allow some flowering stems to grow, though, so you have flowers to use in salads and to dry.

Some perennials, such as sweet bay and tarragon, need winter protection in cold areas. You can also force tarragon and mint into growth in winter by potting them up and bringing them into a warm room or greenhouse.

Thymes need light pruning to keep their shape and prevent upright types becoming too woody. Clip them back in early spring and again after flowering is finished.

Chives and garlic chives should be lifted and divided in autumn or early spring. Cut them back after flowering and remove any slimy leaves in winter.

A mint wheel

1 sage
2 parsley
3 chives
4 thyme
5 chervil
6 garlic
7 marjoram
8 basil
9 rosemary or bay

plants
OF THE
month

Musk Mallow

MUSK MALLOW
(*Malva moschata* – Malvaceae)

Musk mallow, once used in herbal medicine, is now prized for its strongly scented summer flowers and attractive, deeply cut foliage.

type	Hardy herbaceous perennial
flowers	Pink-tinged fragrant white flowers from summer to early autumn
leaves	Lower leaves are rounded, while upper leaves are finely cut. They have a musky fragrance when crushed
height	90cm (36in)
spread	30cm (12in)
planting	Plant seedlings in mid-autumn from a spring-sown nursery bed
position	Sun or partial shade
soil	Well-drained, average garden soil. In moist, rich soil it grows larger
care	Stake large, bushy plants. Cut back in autumn
propagation	Sow seed in late spring in trays in a greenhouse or cold frame at a temperature of 16°C (62°F). Take cuttings in autumn and plant into the growing site once rooted
species and varieties	*Malva moschata* 'Alba' has pure white flowers, *M.m.* 'Rosea' has pink flowers
harvest	Leaves and seeds are edible, and flowers or seed heads are useful in dried arrangements. Pick when flowers are just opening and once seed heads have formed
herbal value	Attractive as indoor dried flower decoration. Leaves can be cooked and eaten as a green vegetable

MYRTLE
(*Myrtus communis* – Myrtaceae)

Myrtle's delicate, white-scented flowers and aromatic, evergreen leaves provide ornament in the garden and have many culinary and household uses, both fresh and dried.

type	Half-hardy evergreen shrub
flowers	Fragrant, creamy-white flowers with large gold-yellow stamens from summer to autumn
leaves	Small, dark green, shiny leaves with a strong citrus aroma
height	2.4–3m (8–10ft), but if grown in a container not more than 60–90cm (2–3ft)
spread	60–90cm (2–3ft)
planting	In mild climates, plant outdoors in spring and protect from frost if necessary. Grows well in containers and indoors
position	Full sun but sheltered. Indoors or in a heated greenhouse in winter
soil	In containers, needs good loam soil with added grit to improve drainage, otherwise well-drained garden soil
care	Can be clipped into formal shapes, but no pruning necessary. Water container-grown myrtle frequently
propagation	Take 5–7.5cm (2–3in) stem cuttings in summer or layer one or two stems
species and varieties	*Myrtus communis* 'Variegata' has prettily mixed cream and green leaves, while *M. c. tarentina* has a shorter, more compact habit and smaller leaves
harvest	Pick buds and flowers in season, and leaves all through the year
herbal value	Use buds fresh in salads, flowers and leaves dried for pot-pourri.

ROSE
(*Rosa* species – Rosaceae)

Old roses offer fragrant and colourful flowers for ornament in the herb garden. In the home, their petals can be used fresh to flavour food or dried to add perfume and colour to pot-pourri.

type	Hardy deciduous shrub or climber
flowers	White, crimson, pink or bi-coloured depending on species and variety. From late spring until midsummer
leaves	Light to greyish-green with five to seven leaflets
height	90cm–3m (3–10ft) depending on individual species
spread	Up to 3m (10ft)
planting	Plant container-grown roses any time during the year and bare-root stock from early winter to spring. Dig in compost
position	Full sun or partial shade
soil	Fertile, well-drained loam
care	Remove spent flowers unless the fruit, or hips, that follow are ornamental
propagation	Usually bought as plants
species and varieties	There are many species and varieties to choose from
harvest	Pick rosebuds at late bud stage, with stems attached. Hang three to five stems. Bunch to air dry, upside down. Pick hips when fully ripe. Use fresh or dried.

herbal value Rosehips and petals have many culinary uses (p64-5). Rose buds are dried and used in pot-pourri (p127).

SCENTED PELARGONIUM
(*Pelargonium* species – Geraniaceae)

Scented pelargoniums have delicately cut and softly textured leaves full of aromatic oils. Their fragrance is released when crushed or brushed against.

type	Tender evergreen perennial
flowers	Small mauve, purple to pink, red and white flowers bloom in summer and autumn
leaves	Softly textured with finely cut or wavy edges. Fresh green, variegated white and green, dark and light green in colour, depending on species
height	Usually 30–60cm (12–24in)
spread	Usually 30–60cm (12–24in)
planting	Plant outdoors in the ground or in containers in summer, but bring indoors in winter in cold climates
position	Sun or partial shade
soil	Well-drained potting compost or loamy garden soil
care	Pinch out growing points to make plants bushy and leafy. If allowed to flower, deadhead afterwards. Water container-grown plants frequently and cut back before overwintering indoors
propagation	Sow seed in spring or take cuttings in late summer or autumn
species and varieties	*Pelargonium radens* has a mixed rose-citrus scent and finely cut leaves; *P. crispum* 'Variegatum' has curly white-edged leaves with a lemon balm scent; *P. graveolens* has a peppermint scent
harvest	For best fragrance pick leaves before flowering, or if flowers are nipped out, pick through the season. Dry individual leaves on a drying frame. Can be used fresh

herbal value Use leaves fresh to make fragrant ice cream, to flavour butter and sugar, and in sauces. Crystallise for cake decorations, lining base and sides of cake tins with leaves. Use flowers in salads. Add dried leaves and flowers to pot-pourri

THYME
(*Thymus* species – Labiatae)

Thyme, whether upright or creeping in form, provides aromatic leaves and dense clusters of pink, white or mauve flowers.

type	Hardy evergreen sub-shrub
flowers	Pink, mauve, white flowers in early to late summer
leaves	Has small, spike-shaped or round aromatic leaves, varying in colour
height	Varies from 2.5–30cm (1–12in)
spread	From 10–45cm (4–18in)
planting	Plant low-growing thymes on paths, rockeries or between stepping stones 10cm (4in) apart. Upright thymes grow well as edging or specimen plants
position	Full sun
soil	Well drained
care	After flowering, cut back to promote new growth. Prune frequently during the growing season. Replace plants after three to four years if woody. Protect in very cold areas in winter and bring woolly thyme (*T. lanuginosus*) indoors
propagation	Take heel cuttings from stems in spring, summer or autumn. Divide mat-forming clumps or layer stems in spring or autumn. Sow seed of species such as *T. vulgaris* into seed trays in early spring, prick out and plant in autumn
species and varieties	There are many species and varieties to choose from
harvest	Use fresh throughout the year. In winter, use dried thyme as it has more flavour than fresh leaves. Hang small bunches to air dry in a warm, dark but airy shed
herbal value	Use for cooking to make *bouquet garni*, stuffings (see p65), chop into salads, and add to apple jelly to serve with meat dishes. Use to flavour oils and vinegar, to scent baths and to make a hair rinse. Add to pot-pourri

Myrtle

Old rose

JULY

In midsummer, growth in the herb garden is at its peak. Plants outgrow their allotted places and supports and, as they sprawl and bump into neighbouring plants, make their own patterns and associations, playing tricks with the eye.

Take advantage of this natural surge of activity and turn leaves, flowers and seeds into herbal produce. Flowers are ready to pick for use in fragrant bath bags, floral waters and aromatic shampoos. Many flowers can still be used to flavour salads and other dishes, while the first seeds are ready to harvest.

Part of the cut-and-preserve activity of midsummer is directed towards increasing your stock of plants by taking cuttings, especially from tender shrubby herbs such as lemon verbena, scented pelargoniums and some lavenders. Now is also the time to start thinking about your indoor herb garden to keep you in fresh herbs over the winter.

If your herb garden is centred around plants to produce colourful dyes, this will be a busy time controlling growth, drying plants and getting ready to use them to dye wool or fabric.

At this time you may wish to increase your stock of plants to use for the creation of a new herb area, to offer as gifts to friends, or to sell. It is also useful to take cuttings from herbs that may be tender in your climate, such as lemon verbena, some lavenders and scented pelargoniums.

In midsummer take a dispassionate look at the herb garden when the plants are growing well. It is a good time to see where you may have made mistakes. You can tell if you have planted too closely or if tall plants are in the wrong place, obscuring their shorter neighbours. Make notes of any changes you would like to make, but wait until autumn to carry them out.

tasks

FOR THE

month

CHECKLIST

- Continue taking softwood cuttings, especially from tender plants
- Start taking semi-ripe cuttings and layering stems
- Continue outdoor sowing of winter salad herbs
- Continue to pinch out flowering stems of herbs for the leaf harvest
- Remove spent flowers to encourage more for the flower harvest
- Harvest leaves and flowers of dye plants and of other herbs for salads and to dry for pot-pourri
- Start planning and sowing for the indoor herb garden
- Begin making moist pot-pourri

MAKING NEW PLANTS: CUTTINGS

As the year progresses you may need extra herb plants. You may wish to use them as replacements for damaged or over-picked plants, as additional plants to make a formal edge or neat hedge, or as gifts at the end of the year. Whatever the reason for needing to increase your stock, the most satisfying, relatively inexpensive and easy way to do this is by taking cuttings from existing plants.

Taking cuttings is also a plant insurance policy. It is always wise to take cuttings of plants that may be tender in your climate, such as scented pelargonium and lemon verbena. Then, if the parent plant doesn't overwinter well despite protection, you have new plants ready to grow away as soon as the temperature rises.

This form of plant reproduction is called 'vegetative' and it ensures that new plants with exactly the same growth habit and flower colour as the parent plant are produced. Uniformity is especially useful in a formal herb garden. Lavender grown from seed, for example, may have a range of flower colours and shapes.

Always use material from healthy, strong plants. There are several types of cutting, and certain times of the year when it is best to take them. The names indicate their stage of growth when taken.

- *Softwood cuttings* have soft, rather green stems and leaves They are taken from fresh shoots made from the first new bursts of growth in spring, or just after flowering.

- *Semi-ripe* or *semi-hardwood cuttings* are taken, as their name suggests, from slightly older growth. Their stems are just beginning to harden at the base, while the tips of the shoots are soft. They are best taken from midsummer through to the end of summer.

The method for taking the cuttings is the same for all types, except that they vary in length and the way you prepare them.

TAKING CUTTINGS

Never take more cuttings than you can deal with in one session, or they will wilt completely before you can get them potted up. Keep cuttings moist and in the shade until you can prepare them.

- Always use a sharp, clean knife to take cuttings. Cut off a healthy-looking non-flowering side shoot.

- For softwood cuttings, the best length is between 5–10cm (2–4in); for semi-ripe cuttings 10–15cm (4–6in).

- Cut the stem just below a set of leaves. If the cutting has a 'heel' or jagged part of the parent stem, trim this to a manageable size. Semi-ripe cuttings seem to root better if they are taken with heels.

- Remove the lower leaves as shown. You can dip the end of the cutting in hormone rooting powder, but most herb cuttings root well without such treatment.

Rooting

■ Fill a plant pot with a seed-sowing compost or a mixture of sharp sand and peat or peat alternative. No nutrients are necessary at this stage.

■ Moisten the growing medium and insert the cuttings around the edge of the pot. If you are taking cuttings in great quantity, use larger containers such as wooden boxes.

■ Once the cuttings are in place, allow them to recover before providing under-pot warmth and humidity. Heat encourages rooting and moist air keeps the cuttings from wilting and dying before roots are formed. The least complicated way to do this is by covering individual pots with polythene bags to make a moist and warm environment.

■ Use small stakes to keep the polythene off the cuttings and check their water needs daily. Place the pots in a warm but shaded site.

■ If you have a small electric propagating unit, where under-pot heating can be provided easily, rooting will be quicker. Cover the cuttings with the plastic dome of the propagator and mist them daily with water from a sprayer.

■ Avoid misting or enclosing in polythene herbs from hot countries such as rosemary, thyme and lavender, or herbs with felted, silvery or textured leaves. If their leaves are too moist, they are likely to develop mildew.

Potting on

Cuttings have taken root when you see signs of new growth above ground. New shoots and leaves indicate that the young plant is ready to be potted up individually and that you need to give it nutrients to keep it growing healthily. Remove the cuttings from their pot, taking care not to disturb their roots. Pot them into individual pots using a good potting compost. Grow them on in these pots until you can plant them out in the herb garden, bring them indoors to use in winter, or you are ready to offer them as gifts.

MAKING NEW PLANTS: LAYERING

Layering is another way to reproduce plants vegetatively. There is no need to separate the plant material from the parent plant at the beginning of the process. Simply pull down a strong-growing stem, and where it touches the ground dig a small hole, fill it with compost and peg the stem down into it with a stone or piece of wire. Cover the stem with soil, water it well and by the end of the growing season new roots will have developed on the stem. Either leave the daughter plant *in situ* until the following spring, or sever it in autumn and replant in a new position or into a container.

Layering can be done all through the growing season from spring until early autumn, but the earlier you start the sooner you will have new plants.

PLANNING AN INDOOR WINTER HERB GARDEN

With so much harvest activity, maintenance and cuttings preparation in high summer, it is easy to overlook plans for a winter herb garden. If you wish to have fresh, home-grown herbs over winter, however, you must take time to make plans. Of course, you can simply buy herb plants late in the season to grow in the kitchen, but it is more fun to prepare plants yourself. Sow annuals such as basil or biennials like parsley and chervil in late summer, or pot up herbs such as chives and keep them growing through the winter. Place them in a cool, shady site for a few weeks to simulate their winter dormant period. Take softwood cuttings of sage and tarragon in late summer to pot up for winter use.

THINGS TO DO

Harvest

Leaves: almost all herbs
Leaves for dyeing: dyer's greenweed, weld, woad
Flowers for drying: anise hyssop, chamomile, cotton lavender, dyer's chamomile, French marigold, German chamomile, hyssop, lavender, roses, safflower, scented pelargonium
Flowers for dyeing: agrimony, coreopsis, dyer's chamomile, safflower, weld
Roots: madder (in its third year), orris
Seeds: nasturtium (unripe)
Fruit: wild strawberry

Pot up

New sage and thyme plants from layered stems

Routine maintenance

■ Pinch out basil flowers to encourage bushy growth
■ Cut back flowering stems of lady's mantle
■ Prune box
■ As you harvest leaves and flowers, remove any dead or damaged shoots, and spent flowers and leaves
■ Water herbs in containers and hanging baskets

RELATIVE ROOTING TIME
Box and bay are slow to root and may take anything up to a year. Mint is relatively quick, taking up to a week; rosemary, sage or lavender take up to three weeks. Most semi-ripe cuttings take four to six weeks to root.

HARVESTING FOR POT-POURRI
Pick roses to use in moist pot-pourri. Harvest flowers for dry pot-pourri as they begin to open each month during summer. For colour accents use garden flowers such as golden rod, marigold, pansy, globe amaranth and larkspur.

practical project

THE DYER'S HERB GARDEN

FROM THE HERB GARDEN

FLOWERS FOR YELLOW OR ORANGE
(use alum and cream of tartar as mordant)

Chicory • Coreopsis •
Dyer's chamomile • Elecampane •
Feverfew • Honeysuckle •
Poppy • Roses • Tansy

LEAVES AND STALKS FOR SHADES OF GREEN
(mordant with iron)

Alexanders • Angelica •
Coriander • Dill • Fennel •
Lovage • Parsley • Sweet cicely

SURPRISE COLOURS
Be prepared for surprises along the way when using material from your own dye garden. Diversity of colour in the end product is part of the fun. Many factors influence the final colour of the dye: the age and maturity of the plant, the parts used, the weather conditions and soil that it has grown in, the type of mordant, and whether you are using it on wool, cotton or silk.

Madder, woad, weld, safflower and agrimony are the magical names of plants traditionally used to produce dye colours for wool and fabric. If you are keen to make your own dyes from home-grown dye plants, you need space for a separate dyer's herb garden area. You will need a basic minimum quantity to produce sufficient plant material for dye-making and many dye plants are thuggish in the way they grow; if allowed, they also self seed abundantly.

In the dyer's garden design illustrated here, the flower colours provide an overall yellow and green effect, which would be pretty in itself, although a working dyer's garden is not necessarily planted for its ornamental qualities as it grows.

Site the dye-plant garden in full sun, in fertile soil. If necessary, enrich the soil with herb compost when digging the ground over in early spring or autumn. To produce good material, many of the dye plants need frequent watering, so make sure you can get sufficient water to the site easily.

MANAGING THE DYER'S GARDEN

Plant woad and weld along the front of the garden. Both plants are biennials that produce flowers and seeds in their second year of growth. Normally, they would be too tall for the front of the bed, but for dyes you need leaves from the mounded rosettes of foliage that they produce in their first year. The basal rosettes are up to 30cm (12in) wide.

Neither plant grows well if transplanted, so it is best to sow seeds *in situ* in spring and cover with 1cm (½in) soil. Water well, and as the seedlings develop, thin out to 30cm (12in).

Harvest the leaves as you need them through their first summer. You will get in two to three cuts during the first growing season. At the end of the summer, either use all the remaining leaves for a big dyeing session, or dig the plants up and put them on the herb compost heap. In their second year the leaves of woad do not provide good colour.

If you want to grow woad to produce your own seed, sow just one plant in spring at the back of the garden. Allow this to continue growing in its second year, to flower and set seed. Make sure you harvest the seed from its abundantly filled seed pods before they burst and self sow over the garden. If not, woad will become a garden weed.

Sow annuals such as safflower and coreopsis in spring, in their permanent positions and thin out when the seedlings are large enough to handle. Plant perennials such as agrimony, dyer's chamomile, dyer's green-weed and madder in spring or autumn.

You can also grow agrimony and dyer's chamomile from seed. Sow them in spring when you sow annuals. Sow them all direct into their growing sites and thin out if necessary. Dyer's chamomile planted closely will later support each other. Similarly, closely-planted safflower will provide mutual support, but if the dyer's garden is in an exposed site, staking is essential for both.

Although dyer's greenweed can be grown

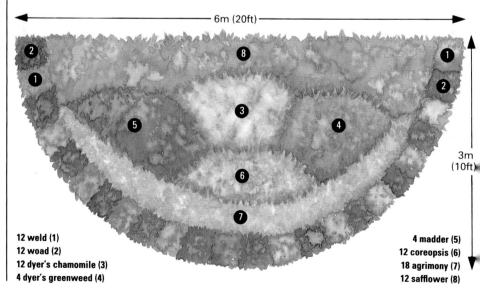

6m (20ft)

3m (10ft)

12 weld (1)
12 woad (2)
12 dyer's chamomile (3)
4 dyer's greenweed (4)

4 madder (5)
12 coreopsis (6)
18 agrimony (7)
12 safflower (8)

from seed, it will take one growing season before it flowers and at least that before it has made enough leafy growth for you to harvest for dye material. Buy sturdy young plants from specialist nurseries and set them into their final growing site, as they dislike root disturbance. Lightly prune stems in spring to stimulate lots of new stem growth for harvesting in summer.

Keep the dyer's garden weeded and water the plants frequently, especially in dry summers. Water is one of the main factors affecting the quality of dye produced from the plants.

Planting madder

When planting madder, mark out the planting area and dig in well-rotted herb compost to a depth of 30cm (12in). Set the plants 30cm (12in) apart. When the tops of the plants have grown to a height of 30cm (12in) pull the stems down to ground level and hold down with a little soil. This layering process encourages new stem and root production. Repeat two to three times during the growing season, and over the three years. By the time the madder bed is ready for harvest, the ground under the plants will be a mass of orangey-red roots, each the thickness of a pencil.

In the third autumn after planting the first madder bed, harvest the plants. Dig them up, cut off the roots and put the remaining plant material on the compost heap. If you wish, save a few plants to start off a new bed.

Before using the roots, wash them thoroughly and use fresh, or dry them. Once dry, grind them into powder and store for later use. Madder is non-toxic, but you will want to keep a blender specially for using with dye plants.

Using madder roots

If fresh madder roots are used, they must be soaked in hard water over night. The next day add the mordanted wool and slowly raise the temperature of the water. It is important not to boil madder at any stage in the dye process. If you do you will lose its strong red colour and the resulting dye will be dull and brown. Use a thermometer to check the water temperature and raise it to just under boiling point, 90°C (160°F). Simmer the wool for about 30 minutes, checking to see if it has taken up the colour well. Leave the wool to cool in the dye bath, then rinse it several times in warm water, then cool water, before squeezing water from wool and hanging it to dry in the shade.

MATERIALS AND MORDANTS

Wool is the easiest natural material to dye. Use white or 'natural' wool and wind into skeins weighing 60–120g (2–4oz). The wool must be clean for the dye to be taken up evenly, so wash it in warm water before you start.

Mordants are metallic salts that fix and intensify the colour in the fabric. They should be treated with respect, and be kept labelled and out of reach of children. Using different mordants, you can extract several colours from one plant. Madder, for example, produces vermilion with alum, bright red with chrome, chocolate-brown with iron, and orange with tin as the mordant.

Alum (aluminium potassium sulphate) is probably the best and safest mordant to use. It is also readily available from craft shops and chemists.

TIME FOR MADDER
It takes time – at least three growing seasons – and special treatment to encourage madder to produce the mass of roots necessary for dye. So start a new bed each year, to ensure a good supply in the future.

COLOURS ACHIEVED WITH DIFFERENT MORDANTS AND PLANTS

plant	alum	chrome	iron	tin
WELD				
(*Reseda luteola*)	clear lemon yellow	yellow	olive green	bright lemon-yellow
DYER'S CHAMOMILE				
(*Anthemis tinctoria*)	bright yellow			
AGRIMONY				
(*Agrimonia eupatoria*)	yellow	gold	khaki	bright yellow
MADDER				
(*Rubia tinctoria*)	ruby red	purplish-red	brown	bright orange
DYER'S GREENWEED				
(*Genista tinctoria*)	light yellow	warm yellow	olive green	bright yellow
SAFFLOWER				
(*Carthamus tinctorius*)	yellow			
WOAD				
(*Isatis tinctoria*)	pink			

plants
OF THE
month

Madder

Coreopsis

COREOPSIS
(*Coreopsis tinctoria* – Compositae)

Coreopsis provides a good display of bright yellow and burnt orange flowers in late summer and autumn. The flowers yield a strong yellow to orange dye.

type	Hardy annual
flowers	Flowers vary from golden yellow, rusty brown and terracotta to bronze-red. They appear from late summer through to early autumn
leaves	Mid- to dark green strappy, lance-shaped leaves with cut edges
height	60–75cm (24–30in)
spread	20cm (8in)
planting	Sow in spring into the growing site, or in early autumn and protect with cloches during winter. Thin in spring
position	Full sun
soil	Fertile, well drained
care	Cut back flowering stems after the first flush of flowers to encourage a second flush
propagation	Sow seed in spring, or in autumn with winter protection
species and varieties	Many different species for ornamental use. *Coreopsis tinctoria* is best for dyeing
harvest	Pick flowers as they bloom
herbal value	To obtain a yellow dye, simmer about 1kg (2.2lb) flowers in 1.5L (3 pints) water for 30 minutes or until the flowers are bleached out. This should be sufficient to dye 120g (4oz) mordanted wool. For a deeper colour, repeat the dip. For a more pastel colour use more wool

DYER'S CHAMOMILE
(*Anthemis tinctoria* – Compositae)

Aromatic leaves and bright yellow daisy flowers are the ornamental attractions of dyer's chamomile, but dyers enjoy it for the fresh yellow dye its flowers yield.

type	Hardy herbaceous perennial
flowers	Yellow flowers from summer through to autumn
leaves	Deeply cut, ferny, dark green aromatic leaves
height	1m (3ft)
spread	1m (3ft)
planting	Plant at the back of a border if mixing with other ornamentals. Plant 45cm (18in) apart so that

	plants can support each other
position	Full sun
soil	Well drained
care	Cut back severely after the first flush of flowers to encourage basal growth and continuity of flowering
propagation	Take basal cuttings in spring or divide plants in autumn. Plants will self sow abundantly if allowed
species and varieties	For an ornamental border rather than a dyer's garden, grow *Anthemis tinctoria* 'Alba' with white flowers. *A.t.* 'E.C. Buxton' has lemon-coloured petals
harvest	Pick flowers as they open to dry for winter flower arrangements. Dry leaves for pot-pourri and use flowers fresh to make yellow dye
herbal value	Flowers yield yellow dye if alum and cream of tartar are used as a mordant, and greenish dye if copper and acetic acid are used

DYER'S GREENWEED
(*Genista tinctoria* – Leguminosae)

Dyer's greenweed produces bright yellow flowers on arching stems. Use the flowers, stems and leaves for a greenish-yellow dye.

type	Hardy deciduous shrub
flowers	Heads of small yellow flowers over a long period in summer
leaves	Small oval, glossy green leaves on smooth green stems
height	1m (3ft)
spread	1m (3ft). Spreads in a fairly compact, mounded shape
planting	Plant into its final growing site as it dislikes root disturbance
position	Full sun
soil	Well-drained, light sandy soil
care	Prune in early summer to encourage new growth for dyeing material
propagation	Seeds require stratification (see page 88). Sow in autumn or spring. Several seasons growth is needed before you can expect a good harvest. Take cuttings from established plants in autumn
species and varieties	*Genista tinctoria* 'Flore Pleno' has double flowers and *G.t.* 'Royal Gold' has strong yellow flowers
harvest	Pick leaves, stems and flowers as required and use fresh, or freeze
herbal value	Makes a fresh yellow dye and when combined with woad produces a green pigment

GERMAN CHAMOMILE
(*Matricaria recutita* – Compositae)

For droopy daisy flowers and a soothing tea, grow German chamomile. The leaves and flowers can also be used dry in pot-pourri.

type	Hardy annual
flowers	Flowers with white petals around a yellow centre all summer
leaves	Fern-like, deeply cut, feathery foliage mid-green leaves
height	60cm (24in)
spread	30cm (12in)
planting	Sow into the growing site and thin out to 20cm (8in) apart
position	Full sun
soil	Average, well drained, light
care	No special care
propagation	Sow seed in early spring. Will self seed if flowers are left on the plant
species and varieties	German chamomile is traditionally used for making tea
harvest	Pick flower heads as they open and dry in a well-ventilated, airy and shady situation. You can also hang complete stems upside down in shade
herbal value	Use the flower heads to make a soothing tisane. They are also useful as a hair rinse to lighten naturally blonde hair. Dried leaves and flowers are used in pot-pourri

MADDER
(*Rubia tinctoria* – Rubiaceae)

Growing madder for dyes takes time and patience, but the red dye it produces makes it well worth the effort. Be prepared to grow it in a separate part of the herb area.

type	Hardy herbaceous perennial
flowers	Small, yellowish-green flowers in summer
leaves	Lance-shaped light green leaves grow in whorls around the stems and have prickly surfaces
height	90cm (36in)
spread	45–60cm (18–24in)
planting	Plant 45–60cm (18–24in) apart and when the plant has grown to 30cm (12in), pull the tops to the ground and cover with soil so the plant makes more roots and stems
position	Full sun
soil	Prefers well-drained, fertile soil
care	Keep layering stems to encourage root and stem development over the season. Start a new madder bed each season with a few roots from the existing bed
propagation	Divide in autumn or sow seed in spring or autumn
harvest	Leave plants undisturbed for three years. Dig up roots and wash off all soil. Dry in full sun for more intense colour. Store dry roots whole or grind into powder
herbal value	Red-brown dye

MEADOWSWEET
(*Filipendula ulmaria* syn. *Spiraea ulmaria* – Rosaceae)

Creamy white and downy, meadowsweet's flowers perfume the garden in midsummer and can be used for pot-pourri, for scenting linen and for flavouring herb jellies.

type	Hardy herbaceous perennial
flowers	Spires of small, fragrant, creamy white flowers in summer
leaves	Dark green oval leaves with toothed edges and greyish undersurfaces
height	90cm (36in)
spread	30cm (12in)
planting	Sow seed in spring
position	Grows best in partial shade
soil	Needs a moist, enriched soil
care	Keep moist in dry conditions. Will grow in full sun if soil is moist
propagation	Divide existing plants and replant in autumn
species and varieties	*Filipendula ulmaria* 'Aurea' is a smaller plant growing to 45cm (18in), with yellow-gold leaves that lighten to a pale green during summer
harvest	Pick fresh young leaves before flowers bloom. Pick flowers as they begin to open along the spire. Harvest roots when you divide plants in autumn. Dry flowers and leaves and use roots fresh or dried
herbal value	Use flowers fresh in arrangements to perfume a room. Dry flowers and leaves to use in pot-pourri and to strew in drawers or in sachets to add fragrance to linen. Flowers used fresh add a good nutty flavour to herb jellies. Use flowers with water to make a refreshing face tonic. Roots provide a black dye and the leaves, a blue pigment

Meadowsweet

practical
project
2

PLANTING AND USING COSMETIC HERBS

1 **lavender**
2 **southernwood**
3 **eau-de-Cologne mint**
4 **marsh mallow**
5 **rosemary**
6 **rose**
7 **fennel**
8 **lovage**
9 **borage**
10 **thyme**
11 **parsley**
12 **peppermint**
13 **soapwort**
14 **purple sage**
15 **marjoram**
16 **valerian**
17 **pennyroyal**
18 **pot marigold**
19 **chervil**
20 **chamomile**

Herbs have a long tradition of use in beauty preparations that calm, soothe, refresh and restore. You don't have to be a cosmetic chemist to use many of the plants in your herb garden to make your own aromatic shampoos, hair rinses, floral waters and bath bags. There are many simple recipes that require just a few leaves, flowers or seeds.

Use cool peppermint leaves to make a footbath to soothe aching feet. A bath infused with chamomile flowers helps you sleep, while lemon grass, thyme and fennel seeds can be combined for a revitalising morning bath. Use pungent rosemary leaves to make a hair rinse, and the leaves and stems of soapwort to make a gently cleansing shampoo. Enjoy the plants in the garden as they grow, and harvest as you need them to use in these gentle homemade preparations.

CREATING A COSMETIC GARDEN

If you have space, you could create a special crescent-shaped herb border like the one shown here specially for herbs to use in the bathroom. If space is limited, grow the plants in containers on a sunny patio or mix them with other herb plants. Some of the most useful cosmetic herbs such as scented pelargonium, lemon verbena and lemon grass are not hardy in all climates. They can be grown indoors on sunny windowsills, extending your harvest and cosmetic enjoyment.

To emphasise the ultimate watery use to which many of the herbs will be put, include a small, informal water feature in your planting plan. A bench positioned close to the pool completes the picture and provides the perfect spot to sit and enjoy the cosmetic garden as it grows. With soapwort dipping its leaves into one side of the pool and creeping pennyroyal the other, you will be tempted to enjoy a cleansing and cooling foot bath.

To make the pool
■ Dig a hole 32.5cm (13in) deep and about 30 x 30cm (12 x 12in) square. Line it with a 2.5cm (1in) layer of sand. The exact dimensions (width and length) of the hole are

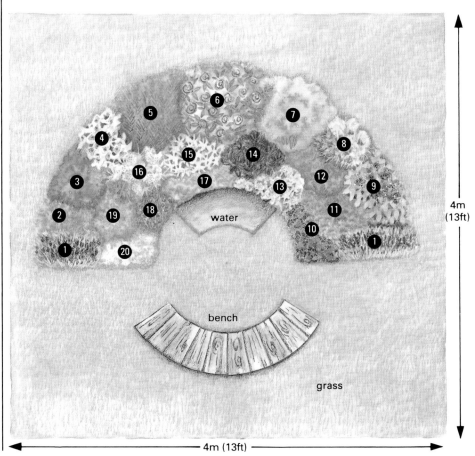

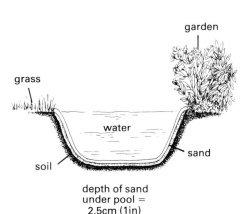

depth of sand
under pool =
2.5cm (1in)

dictated by the shape of the preformed pool, which is then lowered into it. The layer of sand keeps the pool in position and allows you to get it level with the ground.

■ Check the pool is level by filling it with water. If the water line is an even distance from the rim all round, there is no need to adjust it; if water runs out on one side you will need to correct the level.

■ Reposition the pool and tamp down the soil around the edge using a small border spade and broom handle. Take care not to move the pool or lower the ground level.

■ Level the earth around the edges. You can either plant up to the pool, or sow grass.

Plant choice

Restrict the growth of mints and lemon balm or they will swamp neighbouring plants. Sink their roots into the ground in pots or old buckets. Grow fragrant lavender, thyme and chamomile at the front of the garden. Annual sowings of borage, pot marigold, chervil and parsley will provide a good selection of middle and back-of-the-border plants to use in cosmetic preparations.

When to harvest

Pick material to use fresh as you need it, or dry it for later use. Pick in dry weather, early in the morning after sun has dried the dew but before the flowers are fully open, to conserve their fragrant oils for your cosmetics. Hang them in a warm, dry, dark and well-ventilated place to dry. Use fresh herbs on the day of picking, and remember that the homemade products you create do not contain preservative. Use them within two weeks.

MAKING HERBAL BEAUTY PREPARATIONS

Bathing with herbs

The simplest and most effective way to enjoy the fragrant and relaxing properties of herbs is to use them in the bath.

Herb or floral water

Depending on the strength you require, make a floral water either by infusing or decocting the herbal material.

■ Use 25g (1oz) or a small handful of fresh herbs. Halve the quantity if you are using dried herbs. Put the chopped leaves and flowers into a bowl and pour on 580ml (1pt) boiling water.

■ Leave to steep for up to two hours, then strain off the leaves and flowers. Either bottle the infused liquid or pour it straight into your bath.

A decoction provides a stronger mixture and is the best method to use when dealing with herb roots or seeds.

■ Place 25g (1oz) of plant material into a saucepan. Add 1L (2pt) cold water to the pan. Bring the liquid to the boil. Reduce the heat and simmer until the liquid has reduced by half its volume. Strain, use hot or leave to cool before bottling.

Make infusions or decoctions in small quantities to use fresh. You can keep them, bottled, in a refrigerator for up to two weeks.

Bath bags

Bath bags are lovely to use and simple to make as gifts all year round.

■ Place a handful of fresh or dried herbs, together with a small quantity of oatmeal or powdered milk (skin softeners), in the centre of a square of fine mesh cotton or muslin.

■ Gather the edges together and secure the top with string. The string should be long enough to keep the bag in the water as you fill the bath.

When you use a bath bag, tie it to the hot tap so that the heat draws out the essential oils of the herbs. Leave the bag in the water while you bath. You can also use the bag as a sponge, softening and cleansing your skin. Bath bags are reusable until the fragrance fades. Dry them out between use.

BATH HERBS

REVITALISING LEAVES

Apple mint • Basil • Bay • Eau-de-cologne mint • Eucalyptus • Lemon grass • Lemon verbena • Pennyroyal • Peppermint • Pine • Rosemary • Sage • Scented pelargonium • Tansy • Thyme.

Add hyssop or eucalyptus if you are suffering from a cold

SOOTHING FLOWERS

Chamomile • Hop • Jasmine • Lavender • Pot marigold • Rose • Yarrow

SOOTHING LEAVES

Angelica • Comfrey • Lady's mantle • Lemon balm • Scented pelargonium • Valerian • Yarrow

SOOTHING ROOTS

Valerian

HERBAL HAIR CARE

The leaves, stems and roots of Soapwort *(Saponaria officinalis)* contain saponin, a soapy sap that acts as a gentle skin and hair cleanser.

SOAPWORT SHAMPOO

25g (1oz) finely chopped soapwort leaves, stems or roots
580ml (1 pt) boiling water
large handful of herbs (choose from the list, depending on hair colour)

Pour boiling water over soapwort and herbs. Leave for half an hour, strain and cool before using.

HERBS FOR SHAMPOOS

Flowers for fair hair:
Chamomile • Hollyhock • Mullein

Leaves for dark hair:
Rosemary • Sage

Flowers for red hair:
Pot marigold

plants

OF THE

month

German chamomile
(see p81)

NEW JERSEY TEA PLANT

(*Ceanothus americanus* – Rhamnaceae)

Low-growing and shrubby, New Jersey tea plant is an attractive herb for a border. Use its leaves to make a distinctive alternative to China tea.

type	Hardy deciduous shrub
flowers	Upright heads of tightly clustered, small white flowers in summer
leaves	Dark green oval-shaped, with pointed ends and prominent veins
height	90cm (3ft)
spread	1.2m (4ft)
planting	Plant in spring or autumn, disturbing roots as little as possible. Makes an attractive smaller plant if grown in a tub
position	Prefers full sun, but will tolerate shade
soil	Light, well drained
care	Cut back hard in spring
propagation	Seed needs stratification over winter (see page 88). Take softwood cuttings in summer
species and varieties	There are many hybrid ceanothus It is also known as wild snowball and red root
harvest	Pick leaves to dry for tea in spring and summer. Bark was used to treat respiratory problems by the Shakers, an eighteenth-century North American religious group, who were the first commercial herb producers of that continent
herbal value	Decorative in the herb garden, and leaves are a substitute for China tea

PERILLA

(*Perilla frutescens* – Labiatae)

Perilla's deeply frilled, purple leaves make an attractive display in the herb garden, and their strong flavour is useful in soups, salads and rice dishes.

type	Annual, half-hardy in cold areas
flowers	Short flower spires of closely clustered, small pinkish-white or light violet flowers from summer through to mid-autumn
leaves	Ruffled, frilly-edged leaves, purple or green depending on variety
height	60cm (24in)
spread	38cm (15in)
planting	In cold areas sow indoors in spring, barely covering the seed with sowing compost. Plant out after danger of frost is over. In mild areas sow into the growing site, just pressing the seed into the soil
position	Full sun, but will grow in part shade
soil	Well drained, light
care	Keep young plants fairly dry and pinch out growing tips to make the plants bushier
propagation	Perilla self sows abundantly and mature seed will survive in the ground even in cold winter areas. Thin out and transplant in spring, if necessary
species and varieties	Green-leaved varieties are grown in Japan where is it called shiso. *P.f* var. *nankinensis* has even more deeply divided and frilled leaves. Also known as Chinese basil
harvest	Pick leaves to use fresh in cooking before flowers appear. Harvest flowers for pot-pourri and use seed heads dried. Pick leaves and seeds to use in dyeing. Leaves are best used fresh but can be frozen. Wear gloves when harvesting, as leaves can cause dermatitis
herbal value	Use leaves fresh in stir-fried oriental dishes, to flavour and colour rice a pale pink, and in soups and fish dishes. Dried flowers and leaves are useful in pot-pourri. Use seed heads as accents in festive wreaths. Seeds and leaves produce a red dye with alum. In the garden, perilla is a useful and shapely plant that provides focal accent. It looks particularly good combined with silver-leaved herbs such as artemisia or next to mints in flower

Perilla

SAFFLOWER

(*Carthamus tinctorius* – Compositae)

Safflower's prickly encased yellow flowers are good to dry for winter decorations, to use in pot-pourri and can be used to make a strong yellow dye.

type	Hardy annual
flowers	Thistle-like flower heads with orange to yellow flowers in late summer
leaves	Light green, prickly leaves are long and oval-shaped
height	1m (3ft)
spread	1m (3ft)
planting	Sow direct as safflower does not transplant well. Thin seedlings to 45cm (18in) so that mature plants keep each other upright and staking is avoided
position	Full sun
soil	Well drained, average
care	If necessary, stake plants in exposed sites
propagation	Sow in spring into the growing site
harvest	Harvest flowers for use in dried arrangements before they open fully. For use in dyeing, allow flowers to open fully and dry in full sun
herbal value	Decorative in dried flower arrangements, useful as a colourful accent in pot-pourri. For dyeing, wash in cold water first to get rid of a 'fugitive' yellow dye. Useful for a good shade of orange and red on linen and cotton

WELD

(*Reseda luteola* – Resedaceae)

Grow weld for its rosettes of strap-like leaves that provide a strong yellow dye. If you allow it to flower, keep it at the back of the border as it will grow up to 1.5 metres.

type	Hardy biennial
flowers	Tall spikes of small greenish-yellow flowers are carried in the second year of growth
leaves	Large rosettes of long, strappy mid-green leaves
height	Flowering spike up to 1.5m (5ft)
spread	Leaf rosettes spread up to 38cm (15in)
planting	Sow direct in rows as weld does not like root disturbance
position	Full sun
soil	Average, well drained
care	If you are allowing plants to flower, grow at the back of the border; otherwise grow as edging plants
propagation	Sow seed in spring direct into the growing site
harvest	Pick leaves as you need them from a number of plants, or uproot whole plants. If you allow weld to flower, pick just after the flowers have finished and before seed is set
herbal value	The whole plant gives useful yellow pigment, but leaves provide the best colour. Best to use fresh, but can be dried for later use. Chop up leaves using a sharp stainless steel knife, then steep in water for several hours. Leaves from six plants will be sufficient to dye 450g (1lb) wool

Weld

WOAD

(*Isatis tinctoria* – Cruciferae)

Woad can become a garden weed if you let it self seed, but for the dyer it provides a rich blue pigment. Mixed with weld it produces green.

type	Hardy biennial
flowers	Yellow flowers on tall spikes in spring of the second year
leaves	Strappy, lance-shaped leaves that make a soft mound of fresh green
height	Flowering spike up to 1m (3ft)
spread	Basal leaf rosette spreads to 50cm (20in)
planting	Sow in early spring direct into the growing site and thin to 30cm (12in)
position	Full sun
soil	Does well in enriched, well-drained soil
care	If you let it flower, plant at the back of a bed and cut down flower spikes before seed sets
propagation	Sow annually in spring
harvest	Pick leaves during the first growing season. Woad leaves do not provide good blue pigment in their second year
herbal value	Woad gives a rich blue dye, but the process is lengthy and blue only appears once the fabric comes out of the dye-bath and is exposed to air

Woad

AUGUST

In late summer, flowers in the herb garden give way to shapely
seed pods and ripening seed. Many herb seeds have kitchen uses,
and can also be sown to grow next year's herb crop.

A number of herbs self sow abundantly at this time, quite often
before you have a chance to harvest their seed. Take advantage of
the bounty and leave them to grow over autumn and winter. Then
thin or transplant them in spring.

Late summer calls for another burst of seed sowing – of biennials
and winter salad herbs. Still thinking ahead to future harvests,
continue planning your indoor winter herb garden. Select rooted
cuttings to pot up, and grow them on in a sheltered position until
you are ready to bring them indoors.

The harvest of leaves and flowers has its own steady momentum
through the summer, and now seeds are added to the list. Freezing
and drying are not the only methods of preserving the flavour of
herb leaves: pack them into jars with vinegar and oil, and a few
months later you will have herb-flavoured dressings to use in
salads or to give as festive gifts.

As you harvest, you will find yourself simultaneously beginning
the task of maintenance. Herbs that have grown too tall or have
flopped over in storms can be cut back. Tarragon will make a new
flush of growth from the base, giving you shoots to use and take
cuttings from. Cut back mint and artemisia, and pot up daughter
plants of Alpine strawberry to keep them in order.

Fragrance is the keynote of the herb garden in high summer, and
by harvesting the scented blooms now you can preserve them to
enjoy in the darker, less aromatic days of autumn and winter.
But for now you may wish simply to enjoy the perfumes of the herb
garden as it grows. Plant an aromatic lavender border at the edge
of the patio, then relax at the end of the day's harvest and savour
the pleasures of the herb garden.

tasks

FOR THE

month

DRYING SEED
It will take up to three weeks for harvested seed to dry fully. Prepare it for drying in a warm, well-ventilated place. Hang seed heads upside down in paper bags to release the seed, or hang them over newspaper or cloth. You can also lay them down on drying trays and cover the trays with paper to catch the seed.

STORING HERB SEED
Obviously, fresh seed is best sown as soon as possible. If the seed needs a period of cold to break dormancy (stratification), either provide this outdoors or store the seed and give it a cold start in early spring. Keep seed in small containers such as envelopes, old film boxes or pill bottles. Keep them airtight in dark, well-ventilated, dry conditions. Always label and date seed containers. Use as soon as possible: old seed is likely to germinate erratically.

CHECKLIST

- Collect seed from healthy plants and prepare it for sowing or storage
- Harvest seed for kitchen use, drying and storage
- Sow biennials, such as parsley, and continue to sow winter salad herbs outdoors
- Continue taking cuttings
- Cut back soapwort and mint
- Continue the harvest for pot-pourri

HARVESTING HERB SEED

Herb seeds are the last bounty from the herb garden. Many have culinary uses and most will provide you with a source of next year's plants.

You may have to be quick to catch the seed from some of the prolific self seeders such as angelica, borage, tansy and parsley. They will provide you with copious plants – probably in places you don't want them – but follow their example and sow the ripe seed at the time that it would naturally fall to the ground. If this is not practical, you can store the seed and later trick it into germinating naturally through the conditions of first cold, then warmth, light and moisture that you provide.

Herb seed that you buy from seed suppliers behaves pretty much as naturally occurring seed. For that reason, germination from both your own home-collected seed and that from suppliers may be erratic. Do not give up on sowings if some seed takes a long time to appear.

If you plan to save seed to sow for next year's plants, select it carefully. Earmark plants that are strong and vigorous in their growth, and produce good leaves and flowers. As the flowers fall and the seeds begin to develop, note which look the largest and strongest. This is the seed to collect first for sowing.

When to harvest

Harvest seed before it is fully ripe, and finish off the ripening process in paper bags or on drying trays so that you can control the number of seeds that fall to the ground. As seeds mature their moisture content lessens, and they become browner and harder to the touch.

When harvesting seed, it is helpful to know which of the botanical families a particular plant belongs to. Family characteristics (see table) help tell you when to harvest the seed.

WHEN TO SOW

Annuals
Sow hardy annuals in their permanent positions in spring when the soil has warmed up. Sow half-hardy annuals in trays in a heated greenhouse or on a sunny windowsill in spring.

Biennials
Sow biennials in late spring, summer or autumn as their seed ripens. Biennials die in their second growing season after seed has set. Parsley does best from a late summer sowing into warm soil. Otherwise, of course, sow it indoors in spring with bottom heat of 21–27°C (70–80°F).

Perennials
Sow perennials in late spring and early summer. Sow tender perennials into trays in a heated greenhouse or on a sunny windowsill in spring.

STRATIFICATION

Natural
With plants that self seed, dormancy ensures that the seed will survive until conditions are right for the subsequent seedlings to grow. The seed falls to the ground, is covered by autumn leaves or soil moved by garden animals, insects and birds, and stays dormant over the winter. Then, after a number of days at higher temperatures, the dormancy mechanism is broken, and the seed begins to germinate.

With your own harvested seed, not only can you control the number of seedlings produced by sowing just sufficient for your needs, but you also get better results than with bought seed as yours will be fresh.

You can stratify seed in similar conditions to those that would occur naturally by treating it in an outdoor site or cold frame. Fill a seed tray with moist peat or compost and sow the seeds into it. Spread a thin layer of sand over the surface and cover with glass or plastic to keep out mice, birds and slugs. Place the tray and its cover in a shady site outdoors, preferably in a cold frame. Keep an eye on the tray through the winter and transplant any seed that germinates too early. In spring, remove the treated seed and sow it in place.

Artificial
To break seed dormancy artificially, you need to provide the period of cold and moisture in the refrigerator, and follow it with the warmth of a heated propagator or spring-warmed soil. Mix the seeds with moist sand and/or peat in a container covered with a polythene bag, and place in the fridge for four to six weeks.

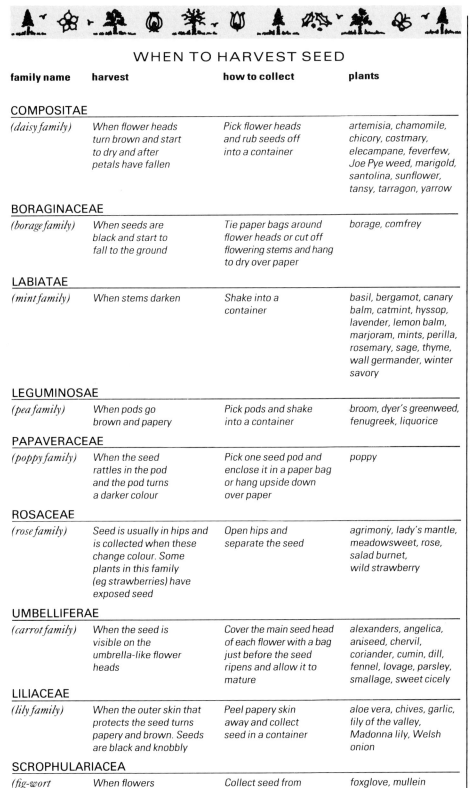

WHEN TO HARVEST SEED

family name	harvest	how to collect	plants
COMPOSITAE			
(daisy family)	When flower heads turn brown and start to dry and after petals have fallen	Pick flower heads and rub seeds off into a container	artemisia, chamomile, chicory, costmary, elecampane, feverfew, Joe Pye weed, marigold, santolina, sunflower, tansy, tarragon, yarrow
BORAGINACEAE			
(borage family)	When seeds are black and start to fall to the ground	Tie paper bags around flower heads or cut off flowering stems and hang to dry over paper	borage, comfrey
LABIATAE			
(mint family)	When stems darken	Shake into a container	basil, bergamot, canary balm, catmint, hyssop, lavender, lemon balm, marjoram, mints, perilla, rosemary, sage, thyme, wall germander, winter savory
LEGUMINOSAE			
(pea family)	When pods go brown and papery	Pick pods and shake into a container	broom, dyer's greenweed, fenugreek, liquorice
PAPAVERACEAE			
(poppy family)	When the seed rattles in the pod and the pod turns a darker colour	Pick one seed pod and enclose it in a paper bag or hang upside down over paper	poppy
ROSACEAE			
(rose family)	Seed is usually in hips and is collected when these change colour. Some plants in this family (eg strawberries) have exposed seed	Open hips and separate the seed	agrimony, lady's mantle, meadowsweet, rose, salad burnet, wild strawberry
UMBELLIFERAE			
(carrot family)	When the seed is visible on the umbrella-like flower heads	Cover the main seed head of each flower with a bag just before the seed ripens and allow it to mature	alexanders, angelica, aniseed, chervil, coriander, cumin, dill, fennel, lovage, parsley, smallage, sweet cicely
LILIACEAE			
(lily family)	When the outer skin that protects the seed turns papery and brown. Seeds are black and knobbly	Peel papery skin away and collect seed in a container	aloe vera, chives, garlic, lily of the valley, Madonna lily, Welsh onion
SCROPHULARIACEA			
(fig-wort family)	When flowers have turned brown	Collect seed from capsules	foxglove, mullein

PLANTS THAT NEED A COLD START

Dyer's greenweed
Juniper
Lily
Marsh mallow
New Jersey tea
Poppy
Rose
Soapwort
Sweet violet
Sweet woodruff

ALL UMBELLIFEROUS HERBS INCLUDING:
Angelica
Chervil
Coriander
Dill
Fennel
Parsley
Sweet cicely

THINGS TO DO

Sow seed
Outdoors: alexanders, chervil, coriander, Joe Pye weed, lamb's lettuce, landcress, parsley, poppy, traveller's joy, winter purslane

Propagate
Take cuttings: honeysuckle, jasmine, Joe Pye weed, juniper, pinks, rue, scented pelargonium
Layer: honeysuckle

Harvest
Leaves: as needed
Flowers: as needed to dry for seeds, including sunflower
Seeds: aniseed, caraway, coriander, cumin, fenugreek, nasturtium, poppy
Fruits: wild strawberry

Routine maintenance
- Choose strong-growing rooted cuttings to pot up and bring inside for an indoor winter herb garden
- Water herbs in containers
- Cut back spent flowering stems and generally tidy up as you harvest
- Trim lavender plants, add trimmings to pot-pourri

practical project

MAKING HERB OILS AND VINEGARS

When you feel that you have dried and frozen enough herbs to supply your winter needs, try one of the simplest and most effective methods of preserving herb flavours: making herb oils and vinegars.

These have a wide range of culinary uses. Use them to enliven both salad and cooked dishes, and to marinate, baste and tenderise meat, poultry and seafood. Add a spoonful to soups and stews in the last few minutes of cooking and use as a substitute where oil or lemon juice is called for in a recipe.

The basic method is the same, whichever herbs you use. You can experiment with different combinations and amounts of herb, and with various grades and types of oil and vinegar for the base. Avoid using distilled wine vinegar as it tends to be a bit sour. Choose mild-flavoured oils and vinegars as they won't overpower the herb, but will be enhanced by its addition. White wine, rice and cider vinegar; sesame, sunflower and safflower oils are the best choices.

HERB OILS

Basil and lemon balm both flavour oil well. Use them just before they come into flower, when their aromatic oils are at their most intense.

Add parsley to extra-pungent herbs such as rosemary, winter savory and thyme. Parsley will soften their flavour and produce a milder oil.

■ Pick the herb leaves or flowers early in the day, as usual, when the oils are most concentrated and have not begun to evaporate in the hot sun.

■ Rinse them, pat dry with absorbent kitchen paper and lightly crush them in your hands to accelerate the release of flavours. You can also use seeds and soft green stems, but discard woody stems as they will leave a bitter flavour.

■ Fill a wide-necked jar with the crushed herbs, then pour on the oil until the herbs are covered. Stir well and close with an airtight lid. Stand the jar on a sunny windowsill and stir daily, occasionally pressing the herbs with a wooden spoon to keep releasing their aromas.

■ If the herb material floats to the surface of the jar, push it down and wedge in place with small wooden skewers. The higher the ratio of herbs to oil, the less they will be able to float to the surface.

■ Leave to steep for three weeks. Taste the oil to see if the flavour is at the strength you like. If so, strain the oil through a piece of muslin and discard the used herbs. Bottle, label and store ready for use or to offer it as a gift.

Garlic in oil

Use this method to preserve the flavour of your own home-grown heads of garlic. You can also use the garlic cloves in marinades and in stuffings, stews and soups.

- Remove as much of the outer, papery skins of the garlic cloves as possible, trying to keep the head intact. If you have to break it up into individual cloves, don't worry, as they will still look attractive in the bottle and flavour the oil wonderfully.

- Lightly brush a sheet of kitchen foil with oil. Place the garlic on the foil, wrap it up and place the foil parcel in a roasting dish in the oven.

- Bake at gas mark 5 (190°C/375°F) for 20 minutes until the cloves are soft and juicy.

- Pack the garlic into a wide-necked glass jar. You can also add black or green olives.

- Insert sprigs of thyme and bay leaves between the garlic and the sides of the jar.

- Fill the jars with oil. Seal and store in a cool place for two months before using. This wonderful oil can be used to flavour salads or sauté potatoes, and the garlic is delicious in soups or stews.

HERBAL VINEGARS

Herb vinegar is made in a very similar way to herb oil.

- Gather the herbs of your choice – leaves, stems, flowers and seeds – wash them and pat dry. Discard any woody stems.

- Pack the herbs into a wide-necked glass jar.

- If using seeds, lightly crush them to release their aroma. Add seeds, garlic or spices first, so that the weight of other herb material keeps them submerged.

- Pour over the vinegar, stir gently to remove any air pockets and seal with a non-corrosive lid.

- Leave the vinegar to steep in a warm, dark place. Sunlight causes the herb material to fade and this can alter the taste of the vinegar.

- After 24 hours, open the jar and check that the vinegar is still covering all the herb material; if not, add more vinegar. Herb vinegar is ready to use in a few days. Whether you are making it for home use or to offer as a gift, strain it through muslin and pour into a bottle.

- Add a sprig of the predominant herb to decorate. Label and store in a cool, dark place.

> ### TIPS
>
> - *Use cork stoppers or non-corrosive lids for vinegar products.*
>
> - *Keep old olive oil, wine vinegar and salad dressing bottles for recycling as containers for delicious herb vinegars and oils.*
>
> - *When using leaves or flowers there is no need to heat the vinegar, but for seeds, warm it slightly.*
>
> - *Make sure you use a good quantity of herbs so that the flavour is passed into the vinegar.*

Floral vinegar

Use lemon balm, chive, lemon verbena and scented pelargonium flowers to flavour vinegar for use in spicy fruit salads. Add lavender flowers sparingly, as their fragrance can be overwhelming. For more information on making floral vinegars, see page 59.

Herb vinegar for fish dishes

To a white wine vinegar base add dill seed, leaves and stems, lemon thyme and lemon balm leaves, a bay leaf and some lemon peel. Use the lemon peel and bay leaf to keep the rest of the herb material submerged.

Herb vinegar for roasts, barbecues and marinades

Use a red wine or cider vinegar as the base. Mix in garlic, parsley, sage, juniper berries, thyme, rosemary, black peppercorns, coriander, caraway and cumin seed and a bay leaf.

Lemon chilli vinegar

Use white wine or cider vinegar as the base. Add the peel of a lemon and a lime, a handful of chillies, 2–3 cloves of garlic chopped into small slivers. Mix in 25g (1oz) each of whole coriander and cumin seed. Top the mix with 4–6 bay leaves. After steeping for two days, strain through muslin and bottle, then add lemon peel and thyme to decorate.

RECOMMENDED HERBS FOR SAVOURY OILS:

Basil • Bay • Fennel • Garlic • Hyssop • Marjoram • Mint • Rosemary • Tarragon • Thyme • Sage • Summer savory • Winter savory

RECOMMENDED HERBS FOR SWEET OILS:
Almond oil is the best choice for the base:

Clove pink flowers • Lavender flowers • Lemon balm • Lemon verbena • Rose petals • Scented pelargonium

RECOMMENDED HERBS FOR VINEGARS

Basil • Bay • Caraway • Chervil • Chives • Coriander • Cumin • Dill • Fennel • Garlic • Horseradish root • Lemon balm • Lemon verbena • Marjoram • Mint • Parsley • Rosemary • Sage • Salad burnet • Savory • Tarragon • Thyme

RECOMMENDED FLOWERS FOR VINEGARS

Basil • Chive • Dill • Elder • Fennel • Lavender • Lemon balm • Lemon verbena • Marjoram • Marigold • Mint • Nasturtium • Clove pink • Primrose • Rosemary • Rose petals • Sage • Scented pelargonium • Sweet violet • Thyme

plants
OF THE
month

Aniseed

ANISEED
(*Pimpinella anisum* – Umbelliferae)

Delicate, feathery aromatic leaves and highly flavoured seeds are two of the culinary attractions of aniseed. Grow this annual herb as a frothy edging to a path.

type	Half-hardy annual
flowers	Clusters of small white flowers in summer
leaves	Basal leaves are rounded and toothed, while leaves on flower stems are feathery. All are aromatic
height	45cm (18in) when in flower
spread	25cm (10in)
planting	Does not transplant well, so sow into the growing site and thin out
position	Very hot, sunny, but also needs shelter
soil	Light, well drained
care	Needs maximum sun for seeds to ripen fully
propagation	From seed only. Sow into the growing site in late spring when danger of frost is over. Thin to 20cm (8in)
harvest	Cut leaves through the growing season as you need them to use fresh. Use flowers fresh in salads or fruit dishes. Harvest seed in late summer when tips of fruits are turning from green to grey. Cut stems long, tie into bunches and hang upside down in a cool, dark place, over a bowl or sheet of brown paper to collect the seed, if it falls
herbal value	All parts of aniseed are aromatic and useful in many ways. Add leaves to salads, both sweet and savoury. Use seeds to flavour Indian and Middle Eastern dishes, cakes and biscuits, puddings, pickles, and to enliven preserved fruit dishes. Seed is used to flavour commercially made liqueurs and to make five-spice powder, but star anise may be substituted if necessary

CARAWAY
(*Carum carvi* – Umbelliferae)

Enjoy caraway's ornamental qualities of finely cut, ferny leaves and small white flowers before you harvest its aromatic and useful seeds in late summer.

type	Hardy biennial
flowers	Tiny white flowers carried in flat clusters in summer
leaves	Finely cut, feathery mid-green leaves with good flavour
height	Grows to 25cm (10in) in the first year and in the second year flower stems grow to 90cm (36in)
spread	30cm (12in), and dies back in winter of the first year
planting	Sow in rows and thin to 30cm (12in). Mark rows so that you don't dig it up in spring, before it comes into growth
position	Full sun
soil	Likes well-drained, rich loamy soil
care	Can transplant seedlings if necessary but only when very small, otherwise they will bolt
propagation	From seed only
harvest	Pick fresh young leaves to use in salads. Hang seed heads upside down over a receptacle to collect seed. Dry in a cool, shady, well-ventilated site. Seed explodes from the capsules when ripe and brown
herbal value	Seed provides aromatic flavour in Middle Eastern dishes, bread and biscuit making. Used in production of the liqueur Kümmel

CORIANDER
(*Coriandrum sativum* – Umbelliferae)

Coriander's highly aromatic leaves provide delicate ornament in the herb garden. Dainty white flowers are followed by round, bead-like seeds.

type	Hardy annual
flowers	Wide, flat clusters of small white or pinkish flowers are carried in late summer
leaves	Lower leaves are divided into two or three leaflets with toothed edges, and upper leaves are finely cut and feathery. Foliage is dark green, and very spicy to taste and smell
height	60cm (24in)
spread	20cm (8in)
planting	Grow some in part shade for good leaf production. For best seed production, choose a drier, warmer situation
position	Full sun or partial shade
soil	Average, but needs to be moist
care	Water young seedlings well

propagation	Sow indoors in early spring and transplant into the growing sites in late spring. Sow direct into growing sites in late spring and make successive sowings through the summer
harvest	Pick young leaves to use fresh as you need them. Harvest seeds when they have started to turn brown. Finish the ripening process in a dark, airy, cool site. Once the seeds are dry, store them in an airtight container
herbal value	Use fresh leaves in Indian, Turkish, Greek and Lebanese cuisine. Seeds enliven both sweet and savoury dishes. In Mexico and Latin America, coriander or *cilantro* is popular in a wide range of dishes. Never add it at the end of cooking – always use it through the whole cooking time. Use seed for pot-pourri

CUMIN
(*Cuminum cyminum* – Umbelliferae)

Grow cumin in the hottest part of the herb garden to provide it with a long, warm growing season to ripen its spicy seeds.

type	Tender annual
flowers	Flat clusters of pink to white flowers in summer
leaves	Small, deep green, thin leaves with deeply cut, feathery edges
height	25–30cm (10–12in)
spread	25–30cm (10–12in)
planting	Sow seed in a warm greenhouse in spring, then plant out into a sun-drenched bed for best seed production
position	Full sun
soil	Well-drained loam
care	Needs a long, hot period for seeds to mature fully
propagation	Sow into pots or trays in a heated propagator in spring. Transplant seedlings into their growing sites when danger of frost is over and soil has warmed up
harvest	Pick the whole plant as seeds ripen and change colour in midsummer. Hang to dry in a well-ventilated, shady, but cool site. When dry, rub seeds off the plant
herbal value	Use hot and aromatic seed sparingly in Indian and Arabic cooking

FENUGREEK
(*Trigonella foenum-graecum* – Leguminosae)

Grown as cattle fodder by the Romans, fenugreek has long held a place in the kitchen for its spicy leaves and aromatic seeds.

type	Tender annual in temperate climates
flowers	Small, creamy yellow to white pea-like flowers, sometimes violet-tinged, blooming in summer
leaves	Mid-green leaves are divided into three rounded, clover-like leaflets with slightly toothed edges. They have a spicy flavour if sprouted or when young
height	30–60cm (12–24in)
spread	May sprawl into a prostrate habit. Thin to 20cm (8in)
planting	Sow in rows, so that plants can support each other, or 'sprout' seeds in a sprouting jar as you would mung beans
position	Full sun
soil	Prefers a light, well-drained chalky soil
care	Sow thickly so that plants can support each other, and stake with light twigs
propagation	Sow seed in spring for seed production and sprout seeds as you need them through the season. Sow in succession, too, to provide fresh young leaves. When sowing, press seed into the soil and cover lightly
harvesting	For seed harvest, pick plants when two-thirds of the seed is ripe. Hang stems upside down in bundles over a receptacle in a cool airy place. Pick young leaves to use fresh from successionally sown plants
herbal value	Use leaves for a curry flavour in salads, stews and soup. Use seed in spice mixtures. Toast it to bring out the flavour, but do not overheat as this will have the opposite effect. Use seed ground in curries and Middle Eastern dishes

Coriander

Fenugreek

practical
project
2

GROWING AND USING LAVENDER

LAVENDERS SUITABLE FOR CONTAINERS
(All the lavenders below need frost protection)
Lavandula canariensis
L. dentata
L. dentata candicans
L. lanata
L. pinnata
L. stoechas
L. stoechas pendunculata
L. viridis

Lavender is one of the most satisfying flowering and aromatic herbs to grow in the herb or ornamental garden. Its soft grey foliage and blue, mauve, pink or white flowers contrast with its rather stiff and formal look. It is a useful plant to use as a bridge between the patio edge and the beginning of the lawn, softening the hard edge of the paved area and acting as a shapely foil to the lush green of grass. Once lavender is growing well, it provides an almost endless harvest of flowers to use in the kitchen and to perfume the home.

The right conditions

Lavender comes originally from the Mediterranean and prefers a well-drained, light soil in a sunny site. If your soil is heavy and moist, either incorporate sand or grit to open up the texture when you prepare the bed, or raise the bed to improve drainage.

When planting lavenders for edging, use pegs and string to help you plant in a straight line. Space the plants evenly, set them in so that they are upright and water in well. The planting may look gappy and sparse at first, but lavender grows away quickly and will soon fill the space.

During the summer you will be harvesting lavender flowers to use in many projects. In late summer, trim the plants to neaten their shapes and remove all spent flower heads. If you feel the plants are looking straggly in spring, then cut them back early to encourage fresh growth from the base of each plant. Lavender plants do become leggy with age, so you may need to replace them with young plants grown from your own cuttings every five or six years.

USING LAVENDER

Like many herbs, lavender can be enjoyed just for itself as it grows in the herb garden, as well as used either fresh or dried in a variety of ways in the home.

Lavender water

Lavender water makes use of both leaves and flowers, fresh or dried. Add it to your bath water for an aromatic relaxing effect, use it as a hair rinse or skin toner, or just dab a few drops onto your face and neck to refresh yourself on a hot summer's day.

- Add a generous handful of lavender flowers and leaves to 580ml (1pt) of boiling water.

- Infuse the herbs by pouring the water over them and leaving to steep until cool. Then strain, pour the liquid into bottles and seal.

- For a stronger-smelling mixture, make a decoction by putting the flowers and leaves into a pan filled with 580ml (1pt) cold water.

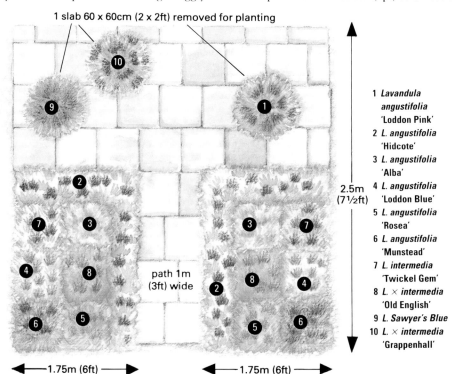

1 slab 60 x 60cm (2 x 2ft) removed for planting

2.5m (7½ft)

path 1m (3ft) wide

1.75m (6ft) 1.75m (6ft)

1 *Lavandula angustifolia* 'Loddon Pink'
2 *L. angustifolia* 'Hidcote'
3 *L. angustifolia* 'Alba'
4 *L. angustifolia* 'Loddon Blue'
5 *L. angustifolia* 'Rosea'
6 *L. angustifolia* 'Munstead'
7 *L. intermedia* 'Twickel Gem'
8 *L. × intermedia* 'Old English'
9 *L. Sawyer's Blue*
10 *L. × intermedia* 'Grappenhall'

- Bring to the boil and allow the mixture to simmer until the liquid is reduced by half.

- To preserve lavender water for any length of time, add a few drops of pure alcohol, vodka or brandy. Pour into pretty glass bottles with stoppers and keep to use in the home, or to offer as gifts.

Fresh lavender in the kitchen

Add lavender sparingly to cream or yoghurt: the flowers have such a strong flavour that they will overpower more subtle tastes. Use flowers and leaves to flavour soups and stews. Just one flower head and three to four leaves will be sufficient to flavour 290ml (½pt) of soup. Add lavender also to jams, jellies, sugars, vinegars and oils to create highly perfumed products used as accompaniments, in baking or desserts and in salads.

Lavender sugar

Cut three to four sprigs of lavender from a plant. Knock them gently to dislodge any scent-drunk or lurking insects. Remove the flowers from the stems.

- Choose a pretty glass jar (so you can see the lavender and sugar) and fill it with alternate layers of sugar and flowers until it is full. Alternatively, you can almost fill the jar with sugar and then insert three to four lavender flower spikes, so that the tops are just above the sugar level.

- Put a lid on the jar and leave for three to four weeks for the sugar to absorb the scent and colour from the flowers.

Lavender bottles or wands

Lavender is most popularly used to perfume linen in drawers. You can use it dried in sachets, but you can also make decorative lavender 'bottles', or wands, from the fresh flower sprigs. Lavender bottles were a favourite Victorian drawer freshener.

- Cut the flowers with stems as long as possible. Use about 20 stems, with the blossoms just beginning to open. Make sure the flower heads are all level at the top and the stems are all the same length.

- Tie a 1m (3ft) length of ribbon or thread around the bunch at the base of the flower heads. Leave one end long to weave through the stems. Hold the bunch in one hand and with the other hand gently bend back each of the stems, so that they enclose the flowers.

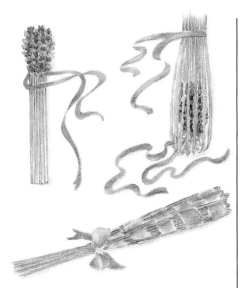

- Pull the ribbon to the outside of the stems and weave it in and out so that the flowers become encased in a cocoon of woven ribbon and stems.

- When the flowers are completely enclosed, stitch the ribbon in place and add a small bow to finish off. Cut the stems that stick out of the end of the bottle to the same length and tie them with a bow or ribbon. As the flowers dry they will fall from the stem and be caught in the cage of ribbons.

MAKING POT-POURRI

- Use one type of lavender, or mix several colours and varieties together for a pretty visual effect.
- Use 240g (8oz) dried lavender flowers mixed with 15g (½oz) each of dried thyme, marjoram and rosemary leaves. To this add 7g (¼oz) each of dried mint and orris root.
- For a spicier, winter mixture add a further 7g (¼oz) of powdered clove and caraway seeds.
- Mix all the ingredients together in a bowl and stir from time to time to release the scents.
- If you have lavender essential oil, sprinkle a few drops in with the powdered orris root for a stronger scent.
- A few drops of essential oil will also revitalise old bowls of pot-pourri that may have begun to lose their fragrance.

WHICH LAVENDER?

COMPACT VARIETIES
(Up to 50cm (20in))
'Hidcote', violet-blue flowers
'Munstead', blue flowers
'Hidcote Pink', pale pink flowers
'Nana Alba', very compact, white flowers

Space plants 23cm (9in) apart. 'Hidcote' and 'Hidcote Pink' work well together

TALLER VARIETIES
(Up to 1.2m (4ft))
Old English *(L. angustifolia)*, purple flowers
'Alba', white flowers
'Hidcote Giant', deep violet flowers

HALF-HARDY VARIETIES
Ideal for pots and containers.
Bring into conservatory or greenhouse in winter

French lavender *(L. stoechas)*, strongly aromatic tufted, deep purple flowers
Woolly lavender *(L. lanata)*, white, woolly stems and leaves

DRYING LAVENDER

- *Gather flowers early in the day, but after the dew has dried*
- *Cut each stem as long as possible when you pick*
- *Remove leaves and dry them separately for adding to pot-pourri*
- *Tie stems into medium-sized bunches and hang to dry upside down in an airy, dark and warm shed or room*
- *If you have space and a fine-mesh wire drying rack, you can dry the stems individually*
- *Lavender flowers keep their fragrance for up to five years. In warm conditions, they will be dry after a fortnight*

plants
OF THE
month

Poppy

LANDCRESS
(*Barbarea verna* – Cruciferae)

Landcress provides sharp-flavoured leaves for salads and soups all through the year and makes an ornamental show of glossy green, deeply cut leaves.

type	Hardy biennial
flowers	Clusters of bright yellow flowers in spring and early summer, depending on time sown
leaves	Glossy, dark green, deeply divided leaves with a sharp and spicy taste grow to form a mounded rosette
height	20–70cm (8–28in)
spread	20cm (8in)
planting	Sow in rows and thin to 20cm (8in). Sow in late summer for a good winter crop and in spring for a summer harvest
position	Prefers full sun, but will grow in shady sites
soil	Rich, moist
care	Keep cutting leaves to use, and nip off flowering stalks to avoid self sowing
propagation	Sow into the growing site in spring or late summer and thin when seedlings are large enough to handle
species and varieties	Wintercress *(Barbarea vulgaris)* is a taller-growing perennial cress native in many parts of Europe and naturalised in northern North America. It has similar uses and is found growing in moist sites
harvest	Pick leaves as needed to use fresh
herbal value	Use leaves as a substitute for watercress in salads or soups. Use chopped in green sauces and cook leaves with butter to serve as a vegetable accompaniment

LEMON GRASS
(*Cymbopogon citratus* – Gramineae)

Grow lemon grass for its tall, ornamental and citrus-scented leaves. Use the leaves in salads, teas and in relaxing aromatic baths.

type	Perennial grass, tender in non-tropical climates
flowers	Does not normally flower in indoor cultivation, but in tropical conditions has clusters of greenish-grey, red-tinged flowers in summer
leaves	Long, green, strappy, fragrant leaves furled around stems
height	Usually 1.8m (6ft), but in a container only to 1m (3ft)
spread	Makes a dense, bamboo-like basal clump
planting	Grow in a frost-free greenhouse or conservatory in winter. In mild areas mulch or cloche in autumn
position	Full sun, but under glass needs shade or leaves will be scorched. Indoors needs to be in a temperature above 13°C (56°F)
soil	Moisture-retentive loam
care	Provide a minimum temperature of 13°C (56°F). Divide large clumps in autumn. Water frequently
propagation	Divide large clumps and grow from offsets to make new plants
species and varieties	*Cymbopogon citratus* is known as West Indian lemon grass. Malabar grass *(C. flexuosus)* is also lemon-scented
harvest	Pick leaves as needed and dry in cool shade. Can also use leaves fresh. Cut some fresh new shoots in spring. Freeze leaves
herbal value	Use dried in pot-pourri. Use new shoots in salads. Leaves can be used fresh in salads or stews, dried to make teas and in Chinese, Indonesian and Indian dishes. Use lemon grass fresh or dried in bath bags or to make scented lemon water for hand bowls after a meal

POPPY
(*Papaver* species – Papaveraceae)

Grow poppies in the herb garden for their ornamental flowers, attractive leaves and seed pods. Use the dried seeds to provide flavour in bread, biscuits and cakes.

type	Hardy annual
flowers	Poppies come in a wide range of colours, including red, mauve and orange. Flowers are single or double and are produced all through the summer
leaves	Field poppy has hairy, toothed leaves, while opium poppy has fleshy grey leaves that wrap themselves round the plant's stem at the leaf nodes
height	30–150cm (1–5ft)
spread	30cm (1ft)
planting	Sow direct into the flowering position, and thin to 30cm (12in)

position	Full sun
soil	Fertile, well drained
propagation	Sow direct in spring or autumn. Poppies self sow abundantly, so thin out plants when large enough to handle
species and varieties	Opium poppy *(Papaver somniferum)* has large flowers and attractive seed pods. In North America it is illegal to grow it without a permit, but it is nonetheless widely grown and has escaped into the wild in many places. Field poppy *(P. rhoeas)* is shorter growing with small seed heads and bright orange to red flowers. There are many ornamental species and varieties of poppy to choose from
harvest	Harvest seed pods as soon as flowers fall to dry for winter arrangements. If harvesting for seed, pick seed pods as they ripen, or birds may get them first. Stand seed pods upright in jars or bottles to dry in a cool, airy, dark site. Hang field poppy stems upside down with paper or cloth under them to catch the drying seeds
herbal value	Use opium poppy seeds to make European poppy seed cakes and biscuits. Seed has to be ground before mixing in with other ingredients. Feed excess seed to birds in winter

TEASEL

(Dipsacus fullonum – Dipsacaceae)

For unusual ornament in the herb garden, and for spiny seed heads in dried flower displays, grow lilac-flowered teasel.

type	Hardy biennial
flowers	Lilac to mauve flowers on cone-shaped flower heads are carried in late summer
leaves	Lance-shaped light green leaves with spiny, serrated edges
height	1.5m (5ft)
spread	30–45cm (12–18in)
planting	Sow into the back of the border as teasel is such a tall plant
position	Full sun
soil	Average
care	No special care needed
propagation	Sow seed 45cm (18in) apart into the growing site
species and varieties	Fuller's teasel *(Dipsacus sativus)* has very strong spines on its seed

	heads and is taller growing. It was specially developed to be used to raise the nap on woollen cloth
harvest	If you want them green, pick teasel just after flowering and hang upside down to dry in the dark. If you leave them later they turn tan, and you may have to compete for them with finches
herbal value	Seed heads are decorative in dried flower arrangements

WINTER PURSLANE

(Montia perfoliata syn. *Claytonia perfoliata* – Portulacaceae)

Sharp and fresh-tasting, winter purslane's leaves and flowers are useful salad herbs in winter and spring. Make several summer sowings for winter harvests.

type	Hardy annual
flowers	Small white flowers in spring and summer
leaves	First leaves are narrow and angular, later leaves are rounded and seem to wrap their edges around the stem. Flower stems grow through these leaves. Both types of leaf are succulent and juicy to eat
height	20–30cm (8–12in)
spread	20–30cm (8–12in)
planting	Sow in rows in spring for a summer crop and in late summer for winter salads
position	Full sun or shade, but plants may need to be covered with cloches in severe conditions in winter
soil	Well drained, fertile
care	Cover with cloches in severe winters
propagation	From seed only. Sow in late summer for a winter crop and in spring for summer salads
species and varieties	Winter purslane is also known as claytonia or miner's lettuce
harvest	Pick leaves as needed. Winter purslane will grow as a cut-and-come-again salad
herbal value	Add leaves and flowers to salads, or use as cress on egg mayonnaise sandwiches. Add chopped just before end of the cooking time to winter soups. Cook leaves as a spinach substitute. Flowers are attractive and tasty additions to summer salads

Teasel

SEPTEMBER

Early autumn is the time to start tidying, clearing and maintaining herb plants and the soil in which they grow. Clear damp leaves and tangled and lax stems that have no harvest value, and add them to the compost heap. By now you will have started a second or third heap, and the first will soon be ready to return to the soil, enriching it for next year's gardening.

Many perennial herbs will have grown too large for their current site. Some that are positively thuggish in their growth, such as soapwort, horseradish and artemisia, should be lifted and divided. This invigorates the plant for the following year and gives other plants around it a little more space. If you have room, move any spare plants into other parts of the garden, or pot them up to offer as unruly herbal gifts to friends who do have space!

Now is the time to begin serious pruning and clipping of hedging herbs such as wall germander, cotton lavender, lavender and thyme – leave it any later and the new stems and shoots may be damaged by frost.

Keep your indoor winter herb garden in mind and pot up chives, parsley and marjoram to acclimatise for indoor growing.

Much of the frenzy of summer harvesting is now over, but there are still herbs to harvest and prepare for drying and later use, while mint harvested in late summer will be almost ready to store either for pot-pourri making or to use in refreshing aromatic teas.

In fact, if you are planning ahead, now is the time to start preparation for next year's tea garden. Mark out the garden and set the trelliswork in place; then plant out hardy herbaceous perennials to form the framework of the garden.

While sleep and pot-pourri herbs are drying, begin making pretty pillows to hold their scents. Use them in bedrooms and cupboards, or offer them as gifts at the end of the year.

tasks

FOR THE

month

ALWAYS LABEL
Always label newly planted herbs and mark their position in the soil and on the herb garden plan. In a few months' time most perennials will have lost their above-ground growth and be totally invisible. If you know where you have planted, there is less danger you will slice through the roots when continuing autumn digging or starting early spring planting.

CHECKLIST

 Divide large clumps of perennial herbs

 Cut back tall stems and foliage of perennials not divided

 Prune edging and hedging herbs

 Deadhead spent flowers and cut back flower stems

 Plant newly bought perennials and shrubby herbs

 Select, pot up and apply fertiliser to herbs for the indoor winter herb garden

 Place newly potted chives and tarragon plants in a cool place before bringing in for winter

 Make garlic ropes

 Tie trimmings of thyme, lavender and sage into bundles to use on winter fires

 Continue to sow salad herbs outdoors

 Pick artemisia stems and bind them into circles to use for festive wreaths

 Continue taking cuttings

DIVIDE AND RULE

In early autumn, herb garden activity turns from frantic harvesting to steady and continuous maintenance.

You will have noticed how some herbs such as tansy, soapwort, comfrey and artemisia have settled in, taken advantage of your hospitality and made a bid for supremacy. Now is the time to remind them sharply that they are welcome – but on your terms.

■ Cut back lax and flopping stems and lift large clumps, ready to divide.

■ Use two forks placed back to back to prise the clump apart (see page 41).

■ Shake off soil and remove damaged roots before replanting in the same site, or relocating the division to a different part of the herb garden.

■ Among the plants that need dividing now are Good King Henry, soapwort, yarrow, elecampane and liquorice.

Large stands of fennel, tarragon and lovage need dividing every three or four years to improve the vigour of the plant and the flavour of its leaves. When you lift them, discard the central and oldest part, and use the younger growths around the edges as your new plants. Replant in a different area of the herb garden into well-manured or fertilised soil.

HEDGE AND EDGE CONTROL

Hedging herbs that you are using to edge borders or to form small hedges in knot gardens should be pruned now. Clipping in early autumn gives them a chance to recover, and to grow new shoots that have enough time to strengthen before the onset of

cold winds and winter weather. Cut back woody herbs such as thyme, sage, lavender and rosemary to half the year's growth to control their size and promote a full and bushy shape.

Even with regular clipping, sage and thyme plants will develop very woody centres and eventually it is best to replace these with young, vigorous plants. Save the woody trimmings and clip them into manageable lengths. Then tie into bundles, store in a dry place and use as fire twigs in winter. As they burn, the resulting aromas will bring back welcome scents of summer.

Finally, cut off unharvested and spent flowers on curry plant, hyssop, santolina and lavender, reducing flower stems to 23cm (9in).

AUTUMN PLANTING

Autumn is the best time to plant perennial and shrubby herbs into a new herb garden, or to replant those you have just lifted and divided. The soil is relatively warm and any newly made compost will quickly enrich it. When you get nursery-bought herbs home, plant them as soon as possible. If you have to keep them on hold for a day or two, water them and stand in a sheltered site.

■ Choose a warm day and plant early, while the ground is still damp from overnight dew.

■ Water the plants thoroughly before you begin.

■ Dig a hole deep enough to accommodate the plant's roots and place a little compost in the hole.

■ Remove the plant from its pot, taking care not to damage the top-growth or roots.

■ Gently loosen any constricted roots and place the plant in the hole.

■ Backfill with the soil you dug out, but do not bury the plant any deeper than it was in the pot.

■ Firm the soil around the plant until the hole is completely filled.

■ Water in thoroughly, and continue to water regularly until the plant is well established.

INDOOR HERB GARDEN

■ Select strong-looking specimens of chives, marjoram and parsley in the garden to lift and pot up for the indoor herb garden.

■ When you dig up herbs, handle them gently to avoid root damage and disturbance but try to remove as much of the garden soil as possible. This will lower the level of weeds, diseases and soil pests that you might bring indoors.

■ Always use clean pots and fill them with a free-draining potting compost mix. Either use a commercial mixture that suits you, or mix together one part potting compost, one part soil and one part sand or perlite.

■ Keep newly potted herbs, such as chives and parsley, in their pots in the greenhouse, porch or summerhouse to acclimatise them to the lower light levels of sheltered living conditions. You could also leave them in a shady site outdoors, but don't forget to water them.

■ Cut back potted chives and grow them on in a warm, humid site. Then move them to a cooler site before bringing them indoors later in the autumn.

■ Outdoors, basil should be harvested now. Save one or two plants and repot them for growing on indoors. At this stage you may find garden centres selling off basil plants to get rid of stock. Buy them for your indoor harvest.

Food for the indoor garden

Plants grown in containers need extra attention in the shape of careful watering, balanced nutrients and a good light supply. Slow-release fertilisers are available for use in containers which provide nutrients to the plant over a long period. Usually in pellet form, they are added to the compost when you fill the pot. You can also add water-holding pellets that will slowly make water available to the plant's root hairs.

WARNING

■ *Before you bring newly bought plants or recently potted up home-grown herbs indoors, begin a quarantine and spraying process to control aphids. Use an insecticidal soap every two to three weeks to prevent a build up of these insects, which will thrive in the warm environment indoors.* ■

MAKING GARLIC ROPES

■ When you harvest garlic at the end of the summer, peel off one or two layers of outer leaves and trim the roots as close to the bulb as possible.

■ Place the trimmed plants on a wire frame and if the weather is warm, leave them to dry outside.

■ If it is a wet end-of-summer, dry them on racks in a warm, well-ventilated shed for up to a week. Check the leaves every few days, and when they have lost most of their moisture but are still flexible, plait them together to make neat garlic ropes.

■ Aim to work with bulbs of similar size and weight, so that the rope has a uniform look, using up to ten bulbs for each rope.

■ Store them in a dry, well-ventilated place until you are ready to use them or offer them as gifts.

■ Keep the ropes out of the warm and humid atmosphere of the kitchen, or they will not remain in prime condition.

OTHER METHODS OF PRESERVING

■ **Freezing** *This preserves the flavour but not the look of herbs, so it is only useful for those that you wish to pop straight into sauces, stews and soups. Parsley, sage, thyme, dill, tarragon, basil, chervil, chives, fennel, mint and lemon balm all freeze well. Frozen herbs keep their flavour for up to six months. Either place several small sprigs into small freezer bags, or chop the herbs small and freeze them in water in ice-cube trays. Remove herb ice cubes from the trays when frozen, bag them up and label.*

■ **Microwaving** *Lay the herbs on absorbent paper. Follow the microwave manufacturer's instructions for heat level. The timing varies with the type and amount of herbs you are drying. Check them every 30 seconds as they may get too dry, disintegrate and ignite. When they are ready, remove them from the absorbent paper and leave in a warm room for a few hours before storing.*

THINGS TO DO

Seeds to sow
Outdoors: alexanders (cold frame), borage, chervil (successional sowings), clary sage, coreopsis (in flowering position), flax (in pots), foxglove (cold frame), herb bennet, lamb's lettuce, mullein, sweet cicely, sweet woodruff
Thin: landcress, winter purslane

Plant out
Bay, box, catmint, chives, clary sage, clove pink, costmary, elecampane, garlic bulbs, jasmine, juniper, liquorice, Madonna lily bulbs, marsh mallow, mullein, orris, pennyroyal, rosemary, sage, spearmint, sweet cicely, thyme, wall germander, Welsh onion, wild strawberry, witch hazel

Propagate
Take cuttings: marsh mallow, rosemary, sage, thyme
Divide: chicory, echinacea, elecampane, Good King Henry, lemon grass, liquorice, soapwort, tansy, yarrow
Layer: peg down stems of honeysuckle and cover with soil

Harvest
Leaves: lamb's lettuce, rosemary, sage
Fruits: wild strawberries
Stems: artemisia
Roots: garlic (bulbs), horseradish, liquorice, marsh mallow, orris

Pot up
New myrtle and pink plants from layered parent. Pot up and overwinter in heated greenhouse

Routine maintenance
■ Cut back peonies.
■ Cut back dyer's chamomile to avoid seeding and to encourage new growth.
■ Remove flowering stems of jasmine.

practical project

MAKING A HERB-FILLED PILLOW

Fragrant home-grown herbs, dried then mixed to produce relaxing, sleep-inducing aromas or stimulating, summer-reminiscent perfumes, are best contained in pretty but simple-to-make decorative pillows. You will need to make a pillow case, a pillow to hold the padding and a small sachet for the herbs.

MATERIALS

for the herb sachet:
muslin or cotton 20 × 10cm (8 × 4in)

dried herbs and flowers

for the pillow:
cotton sheeting (or any closely woven cotton fabric) 50 × 30cm (20 × 12in)

50g (2oz) synthetic wadding (stuffing for children's toys)

for the pillow case:
fabric 60 × 35cm (24 × 14in)

matching sewing cotton

TO MAKE THE SACHET

■ Fold the fabric in half and stitch round the edge. Leave a small gap unsewn. Push the dried herbs and flowers through the gap into the sachet. Stitch the gap closed.

TO MAKE THE PILLOW

■ Fold the fabric in half across its length and stitch together down two sides. Stitch together 10cm (4in) of the third side.

■ Turn the pillow right side out, so that the stitched seams are now on the inside.

■ Loosely fill the pillow with the wadding. Make a pocket in the middle of the wadding and put the herb sachet inside.

■ Stitch up the rest of the third seam of the pillow.

TO MAKE THE PILLOW CASE

■ Make a 1.5cm (½in) fold along each of the 35cm (14in) sides of the material. Iron this in place, then fold in each of these sides again, this time by 2.5cm (1in), and iron.

■ Tack and hem along the folded edges. Overlap the hems, so that the fabric is tube-shaped. Tack the overlap 7.5cm (3in) along from each of the open edges. Stitch this down along both hem edges, making a 7.5cm (3in) long U-shape.

■ Reverse the fabric so that the right side is on the inside. Make sure the stitched-down overlap is roughly in the centre as you work.

■ Tack and stitch down both open edges. Reverse the material once again, so that the right side is outside. Place the inner herb-filled pillow inside the 'envelope' opening you have made.

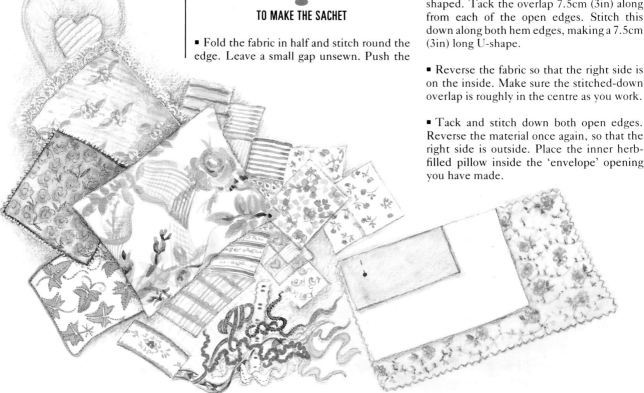

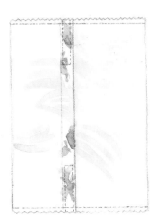

NOTE

■ *The wadding protects you from any hard bits there may be among the dried herbs, and helps stop the rustle of herbs inside the pillow.* ■

HERBS TO USE

A sleep pillow

Hop and chamomile flowers are the most sleep-inducing combination, but their aroma can be overpowering. You may wish to add some other herbal fragrance to dilute and soften their scent. For a fresh and spring-fragrant mixture combine meadowsweet, lemon verbena, sweet clover, heather, marjoram, honeysuckle and lavender flowers, rose petals and mint leaves.

Hops produce male and female flowers on separate plants. Those from female plants are best for sleep pillows. Female flowers are green and large, compared with the small, yellow-green male flowers. Wear gloves when handling hop flowers as they can cause an allergic skin reaction. Hop pillows keep their aroma for up to six months.

A fragrant pillow

The flowers and herbs that you would use in a fragrant pot-pourri are the ones to choose for a scented pillow. To rose petals and lavender add rosemary, myrtle, southern-wood, catmint, sweet clover and sweet woodruff.

Insect-repellent sachets

Make a smaller pillow, but use the same method for making the pillow and outer pillowcase. If the herbs have been well dried they should remain effective for up to two years.

Work in a well-ventilated room when you mix the herbs, so that you are not affected by the strong aromas. Use a sieve to remove any coarse material from the dried herbs, then lay them on brown paper and crush with a rolling pin. Mix the different herbs in a basin and then fill the pillow. Make a sticky label to go on the inner pillow, or note down the herbs you have used. If the combination works well, you will want to remember it for the future.

Muslin squares

If you would rather not go to the bother of making pillows or sachets, you can simply tie the insect-repellent herbs into muslin squares or even use brown paper bags. Several small bags placed in a drawer are more effective and easier to stow than one large pillow. If you wish to use them in a wardrobe, hang the sachets or muslin squares from hangers. You can also strew the herbs on the floor of the wardrobe.

INSECT-REPELLENT HERBS

Bay • Costmary •
Cotton lavender •
Elecampane (root) •
Eucalyptus• Fleabane •
Hyssop • Joe Pye weed •
Lavender • Mugwort •
Pennyroyal • Peppermint
Rosemary • Rue •
Southernwood • Sweet woodruff •
Tansy • Wormwood

LAVENDER BAGS
Lavender-filled bags have a double advantage: not only will they repel moths, but they will also give fragrance to linen and clothes.
Strip dried lavender flowers from their stems and, if the bags are still to be made, store the flowers out of sunlight in airtight containers.
To make the bags, use a small double square of muslin, cheesecloth or fine, coloured cotton. Fold the fabric in half and stitch down one long side and one short side, leaving one end open for the filling.
Turn the bag right-side out, so that the stitching is on the inside. Fill it with the dried lavender, but don't overfill. To close, stitch down the open side. It is easy to adapt the bag to hang from a coathanger inside a wardrobe. Use more lavender and tie up the open end of the bag with a ribbon. Loop the ribbon so that you can hang it from a hanger.

plants
OF THE
month

Artemisia

ALEXANDERS
(*Smyrnium olusatrum* – Umbelliferae)

An old pot-herb, alexanders or black lovage is a large plant best grown in a group where its height and size can be appreciated.

type	Hardy biennial or short-lived perennial
flowers	Yellow flowers appear from mid-spring to midsummer, followed by small black fruits
leaves	Broad, dark green leaves divided into oval leaflets with a celery-like taste
height	60–150cm (24–60in)
spread	60cm (24in)
planting	Plant in spring
position	Sun or light shade
soil	Average, well drained
care	Keep weeded until established. Support with twiggy sticks if necessary. To blanch, cover stems of one-year-old plants with soil or straw for three to four weeks in spring
propagation	Sow seed in autumn or spring direct into the growing site. Alexanders self seed freely
species and varieties	*Smyrnium perfoliatum*, 60cm (24in) high, has light green, perfoliate leaves and striking yellow, euphorbia-like, upper leaves and flowers. It is grown as an ornamental plant
harvest	Pick shoots and leaf stalks, and gather leaves for drying in late spring, just before flowering. Dig up mature roots in autumn
herbal value	Add leaves and shoots to soups and stews. Add fresh young leaves and flower buds to salads. Boiled young shoots make an unusual vegetable, but have a bitter after-taste unless blanched. Grind the seeds as a spice. The upper parts of the roots can be boiled and eaten like parsnips

ARTEMISIA
(*Artemisia* species – Compositae)

Artemisia is a large genus of mainly sun-loving shrubs and perennials. Their aromatic, silvery leaves make attractive accents in the herb garden.

type	Hardy deciduous shrub or herbaceous perennial
flowers	Small white or yellow button flowers appear in summer or autumn
leaves	Often finely divided or thread-like, silvery, aromatic
height	Varies, from 10–120cm (4–48in)
spread	15–120cm (6–48in)
planting	Plant in spring or autumn and cut back in autumn
position	Hot, sunny
soil	Well drained, average or poor, but white mugwort (*A. lactiflora*) needs moist soil
care	Deadhead after flowering. Cut back herbaceous forms in autumn. Protect alpine forms from winter wet. Trim untidy shrubs in early spring. Lift, divide and replant rampant types every two to three years, to retain vigour
propagation	Divide established plants and sow seed in spring, or take semi-ripe cuttings of shrubs in summer (see p76)
species and varieties	Shrubs include *Artemisia arborescens* and southernwood (*A. abrotanum*), both with filigree foliage and 120cm (48in) high and wide. Herbaceous perennials, all 45–90cm (18–36in) tall and 45–60cm (18–24in) across, include wormwood (*A. absinthum*), with silky grey leaves; *A. ludoviciana* 'Silver King', with narrow leaves; mugwort (*A. vulgaris*), with dark-green leaves; and dusty miller (*A. stellerana*), with senecio-like leaves. Rockery forms, 10–15cm (4–6in) high and 25–30cm (10–12in) across, include *A. schmidtiana* 'Nana' and *A. lanata*, both with finely cut leaves
harvest	Cut branches in mid- and late summer and hang upside down in bunches in a warm, airy spot to dry. If using as a backing for festive wreaths, tie long stems into circular shapes
herbal value	Infuse leaves to make a disinfectant, natural insecticide or moth repellent. A few mugwort leaves can be added to stuffings for duck or goose, to counteract the richness. Southernwood and wormwood tea acts as a tonic, but artemisias should not be taken by women who are pregnant or breast feeding

CLARY SAGE

(*Salvia sclarea* – Labiatae)

A big, back-of-the-border plant, clary sage, or bright eyes, creates an impressive haze of pink, purple or white for several weeks in summer.

type	Hardy biennial or perennial
flowers	Small, lilac or light blue flowers, surrounded by pink, purple or white bracts, appear in summer
leaves	Large, wrinkled, oval or heart-shaped
height	120cm (48in)
spread	45–60cm (18–24in)
planting	Plant in autumn or spring
position	Sunny
soil	Well drained
care	Stake if necessary
propagation	Sow seed in early autumn into the growing site
species and varieties	*Salvia sclarea* var. *turkestanica* is a biennial garden form, grown as an annual. It has aromatic, coarse leaves and tall spires of purple and white flowers with lavender bracts in summer. Painted sage (*S. viridis*) is a hardy annual, 45cm (18in) tall, with colourful white, pink, red, blue or purple bracts
harvest	Collect fresh leaves as needed. Collect flowers and leaves for drying just before the flowers open fully
herbal value	Once used to flavour beer, today clary is used to make a soothing eyewash and bath oil. Oil of clary is also produced commercially as a fixative for perfumes. Dip fresh young leaves in batter and fry; use the pineapple-scented dried flowers in sachets or pot-pourri. Make a heady wine from fresh flowers

GARLIC

(*Allium sativum* – Liliaceae)

Garlic's lingering, intensely pungent taste is the most memorable flavour of Mediterranean cooking. Store your crop in traditional, plaited ropes.

type	Hardy bulb, grown as an annual
flowers	Pale pink or white flowers appear in midsummer
leaves	Flat, grassy, dark green
height	30–60cm (12–24in)
spread	15–20cm (6–8in)
planting	Plant cloves with the thin, wispy tip end at the top. Papery outer skin should be undamaged. Plant from early autumn through to late autumn, or in early spring
position	Sunny
soil	Well-drained and open soil is best, but if your soil is heavy, line the trench with well-rotted organic matter or work in sharp sand before planting
care	Mulch in winter in cold areas or severe weather. Keep weeded, and water only in hot, dry spells. Apply liquid fertiliser if the soil is not fertile
propagation	Grow from sets available from seed merchants, or save the best bulb you grow from year to year. You can also use bulbs bought from greengrocers or markets. Use the largest cloves
species and varieties	Garlic is often sold unnamed in catalogues, but North American specialists identify several distinct types according to arrangement of the individual cloves around the central stem. 'Continental' usually has four large cloves, 'Silverskin' has three rows of cloves tightly packed around its centre; 'Rocambole' has several medium-sized cloves in one layer around the centre, while 'Artichoke' has a complicated arrangement of small and large cloves around the centre. The largest, Levant or elephant garlic (*Allium ampeloprasum*), has bulbs that weigh up to 450g (1lb) and are milder than other garlics
harvest	Harvest in late summer, when the leaves turn yellow. Lift the bulbs and dry them in a warm place such as a greenhouse or under cloches out of direct sunlight, as this can scorch the bulbs. Allow air to circulate around the bulbs and turn them daily. You can also dry them in trays on a sunny windowsill. When dry, hang in bunches, plait into ropes or store in net bags
herbal value	Garlic is known for its vitamin A, B and C content and for its antiseptic qualities. In the kitchen, it flavours sauces, oils, soups, meat, poultry, fish and vegetable dishes. *Aïoli*, Mediterranean garlic sauce, is used in many dishes, and as a dip

Clary sage

Garlic

practical
project
2

CREATING A HERB
TEA GARDEN

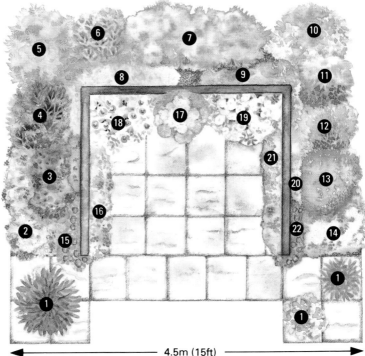

1 half-hardy tea
   plants
2 thyme
3 bergamot
4 purple sage
5 sweet Cicely
6 apple mint
7 fennel (2)
8 golden hop
9 green hop
10 lemon balm
11 peppermint
12 spearmint
13 rosemary
14 chamomile
15 *Rosa* 'Crimson
   Glory'
16 strawberries
17 *Alchemilla mollis*
18 *Rosa rugosa*
19 *Rosa rugosa alba*
20 jasmine
21 alpine
   strawberries
22 *Rosa* 'Etoile de
   Hollande'

← 4.5m (15ft) →

*paving stones for bench and pots/containers with
half-hardy tea plants eg lemon verbena and lemon grass,
basils (planted out in June), New Jersey tea, pineapple
sage, rose-scented pelargoniums*

CAUTION
*Blending is fun, but only use
herbs that you know are safe to
eat or cook with. If you are
pregnant, avoid tea made from
hyssop or pennyroyal*

You can ensure a steady supply of fresh and
dried herbs to use in refreshing herb teas by
planting a pretty arbour with a range of plants
that can be used in tea-making. Furnish the
tea garden with a comfortable bench, and
take a teatime break to relax and enjoy the
scents and aromas of the plants around you –
and in the tea.

PLANTS FOR THE TEA GARDEN

Climbers
Rosa 'Étoile de Hollande' has deep crimson
flowers with a strong scent. It is a vigorous
climber and flowers twice in the summer.
Rosa 'Crimson Glory' has large, dark crimson
flowers that deepen to purple as the flowers
age. It has a strong fragrance and abundant
blooms in early summer, with occasional
flowers later in the year. Combine these
roses with two scented white jasmines, and
two female golden and green hop plants.

Inside the arbour border
Plant alpine strawberries and lady's mantle
to make a mounded edging of attractive and
useful leaves. *Rosa rugosa* will provide wine-
coloured flowers then large red hips. *Rosa
rugosa* 'Alba' has single, white flowers with
orangey-red hips. Both flower over a long
period in summer. For rosehip tea, remove
the hairy bits from the inside of the hip.

Outside edge of the arbour
Use apple mint, bergamot, fennel, German
chamomile, lemon balm, peppermint,
rosemary, spearmint and sweet cicely.

Potted tea plants

Grow tender or half-hardy plants such as lemon verbena, lemon grass, New Jersey tea plant, pineapple sage and scented pelargoniums in pots at the front of the arbour. Plant basil into the tubs in midsummer.

USING TEA HERBS

Herb teas have many health-giving properties, but can also be enjoyed simply for their refreshing flavour. You can use herbs picked fresh in summer, or dried for winter use. Store in airtight jars out of direct sunlight to retain the flavour as long as possible. Keep individual herbs in separate containers, and label them with the date and the herb's name.

Herb teas are good hot or chilled from the refrigerator. You can mix herbs with other orthodox teas to vary the flavour or use them on their own to make a strong, herbal tea.

CHOOSING FLAVOURS

There are so many herbs to choose from, all with different aromas. Experiment with different combinations and with individual herbs. Not all will taste as strong as their aroma or scent, whereas some may be overwhelming. The best way to choose is to think of the flavour that the herb provides when used fresh. Mints offer clean and fresh tasting teas – to refresh you on a hot day. Chamomile and hop flowers, on the other hand, traditionally used in sleep pillows, have a soothing effect when used in teas. Drink this tea at night to help you sleep, or when you need to relax.

Hot tea

Bruise the fresh leaves of the herb so they release their flavour quickly into the hot water. Crumble dried herb material so that its flavours are also quickly taken up in the water. Warm a teapot (or cup, if making an individual tea). Add the herbs. The quantity will vary according to taste, but a teaspoon of dried herbs or tablespoon of fresh herbs per cup of hot water should be sufficient. Pour the boiling water into the container, add the herbs and allow to infuse for five to ten minutes. Strain the tea to remove any floating material, and then sit back and enjoy its herby flavour.

If you are making tea from the seeds of fennel, aniseed or dill, make a 'decoction'. Lightly crush the seed using a mortar and pestle. One teaspoon of seed per cup is sufficient to make a good brew. Bring the water to the boil, add the seeds and simmer for about ten minutes. Strain and serve hot.

Iced tea

Place the herbs in a teapot or cup, depending on quantity, and pour on boiling water. Allow to stand for five minutes, then strain, cool and refrigerate until required.

Sweeteners

Add honey, sugar or lemon to iced or hot teas. Brown sugar, however, will alter the colour of the tea, and some strongly flavoured honeys may overwhelm the delicate flavour of a herb tea.

TEATIME CHOICE

Rose-petal blend

Introduce yourself to herb teas by making a blend or mixture of petals and leaves and adding it to ordinary shop-bought tea. Use large-leaf, mild-flavoured China tea and mix in a few dark red, highly scented rose petals. Make the tea in the usual way. For an Arabic alternative, make a pot of weak China tea using one tablespoon to 1L (2pt) boiling water. Add a handful of mint leaves, roughly bruised and crushed, and sweetener.

Three-mint tea

Make a refreshing mint tea using spearmint, peppermint and apple mint leaves. Mix equal quantities of the three mints. Crush the leaves to release the oils and steep in boiling water for five to ten minutes. Strain, add honey and drink hot, or chill first.

Tea-party tea

Mix equal quantities of bergamot, lemon balm, peppermint and pineapple sage leaves. Crush the leaves and pour on boiling water.

Lemon tea

Use lemon balm, lemon grass or lemon verbena leaves. Crush a few leaves, pour over the boiling water.

Lemon-scented herbs all vary slightly in flavour. Lemon balm has the most delicate flavour and is best used fresh. Lemon grass has a strong, clean flavour and is good fresh or dried. Lemon verbena has the strongest flavour of all and may need a little honey to sweeten it. For a tropical flavour, add pineapple sage leaves to a lemon-scented herb. Use equal amounts of fresh leaves.

HERB FLAVOURS

BERGAMOT
Bergamot makes a tea with a taste similar to fine China tea. Use a few freshly picked leaves to make a highly scented, refreshing herbal tea.

CHAMOMILE
Use the flowers of German chamomile or the perennial Roman chamomile for a delicate apple-scented tea. Sweeten it with honey and drink before you go to bed as a relaxing, sleep-inducing tea. Chamomile tea is also good after a heavy meal as a digestive.

SAGE
Sage tea has a reputation for calming and refreshing. Pour ½L (1pt) boiling water over 25g (1oz) dried or 50g (2oz) fresh leaves. Leave to stand for five to ten minutes, strain and sweeten to taste. Purple- and golden-leaved sages can be used to make tea, and are highly ornamental and colourful in the herb garden.

FENNEL
The seeds and leaves of both green and bronze fennel provide a strong and distinctive-flavoured tea. Fennel tea helps you digest heavy meals and is best drunk hot.

HOPS
Pick and dry female flowers to make tea. Drink at night for a calming effect and in the morning to help clear a fuzzy head. Make in the same way as other herb teas and add honey as an optional sweetener.

plants

OF THE

month

Madonna lily

LIQUORICE

(*Glycyrrhiza glabra* – Leguminosae)

Grown commercially for the confectionary and and medicinal value of its thick tap roots, liquorice offers cool, ferny foliage to enhance the herb garden.

type	Hardy herbaceous perennial
flowers	Blue, purple or white, sweet pea-like flowers appear in summer, followed by reddish-brown seed pods
leaves	Composite, dark-green, slightly sticky
height	60–150cm (24–60in) high
spread	30–60cm (12–24in)
planting	Plant in autumn or spring
position	Open, sunny
soil	Deep, well drained, rich, sandy
care	Keep weeded until established. Cut down foliage in autumn. Mulch annually in spring
propagation	Divide roots in autumn or spring
species and varieties	North American wild liquorice (*Glycyrrhiza lepidota*) is similar, but with yellow flowers
harvest	Lift three-year-old roots in late summer or early autumn, wipe clean and dry. To make liquorice commercially, the roots are macerated and boiled, and the liquid concentrated into a solid extract before being rolled into long, cylindrical sticks
herbal value	In commercial use the root flavours confectionary, tobacco and gives colour and body to drinks such as stout and porter. It is also used to make medicines more palatable. Infuse the root to make a refreshing tea

MADONNA LILY

(*Lilium candidum* – Liliaceae)

The white trumpet-like flowers of the Madonna lily provide sweet fragrance and height in the herb garden. Grow them in containers or in a floral herb border.

type	Hardy bulb
flowers	White, yellow-centred flowers appear in midsummer
leaves	Small, pale green, lance-shaped along the stem with a basal rosette that forms in autumn and persists over winter
height	90–180cm (36–72in)
spread	20cm (8in)
planting	Plant in early autumn, covering the bulb with 5cm (2in) of soil. On heavy soil, plant in a pocket of sand
position	Sheltered, sunny
soil	Well drained, lime rich
care	Keep well watered in dry weather; spray against botrytis if necessary
propagation	Remove plump scales in early autumn and plant up separately
harvest	Use Madonna lily as a fragrant ornamental plant to enjoy in the herb garden
herbal value	Although the bulbs are used in cosmetic manufacture and in ointments for treating burns and inflammation, there are no domestic uses other than for ornamental garden value

MARSH MALLOW

(*Althaea officinalis* – Malvaceae)

So called because of its moist natural habitat, marsh mallow has given its name to the sweet originally made from its powdered roots, sugar and water.

type	Hardy herbaceous perennial, grown as an annual or biennial
flowers	Pale pink or white flowers appear in late summer
leaves	Velvety, grey, lobed and toothed
height	60–120cm (24–48in)
spread	30–60cm (12–24in)
planting	Plant in spring or autumn
position	Open, sunny
soil	Moist, fertile
care	Keep weeded until established. Water freely in dry weather. Stake if necessary and mulch annually if grown as a perennial. Young plants, however, flower best and are more resistant to rust, so grow as an annual or biennial
propagation	Sow seed in spring or late summer, or root softwood cuttings in summer
species and varieties	The rough marsh mallow (*Althea hirsuta*) is a more slender, spreading plant. Garden hollyhock (*A. rosea*, syn *Alcea rosea*) is a popular perennial, up to 3m (10ft) tall, often grown as a biennial or annual. Pink in the species, flowers can be single or double and white, yellow, pink or purple in named forms, such as 'Summer Carnival'

harvest | Pick fresh leaves and flowers as needed. For drying, pick just before flowers open. Collect seeds when ripe in autumn. Dig up roots, wipe clean and dry in autumn

herbal value | Add flowers, young leaves and tops or ripe seeds to salads. Use tea made from the roots to calm and soothe. Use a cold or hot infusion from the leaves and roots to make gentle facial lotions and for face steaming

ORRIS

(*Iris germanica* var. *florentina* – Iridaceae)

For centuries orris root has been valued in perfumery and as a fixative for pot-pourri. In the garden, this iris offers faintly scented flowers and strong leaves.

type | Rhizomatous perennial
flowers | Large, greyish-white, typical flag iris flowers appear in early summer
leaves | Broad, grey, sword-shaped leaves that grow in a fan arrangement from the rhizome
height | 60cm (24in)
spread | 30cm (12in)
planting | Plant in spring or early autumn, leaving the top of the rhizomes exposed. Firm in well
position | Sunny or partial shade
soil | Free draining, neutral, fertile
care | Cut back flower stalks after flowering. Protect against slugs and snails
propagation | Divide every three to four years, after flowering, replanting younger, outer portions. Use second- and third-year growth to make orris root for pot-pourri
species and varieties | *Iris pallida* is also grown for its roots, which are used in a similar way. It has blue or lilac flowers that grow up to 90cm (36in) tall and grey leaves. The gold-variegated form, 'Aureo Variegata', and silver-variegated 'Argenteo Variegata' are first-class foliage plants for the herb garden
harvest | Harvest roots of three-year-old plants when dividing large clumps. Clean, slice into rounds or cubes with a knife or in a food processor, or grate. During preparation, wear gloves and work in a well-ventilated room, as orris root can cause headaches and dermatitis.

Leave in a well-ventilated, dry and warm place for several weeks to dry. Grind into powder or leave in larger pieces. Store in airtight jars for two years while the violet perfume develops

herbal value | The dried root is violet scented, and is used in pot-pourri, pomanders and, as oil of orris, in perfumery, soaps, and to scent linen

SOAPWORT

(*Saponaria officinalis* – Caryophyllaceae)

Soapwort, also known as Fuller's herb or bouncing Bet, is a pretty but potentially invasive plant, valued for its cleansing properties and clove scent.

type | Hardy herbaceous perennial
flowers | Pink or white flowers appear in late summer
leaves | Oval, pointed, pale green
height | 60–90cm (24–36in)
spread | 30–45cm (12–18in)
planting | Plant in autumn or spring
position | Sun or light shade
soil | Moist, rich loam
care | Keep weeded and watered until established. Support stems with twiggy sticks. Cut back after flowering to encourage a second crop of flowers in autumn. Cut back in late autumn. Mulch in spring
propagation | Sow in spring or autumn but provide cold treatment for seed (see page 88). Lift and divide in early autumn or spring. Soapwort self seeds freely
species and varieties | Garden forms include the mat-forming *Saponaria* × 'Bressingham', 7.5cm (3in) high and 10cm (4in) across, with vivid pink blooms; *S.o.* 'Rubra Plena', with ragged, double red flowers; and rock soapwort or tumbling Ted (*S. ocymoides*) 2.5–5cm (1–2in) high and 45cm (18in) across, which makes sprawling mats of pale or deep pink flowers
harvest | Pick fresh leaves, flowers and roots as needed. Dry flowers, leaves and roots in late summer and autumn, for winter use
herbal value | The lather created by boiling leaves in water is a gentle cleanser for fabrics and wool. It can also be used to make soothing and cleansing facial rinses

Marsh mallow

Soapwort

CAUTION
Soapwort is poisonous, and must not be taken internally.

OCTOBER

*You may clean your home in spring, but autumn is the time to
clean, tidy and clear up in the herb garden.*

*If you are planning an entirely new herb garden, now is also the
right time to begin preparation of the site. Clear it of perennial
weeds, dig it over and incorporate fork-loads of organic matter
from your own compost heap or bought, in bagged form, from the
garden centre. Leave the prepared soil to take the winter action of
frost and wind, which breaks down the surface into a crumbly-
textured soil good for growing healthy plants.*

*If you wish to start a formal knot garden, begin its preparation
now. Design it on paper, lay it out and set in place the plants for
the hedges or ribbons of colour that enclose less formal plants. As
the soil is still warm, they will have a chance to establish their root
systems and start growing well before winter begins.*

*Perennial herbs continue to need clearing and dividing. Cut back
old foliage, and lift and divide large clumps that have not been
growing well over the last season. As the night temperatures fall,
bring in tender perennial herbs that have spent the summer
soaking up the sun. Overwinter them in frost-free conditions, and
make sure you have taken cuttings from all tender plants to ensure
stock increase and survival should any be lost in a severe winter.*

*Harvest leaves of rosemary, thyme, sage, parsley and the last of
the basil to add to savoury and sweet autumn jellies, to use over
winter or to offer as gifts.*

*Herb leaves and scented flowers that have been drying in sheds or
an airing cupboard should be prepared for dry storage, or mixed
to use in herb pillows, sachets and pot-pourri.*

tasks
FOR THE
month

HERBS FOR THE COMPOST HEAP

Once cleared from the herb garden the following plants can be used to start next year's compost heap:

ANNUAL HERBS SUCH AS
Cumin • Caraway • Aniseed • Fenugreek • Coriander • Poppy • Summer savory • Borage • Basil • Tagetes • Pot marigold • Dill • Nasturtium • Rocket •

ALSO BIENNIALS LIKE
Parsley • Mullein • Chervil

CHECKLIST

- Plant evergreen herb garden hedges.
- Provide protection for newly planted evergreens and hedges
- Carry out autumn clearance of annual and spent biennial herbs
- Continue tidying up perennial herbs
- Continue lifting and dividing plants
- Fork over and add compost to the soil
- Mulch around perennials with compost
- Bring in tender perennials to overwinter in a frost-free greenhouse
- Continue preparing plants for the indoor winter herb garden

HERB HEDGES

In a herb garden, hedges serve many practical as well as ornamental purposes.

When well established, hedges provide shelter from wind, and therefore increase the temperature of both soil and air around the herb plants. This provides herbs with the warm, sheltered conditions they most enjoy.

The colour of the herb hedge is important as a backdrop for the plants it encloses. The green of slow-growing box or the feathery silver of cotton lavender provides a textured and strong background for a variety of different coloured herbs. Yew, also slow-growing, forms a traditional, dark green herb hedge. Plant it with a good dressing of bonemeal, and water it well to get young plants off to a good start.

Choosing hedge plants
Box and yew hedges are ideal for enclosing large, formal herb gardens. In a small space they have disadvantages, as they tend to be greedy for water and nutrients from the soil, and so are in competition with other herb plants. Instead choose more productive plants as low-growing hedging or edging cover. Chives, alpine strawberry, parsley, thyme, viola and winter savory are all productive, ornamental and effective as 'hedges'. Even though they will still be competing with other herbs for the available moisture and nutrients, they will be providing more than just shelter and background colour.

Hedge plants may also have their own aromatic or floral qualities to offer. There are many low-growing herbs that can be used instead of the slower-growing evergreen hedges: lavender, rosemary, dwarf box and cotton lavender are popular choices. Lavender hedges can be clipped closely and enjoyed solely for their silver-grey foliage, or they can be left to flower, providing extra height, colour and fragrance, as well as useful herb material to dry for pot-pourri or kitchen uses.

Cotton lavender and curry plant offer beautifully textured silver foliage, but need to be clipped regularly to keep compact. Close clipping means, of course, that you have to do without their flowers. Grow extra plants within the herb garden and let them flower, so that you can enjoy their button-like yellow blooms in the garden as well as dried in home-made herbal produce.

Planting a hedge
Plant individual specimens of lavender, box or yew into planting holes dug along a straight line, the length of the border or bed you wish to shelter. Space the plants about two-thirds of their eventual height apart. Make a planting hole large enough to take the roots, fork in a handful of bonemeal or a spadeful of compost, set the plant in, backfill with soil and firm in. Water the plants thoroughly and continue to water until they are well established.

If you are using productive herbs such as parsley or chives for the hedge, sow seed direct into the ground in spring when the soil has warmed up. You can also plant bought chives in autumn or spring. Parsley doesn't always transplant well, so it is best sown direct. If you plan to use basil as your edging plant, sow it direct in early summer, or transplant greenhouse-sown basil in late spring when all danger of frost is over.

NOTE

- *In cold winters it may be necessary to erect a shelter for the young hedge plants to protect them from cold, drying winds. Insert canes into the ground and tie a sacking or fine-mesh netting wind shelter in place on the canes* ■

AUTUMN CLEAN-UP

Begin the autumn clean-up by removing annuals, and biennials that are in their second year and have flowered. Naturally, any annual and perennial weeds that have escaped your attentions before now, must be dealt with vigorously.

Tidy up perennials

Cut back and tidy up perennials such as hyssop, perennial marjoram, mint, sweet cicely, salad burnet, fennel, tarragon, chives and lemon balm. Cut back to young shoots, so that fresh growth has time to strengthen before the onset of frosts.

Continue to lift and divide perennials that have got too large or are losing their vigour.

Enriching the soil and mulching

Once you have cleared up annuals and biennials and tidied up the perennial herbs, lightly fork over the soil around the remaining evergreens and newly replanted perennials. Incorporate some of the well-rotted herbal compost you have made over the year. Layer it thickly around the plants so that it acts as a winter mulch, protecting plant roots from excessive cold. Applied in autumn when the soil is still warm, the mulch layer acts like a blanket. Mulch applied around the base of newly planted herbs will have the same effect.

TENDER TREATMENT

When cool, drying autumn winds begin and night temperatures fall, bring tender herbs such as scented pelargoniums, woolly thyme, lemon verbena, pineapple sage, New Jersey tea plant and ginger, and tender lavenders such as woolly and French lavender, into a frost-free place to overwinter. Young herb plants in containers should also be brought in and protected, as they may not be able to withstand a very cold winter.

Clean up any weeds that might be growing in the potting compost of the tender plants, sink the pots into the soil of the greenhouse beds, and wrap them in newspaper or make straw walls around them to keep them warm. Reduce watering and cut back the stems of lemon verbena and scented pelargoniums.

INDOOR HERB GARDEN

Now is à good time to visit your local garden centre or herb nursery and see what they still have available. Buy small sage, salad burnet, rosemary and thyme plants, acclimatise them gradually to indoor life and use them as the nucleus of your indoor herb garden. Buy new plants of tarragon, or lift some roots of an existing plant. Place them in a cool site for a few weeks, then bring them into the greenhouse to force in heat. Lift a few mint roots too, and put them in pots in a heated propagator. Tarragon and mint will soon develop leafy stems. Grow them on in the greenhouse and bring them indoors for your winter collection once they are established.

THINGS TO DO

Sow seed
Outdoors: honeysuckle, lamb's lettuce

Plant out
Bergamot, lady's mantle

Propagate
Take cuttings: elder (hardwood)
Divide: chives, comfrey, costmary, echinacea, elecampane, Good King Henry, lemon grass, mint, sorrel, tarragon, Welsh onion

Harvest
Leaves: basil, mint, parsley, rosemary, sage, Welsh onion
Bulbs: Welsh onion
Stems and roots: madder, sweet cicely

Routine maintenance
■ Cut back brown leaves of chive plants
■ Cut back comfrey and lady's mantle severely
Indoor herb garden
■ Continue preparing plants for indoors
■ Pot up or buy young rosemary, sage and tarragon plants
■ Root mint and tarragon in pots in a heated propagator

HERB GARDEN HEDGE PLANTS

plant	description	plant	description
DWARF BOX low	90cm (36in) but clipped to 15cm (6in), evergreen	**CURRY PLANT** medium	45cm (18in) evergreen
DWARF CURRY PLANT low	15-20cm (6-8in), evergreen	**ENGLISH LAVENDER** medium	60-120cm (24-48in), evergreen
DWARF LAVENDER 'Hidcote' low	45cm (18in) evergreen	**HYSSOP** medium	60cm (24in), semi-evergreen/deciduous
SHRUBBY THYMES low	30cm (12in), evergreen	**SANTOLINA** medium	30-60cm (12-24in), evergreen
BOX medium	4·5m (4ft) but slow growing, evergreen	**ROSEMARY** medium	Up to 1·8m (6ft), evergreen

practical
project

CREATING
A KNOT GARDEN

YOU WILL NEED

squared graph paper
pencil
compass
ruler

KEY
HEDGES
Santolina 'Lemon Queen'
Santolina rosmarinifolia
Santolina chamaecyparissus 'Nana'

CENTRE
Rosmarinus officinalis 'Miss
Jessopp's Upright'

**HEDGES
ALTERNATIVE**
Buxus sempervirens
Hyssopus ssp. *aristatus*
Teuchrium chamaedrys

The most formal of herb gardens is a traditional low-hedged, geometrically shaped knot garden. Old-fashioned and traditional, it can still be used today to show off individual herbs to best advantage within a network of evergreen, aromatic hedges. The contrast of colours and textures made by the interlaced hedges creates a strong framework for flowering herbs with looser growth and more relaxed foliage.

DESIGNING A KNOT GARDEN

- Draw a square to scale on the piece of graph paper. A square 3 × 3m (3 × 3yd) is a good size to work with. It gives you space to weave the ribbon of the hedges and for infilling with other herbs, but is still possible to maintain easily.

- Experiment with different shapes, but always remember that the simpler the design, the easier it will be to lay out and maintain. Once you are happy with the shape, transfer it onto the graph paper.

- Next, work out how thick the hedges are to be and how many plants you will need. Allow 23cm (9in) between plants. Mark the position of each plant with a dot on the graph paper.

- You may wish to fill the spaces between the hedges with a number of different herbs, or you may want to leave them empty.

- If so, mulch these areas with sand or pea shingle to keep weeds down and make a colour contrast.

PLANTS TO CHOOSE

Different varieties of one particular species can be used to provide contrasting colour and texture. Cotton lavender is a good choice: use the silvery grey of *Santolina chamaecyparissus* 'Nana' with the bright green of *Santolina rosmarinifolia* and the willow green of *Santolina* 'Lemon Queen'. Box (*Buxus sempervirens*) is another good choice and tolerates clipping and shaping well, but it is

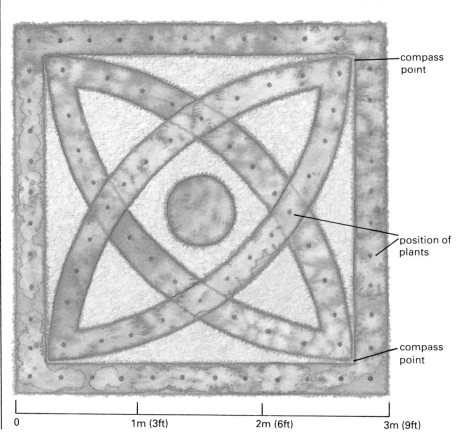

compass
point

position of
plants

compass
point

0	1m (3ft)	2m (6ft)	3m (9ft)

slow growing. Combine green-leaved box with the silver-edged leaves of *Buxus sempervirens* 'Elegantissima' or the variegated gold of the cultivar 'Latifolia Maculata'. For really low-growing hedges use thyme, winter savory, wall germander and rock hyssop.

MARKING OUT THE PLAN

■ First clear the site of all weeds and dig it over. Incorporate well-rotted organic matter and sand or grit into heavy soils to improve drainage.

■ Rake the soil over and level it, before marking out the perimeter of the bed with canes and string.

■ Next, using pegs and strings, mark out the lines of your graph paper.

■ To position the curves of the hedges, use two different materials. For example, use sand to mark the silver 'ribbon' and pea shingle to mark the green 'ribbon'.

■ To distribute the marking material evenly, use a bottle 'pencil' filled with sand or pea shingle with a piece of string 3m (3yd) long attached to it. Tie the other end of the string to a stick, thus making yourself a large 'compass' for marking out arcs on the ground.

■ Place the stick in the ground and, with the string extended, use the bottle to describe the curve that you have drawn on the graph paper. As you do this, tip sand out of the bottle onto the soil.

■ To mark straight lines of hedging, use lengths of string tied securely to pegs. Soon you will have an intricate and complicated pattern of sand, string and pegs. But be patient: it will eventually take shape.

PLANTING THE KNOT GARDEN

Use uniformly sized plants. Buy them at the same time from one source so that there is no variation in size and plant in spring or autumn, so that they have time to establish.

■ If you wish to grow the plants from cuttings, take them in spring, line them out in a cuttings bed for a complete season and transplant into their growing positions in the second spring.

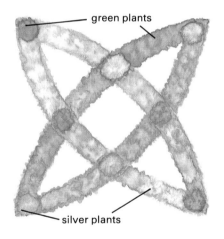

green plants

silver plants

(Continued on page 118)

PLANTS FOR A KNOT GARDEN

HEDGES
Box
Cotton lavender
Curry plant
Lavender species and various cultivars
Rock hyssop
Rosemary 'Miss Jessopp's Upright'
Thyme species and cultivars
Wall germander
Winter savory

SHORT-LIVED KNOTS
Chives
Parsley

GROUND-COVER FILLERS
Alchemilla
Chamomile
Pinks
Primrose
Strawberry
Thymes
Violets

SHORT-LIVED FILLERS
Basil
Flax
Pot marigold

CENTRE OF THE KNOT
Apothecary's rose
Juniper
Myrtle
Southernwood
Standard rose
Sweet bay grown as a mop-head
Rosemary 'Miss Jessopp's Upright'

MARKING AN ARC ON THE GROUND WITH SAND

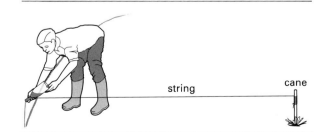

string   cane

cane
string

bottle filled with sand attached to string to mark arc on ground

cane

string tied to a cane

plants
OF THE
month

Box

Curry plant

BOX

(*Buxus sempervirens* – Buxaceae)

Both common box and its dwarf form are traditionally associated with herb gardens. Use them to make hedges and edges, for topiary work and as shaped container plants.

type	Hardy evergreen shrub or tree
flowers	Insignificant yellow flowers appear in spring
leaves	Small, dark green and glossy oval
height	Slow-growing; 4.5m (15ft) if left to develop. Dwarf box grows to 90cm (3ft). Both are kept compact by regular pruning
spread	4.5m (15ft). Dwarf box spreads to 45cm (18in)
planting	Plant pot-grown specimens in autumn or spring
position	Sun or semi-shade
soil	Average; well drained
care	Keep weed free and watered until established. Prune in midsummer and early autumn
propagation	Take semi-ripe cuttings in early summer or when pruning
species and varieties	Garden forms include 'Aureovariegata', with leaves edged and splashed in creamy yellow; 'Elegantissima', compact with silver-edged leaves; 'Rosmarinifolia' with narrow, sage green leaves and 'Suffruticosa', the dwarf or edging box
harvest	Box is grown for its ornamental value alone
herbal value	Box foliage is long-lasting in fresh flower displays and in decorative, festive wreaths

CURRY PLANT

(*Helichrysum italicum* syn. *H. serotinum* – Compositae)

Use curry plant as a contrast in a grey border or as hedging in parterres or knot gardens. Its powerful curry scent may be too strong for some tastes.

type	Hardy sub-shrub, evergreen in mild areas
flowers	Mustard-yellow flowers appear in mid- and late summer
leaves	Narrow, needle-like, grey-green
height	45cm (18in)
spread	45cm (18in)
planting	Plant container-grown plants in mid- or late spring
position	Sunny, sheltered; cold, wet areas are unsuitable
soil	Well drained, light, poor
care	Protect from winter wet, prune in mid-spring, remove faded flowers. Cut back in autumn if using as part of a knot hedge
propagation	Take semi-ripe cuttings in late spring or summer
species and varieties	The dwarf *H. italicum* subsp. *microphyllum*, 15–20cm (6–8in) high, has diminutive, velvety leaves and pink-tinged, white flowers. It is tender. Other forms include the moderately hardy *H. orientale* 'Sulphur Light', 40cm (16in) tall and 30cm (12in) across, with long, felted silver leaves and sulphur-yellow blooms; and the half-hardy *H. petiolare* (syn. *H. petiolatum*), a semi-trailing sub-shrub, 60cm (24in) or more across, with silvery, felted, round leaves. The annual *H. bracteatum*, or strawflower, has red, pink, orange or yellow double daisies, and is one of the easiest everlastings to grow and dry
harvest	Pick the leaves as needed, and the flowers for drying just before they open fully
herbal value	Sprinkle a few leaves of curry plant on to salads, soups, casseroles or stews. Use the flowers in fresh or dried displays, or as everlastings in dried flower arrangements, wreaths or pot-pourri

ECHINACEA

(*Echinacea purpurea* – Compositae)

In the herb garden echinacea offers stately and colourful ornament. In the pharmaceutical world over 240 products are made from its roots, leaves and oils.

type	Hardy herbaceous perennial
flowers	Purple flowers appear from mid-summer to early autumn
leaves	Mid-green, coarse-textured and oval
height	1.2m (4ft)
spread	45cm (18in)
planting	Plant in spring
position	Full sun
soil	Rich, well drained
care	Keep watered and weed free until established. Dead head to extend

the flowering period. Cut down to ground level in autumn

propagation	Divide and replant in autumn or spring. Take root cuttings in late autumn or winter. Sow seed in spring
species and varieties	*Echinacea pallida,* with pale purple to white flowers, and *E. angustifolia,* with narrow leaves, are gardenworthy species. *E. purpurea* is also known as *Rudbeckia purpurea* and its common name is purple coneflower. Garden cultivars include 'Robert Bloom', with intense cerise-mauve blooms; 'The King', crimson pink with a mahogany centre; and the white-flowered 'White Lustre'
harvest	Flowers of purple coneflower, other species and garden cultivars dry well if picked just as they open
herbal value	The plant has great herbal value in the commercial pharmaceutical sector. In today's herb garden, grow it as an ornamental

ELECAMPANE
(*Inula helenium* – Compositae)

Elecampane was a traditional monastic herb garden plant, prized for the medicinal properties of its root. Today, its cheerful daisy flowers are the main attraction.

type	Hardy herbaceous perennial
flowers	Yellow, daisy-like flowers appear in summer
leaves	Long, pointed and dock-like in shape
height	60–150cm (24–60in)
spread	45–90cm (18–36in)
planting	Plant in spring or autumn
position	Sun or partial shade
soil	Rich and moist
care	Keep watered and weed free until established. Cut back to ground level in autumn. Lift and divide clumps regularly to retain vigour
propagation	Sow seed in spring. Lift and divide plants in spring or autumn
species and varieties	Garden species grown for their ornamental value include *Inula orientalis* that grows 45cm (18in) high with large orange-yellow flowers; *I. magnifica,* a larger version of elecampane; and *I. ensifolia* that grows to 30cm (12in) high with narrow leaves and dark yellow flowers on thin stalks

harvest	Dig up two-year-old roots in late summer. Wash, slice into thin rounds and dry. When fully dry they become violet-scented. Store in airtight containers
herbal value	Candy the root to use as a traditional sweetmeat or as pastilles for coughs. Use it in the herb garden as a contrast plant. The yellow flowers look well against stands of bronze fennel or purple orach

LADY'S MANTLE
(*Alchemilla mollis* – Rosaceae)

Prized for its soft, velvety leaves and frothy clouds of small yellow flowers, lady's mantle is used to make gentle skin products.

type	Hardy herbaceous perennial
flowers	Clouds of small, greenish-yellow flowers in late spring and early summer
leaves	Basal mounds of soft-textured, ruff-like light green leaves
height	60cm (24in)
spread	60cm (24in)
planting	Lady's mantle makes good ground-cover, but clumps need to be split every few years
position	Best in sun or partial shade
soil	Well-drained, moist loam. *Alchemilla alpina* grows well on dry banks
care	Cut back after flowering to 2.5cm (1in) above ground
propagation	Sow seed in early spring into seed trays. Transplant into a nursery bed and plant into the flowering position from autumn through to spring. Lift and divide existing plants between autumn and spring
species and varieties	*Alchemilla alpina* grows to 15cm (6in) and has silver-edged leaves with grey undersides. It makes an attractive, low-growing, informal edging to a herb garden
harvest	Pick young leaves to use fresh for a sharp flavour in salads. Pick leaves before flowering to dry in a cool oven or on a drying rack in a shady, well-ventilated site. Pick flowers as they open to dry for winter displays
herbal value	Infuse leaves to make a facial toner. In the herb garden, lady's mantle is used to make informal hedging or edging

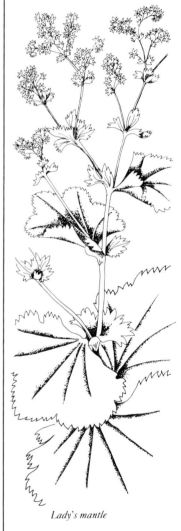

Lady's mantle

(Continued from page 115)

▪ The first plants to go in are the corner plants, to ensure correct spacing.

▪ Next, put in the plants that grow at the junction of two ribbons. Work systematically around the knot (for our design, alternating green and silver plants at each of the crossing points).

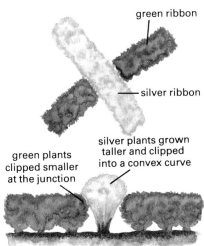

green ribbon

silver ribbon

green plants clipped smaller at the junction

silver plants grown taller and clipped into a convex curve

▪ Then plant the remainder 23cm (9in) apart along the lines of sand or string. Fill in the areas between the hedging with plants or with coloured sand, pea shingle or peat to suppress weeds and give emphasis to hedges.

MAINTAINING THE KNOT GARDEN

Clip the herb hedges in spring to encourage new growth and promote a bushy shape. Through the summer, whenever the hedges get lanky or out of step with each other, clip them back. In autumn, give a final trim so that any new growth is made well before the first frosts.

You can also emphasise the shape of the knot by clipping the plants into more pronounced curves. Where the knot lines cross and a green ribbon seems to go under a silver ribbon, allow the silver plant at that point to grow slightly taller. Then, when you clip it, shape it into a pronounced convex curve. Clip the green plants on either side of it into concave curves.

In spring, lightly dress the ground around the plants with a slow-release fertiliser to encourage good leafy growth during the summer, and weed as necessary.

practical project 2

MAKING HERB PRESERVES

YOU WILL NEED

large saucepan or preserving pan
jelly bag or square of muslin
string
large bowl
ladle
funnel
clean and sterilised jam jars (boil for 10 minutes and dry in a low-heat oven)
wooden spoons
oven gloves (for handling hot jars)
measuring jug
scales

Your herb harvest can also be turned into sweet and savoury preserves, jams and jellies, to use with meat dishes or to spread on bread and biscuits. In autumn, herb jellies and jams are the perfect excuse for using up windfall and surplus fresh or frozen fruit.

Fruit base
Slightly under-ripe windfalls, cookers or crab apples are best for the fruit base. Quince, rhubarb, gooseberry, red and white currants and grapes are also suitable, strained to make the fruit jelly.

INGREDIENTS

fruit of your choice

450g sugar per 580ml (1lb per 1pt) strained fruit liquid

herbs of your choice, water

BASIC APPLE JELLY

Use under-ripe apples as they have a higher natural pectin content than mature apples and the jelly will set better.

▪ Wash the apples and cut them into chunks, leaving cores and pips intact but removing any damaged or insect-infested pieces.

▪ Place the prepared apples in a large saucepan or preserving pan. Add water to cover. Bring to the boil, then simmer until the apples have cooked down to a pulp.

▪ Ladle the apple pulp into a scalded jelly bag, and leave it suspended over a bowl to drip for 24 hours. Avoid squeezing the bag,

Hanging a jelly bag on an upturned stool

as, if you do, the jelly will be cloudy. Next day, measure the strained liquid and pour it into the preserving pan. For every 580ml (1pt) liquid, add 450g (1lb) sugar to the pan.

■ Heat the pan to dissolve the sugar and bring the liquid to the boil. Add the herbs of your choice at this stage. Wrap a good handful of chopped or bruised leaves in muslin and place in the pan.

■ Let the liquid boil rapidly for 15-20 minutes, stirring so that it does not stick. Test the jelly for set on a cool saucer: when ready, it forms little wrinkles on the surface when pushed with a spoon. Remove the muslin bag of herbs. Skim off bubbles and foamy liquid from the surface of the jelly.

■ Leave the jelly to set in the pan for a few minutes, and if you wish add some fresh, clean, unbroken leaves of the herb to the jelly. If you do this while the jelly is cooling in the pot, you will find that the leaves are evenly distributed through the jelly and will not float to the surface.

■ Remove the warmed jars from the oven and stand them on a wooden chopping board. Place a jam funnel on the first jar and ladle the jelly into it. Use oven gloves when handling the jars and avoid splashes from the hot jelly.

■ If you want just a single sprig of herb in the jar, ladle the jelly in as before, but only add the sprig after the jelly has set for a few minutes. Always use clean sprigs of herb to avoid any bacteria getting into the jelly.

■ Place a waxed jelly-sealing disc (wax side

down) on the top of each jar and press it down gently to remove air bubbles. When the jelly has cooled, cover with a cellophane circle and elastic band, and then a metal lid.

Rose hip jelly

Use 900g (2lb) rosehips to 450g (1lb) cooking apples. Cut the apples into rough chunks and place in a saucepan with the hips. Cover with water and bring to the boil. Simmer until the fruits are reduced to pulp, then strain through a jelly bag for 24 hours. For each 580ml (1pt) liquid add 450g (1lb) sugar. Heat slowly until the sugar has dissolved, then boil rapidly until setting point is reached. Skim off foam and pour into prepared jars. Cover with waxed discs and seal when the jelly has cooled.

Parsley or sage jelly

Fill a saucepan with washed and chopped parsley or sage leaves. Just cover with water. Bring to the boil, then simmer for 30 minutes. Strain through a fine sieve and for every 580ml (1pt) liquid add 450g (1lb) sugar, plus the juice of a large lemon. Bring to the boil to dissolve the sugar and boil rapidly until setting point is reached. Pour into jars, cool and seal.

Mint and gooseberry jelly

Cook 1.8kg (4lb) green gooseberries to a pulp in 1L (2pt) water. Strain through a jelly bag. Measure the liquid and add 450g (1lb) sugar to every 580ml (1pt) liquid. Tie several stems of mint into a muslin bag and add to the pan. Bring slowly to the boil until the sugar has dissolved, then boil rapidly until setting point is reached. Remove the mint and pour the jelly into jars. Seal when cool, label and store out of sunlight.

HERBS FOR JAMS AND JELLIES

LEAVES
Basil
Lemon thyme
Meadowsweet (gives almond flavour)
Mints
Pineapple sage
Rosemary
Scented pelargonium
Tarragon
Thyme

FOR PERFUME AND EXTRA FLAVOUR
Fennel (seeds)
Rose (hips and petals)

LEAVES FOR USE WITHOUT FRUIT BASE
Parsley
Sage

MAKING A JELLY BAG
Cut a 35cm (14in) square of muslin, hem the edges and sew on four loops, one at each corner.

PRETTY GIFT

If the preserve is to be offered as a gift, make a gingham or coloured cotton cover to use instead of the metal lid. Cut a circle 5–7.5cm (2–3in) wider in diameter than the jar. Use pinking shears to make toothed edges. Tie the fabric cover in place with a matching ribbon. Label and date, and store out of direct sunlight until ready to give as a gift or use yourself.

plants
OF THE
month

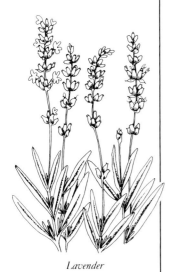

Lavender

LAVENDER
(*Lavandula angustifolia* – Labiatae)

English lavender, with its dainty floral wands and unmistakeable fresh scent, makes excellent hedging, and is attractive in mixed borders.

type	Hardy evergreen shrub
flowers	Fragrant lavender flowers appear in summer
leaves	Aromatic, long, narrow, grey-green
height	60–120cm (24–48in) high, but there are dwarf and shorter-growing forms available
spread	As above
planting	Plant container-grown plants in spring
position	Sunny, warm, open but sheltered
soil	Well drained, light, poor
care	Keep watered and weeded until established. Cut out frost-damaged wood, and cut back straggly plants hard in mid-spring. Trim lightly after flowering
propagation	Take semi-ripe cuttings in late spring or ripe cuttings in summer
species and varieties	Garden forms of English lavender include the compact, violet-purple 'Hidcote' and pale pink 'Hidcote Pink', both superb dwarf hedging; the robust, pinkish-white 'Alba'; the lavender-blue 'Grappenhall'; the blue-purple, compact 'Munstead'; the dwarf, white-flowered 'Nana Alba'; and 'Vera', the late-flowering, so-called 'Dutch lavender'
harvest	Pick the flowers just before they open fully. Pick leaves as needed
herbal value	The flowers and essential oil are an indispensable ingredient in pot-pourri and herb pillows, as well as in perfumery, soaps and cosmetics. Make a lavender rinse to strengthen hair and prevent hair loss. Honey made from lavender is exquisitely scented, as is lavender vinegar, made by infusing a few sprigs in vinegar for a week. Use leaves to make sachets for drawers to deter moths and other insects

SANTOLINA
(*Santolina chamaecyparissus* – Compositae)

Cotton lavender forms pretty, low-growing mounds of aromatic, silvery foliage. Use it in containers or clip it closely to make hedging.

type	Moderately hardy evergreen sub-shrub
flowers	Bright yellow flowers appear in midsummer unclipped on plants
leaves	Silvery, thread-like, woolly
height	30–60cm (12–24in)
spread	30–60cm (12–24in)
planting	Plant pot-grown plants in spring
position	Sunny, hot; cold, wet areas are unsuitable
soil	Light, well drained, poor
care	Cut back lightly, or more severely for formal hedging, in mid-spring. Deadhead and protect from winter wet. Replant every five years or so, dividing existing plants and replanting deeply
propagation	Divide in spring or take semi-ripe cuttings in late spring or summer
species and varieties	The dense, compact form, 'Nana', is ideal for rock gardens or edging. *Santolina pinnata* 'Sulphurea' has finely divided leaves and primrose-yellow flowers; *S. p.* subsp. *neapolitana* has feathery leaves and lemon-yellow flowers; *S. rosmarinifolia* is a dwarf form with thread-like, bright green leaves and lemon-yellow flowers, pale yellow in 'Primrose Gem'
harvest	Pick the leaves as needed. Use the flowers fresh or in dried displays, picking them just before fully open
herbal value	Once used for its stimulant and antiseptic qualities, today its domestic use is mainly in insect repellents or pot-pourri. Use sachets of dried leaves and twigs as an insect and moth repellent, or hang bunches of dried sprigs in cupboards and closets. Add the dried leaves and flowers to pot-pourri to provide a fresh aroma

SMALLAGE
(*Apium graveolens* – Umbelliferae)

Smallage, wild celery or cutting celery has strong-smelling leaves, rich in vitamins. Tall and large-leaved, it should be grown as a central focus or at the back of a border.

type	Hardy biennial
flowers	Flat heads of numerous small greenish-yellow flowers in summer
leaves	Light green, aromatic leaves with toothed and lobed edges
height	30–90cm (12–36in)

spread	30–90cm (12–36in)
planting	Plant or transplant in late summer or autumn
position	Sunny or sheltered
soil	Well-drained, but moist and rich soil is best
care	Keep weed free and watered until established. To extend leaf production, pinch out flower buds as soon as they appear
propagation	Sow under glass in early spring or direct into the garden in late spring
species and varieties	Smallage is closely related to cultivated celery (*Apium graveolens dulce*) and celeriac (*A. graveolens rapaceum*), grown for its swollen, edible root. Fool's watercress (*A. nodoflorum*) grows in shallow water, sometimes alongside watercress, and has been used to flavour meat pies and pasties
harvest	Pick fresh leaves as needed and leaves for drying just as the flowers open in the second year
herbal value	Smallage tea, made from an infusion of fresh or dried leaves, is calming. Use fresh leaves in salads, soups, stuffing, stews or finely chopped as a garnish. Boil and purée the thick stems to serve as a cooked vegetable

WALL GERMANDER

(*Teucrium chamaedrys* – Labiatae)

If left to grow unchecked in a sunny site, wall germander becomes a low, sprawling shrub. If clipped, it makes a good hedge or edge in a knot or formal herb area.

type	Hardy evergreen perennial
flowers	Rosy or purplish-pink flowers appear in summer. If grown as a hedge, flowers will be sacrificed to pruning a neat and compact shape
leaves	Small, oval, hairy and aromatic; mid- to deep green above, grey beneath
height	30cm (12in)
spread	30cm (12in)
planting	Plant in autumn or spring
position	Sunny
soil	Well drained, average
care	Keep weeded and watered until established. Cut back in early spring to keep compact. If using as a hedge, clip again in autumn to keep its shape

propagation	Sow seed or take cuttings in spring. Lift and divide established plants in spring or autumn
species and varieties	Wood sage or sage-leaved germander, *Teucrium scorodonia* grows to 15–30cm (6–12in) and has pale green flowers; it was once used as a substitute for hops in beer-making. *T. pyrenaicum* grows 5cm (2in) high and up to 25cm (10in) across, with flat heads of yellow and purple flowers
harvest	Gather leaves in summer to dry or use fresh
herbal value	Leaves make a tonic tea. Infuse them dried or fresh. Main herbal value is as a hardy hedging plant for knot gardens and as edging for herb gardens

WELSH ONION

(*Allium fistulosum* – Liliaceae)

Also known as bunching onions, green onions or ciboules, Welsh onions are Siberian natives and extremely hardy. Use them as edging in a herb or vegetable garden.

type	Hardy perennial with onion-like bulbs
flowers	Heads of small white flowers appear in summer
leaves	Long, thin, strappy and hollow, onion-like
height	Up to 30cm (12in)
spread	Forms clumps up to 15cm (6in)
planting	Plant in spring or autumn
position	Sunny, sheltered
soil	Light, deep, loamy, enriched with well-rotted organic matter
care	Water in dry weather and remove flower buds as they form to keep the leaves succulent and increase leaf production. Lift and divide clumps every three years
propagation	Sow into the growing site from late winter to late spring or in autumn. Lift and divide offsets in spring or autumn
harvest	Cut the evergreen leaves and harvest bulbous shoots as needed all through the year. Welsh onion leaves can be kept in a refrigerator for a few days but otherwise are not preserved
herbal value	Use the leaves chopped like chives to garnish meat, vegetable dishes and salads. Cook the bulbous shoots as vegetables

Santolina

Wall germander

NOVEMBER

As autumn comes to a close, this is the last opportunity to protect herbs from the cold, drying winds or frost of the winter months to follow. It is also the last chance to clear the site and prepare the ground for new herb gardens for spring planting.

The herb garden's rich summer harvest is all gathered and the garden is no longer the highly fragrant, aromatic place it was in midsummer. The evergreen framework of mature specimens of rosemary, sage and thyme will maintain interest over the winter as they endure the colder weather without special protection, unless it is an extreme season or your climate is particularly cold.

Some herbs and young plants will need some protection: newly transplanted herbs and young hedges or knot garden plants, for example. As you work to protect the various plants, you will find the garden transformed into a sort of shanty town of cloches, hessian wind shelters and woven fleece blankets. No matter what it looks like, however, protecting the plants is worthwhile. It extends their lives, providing you with salad herbs and flavoursome additions to food through the winter, and saves you the cost of replacing plants when winter is over.

By now the indoor herb garden collection is ready to come inside to its winter quarters. If you, too, are driven indoors by bad weather in late autumn, there are few more pleasant occupations than working with the dried flowers and herbs harvested earlier in the year. Rub down dried mints for herbal teas and other herbs to store in airtight jars for kitchen use. Prepare a variety of pot-pourris; moth sachet mixes and sleep pillow herbs to use yourself or offer as gifts. And if you haven't thought about growing plants for their preserved perfumes, plan next year's pot-pourri garden. Choose the plants for their visual and fragrant ornament in the herb garden, as well as in the scented gifts and pot-pourri.

tasks

FOR THE

month

CHECKLIST

- Provide windbreaks for young evergreens and hedge plantings
- Bring tender plants indoors if you have not already done so
- Mulch roots of tender herbaceous perennials and those tender herbs in containers too large to be moved
- Provide cloche or woven fleece protection for salad herbs
- Plant bare-root roses
- Continue cleaning and clearing
- Force chicory
- Bring in herbs for the indoor winter herb garden

WINTER PROTECTION

Shelter for herbs, as in the vegetable or flower garden, increases plant health and productivity. It can also extend considerably the harvest time for fresh herbs for the kitchen.

In the herb garden, permanent shelter is provided by low-growing hedges, similar to those planted for knot garden ornament. In winter, though, some plants need temporary seasonal protection from the effects of cold, drying winds and frost. Windbreaks of netting or hessian, tied to canes or stronger wooden supports, will cut down the wind by 50 per cent.

The hardy evergreen plants that form the framework of the herb garden will survive cold, frost and snow in all but exceptional conditions. Young, autumn-planted specimens of evergreens, though, will need protection while others, such as bay, suffer leaf damage from cold frosty winds. Herbaceous plants such as tarragon need their roots protected.

Bring tender plants inside
The simplest way to protect herbs from the effects of cold, drying winds and frost is to bring tender plants, such as scented pelargoniums and lemon verbena, into a frost-free greenhouse or shed. By now all tender herbs growing in containers should be moved inside (see Tender Treatment p113).

There are several other ways to protect herbs growing outside.

A mulch blanket
If tender plants have to be left in the ground or in containers that are too large to be moved, the best solution is to provide a 'blanket' to protect their roots. Cut back tender herbaceous herbs by half and mound a mulch of fallen leaves, compost or straw around their base. If the mulch is lightweight, keep it in place with a layer of netting over it, pegged or held down with canes or old bricks. If you are using a compost mulch, make sure it is at least 7.5cm (3in) thick to give adequate root protection. If it doesn't, your cuttings will provide insurance.

Windbreak for evergreens
Do not cut back young evergreen herbs such as bay or myrtle. Instead, apply the layer of compost to warm their roots and then insert canes in the ground around the plants. Fix a windbreak of netting or hessian around the canes.

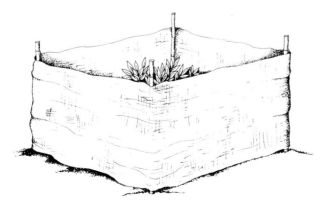

Protecting with cloches

In a conventional vegetable garden, it is fairly simple to provide overwinter protection for row-planted crops. In the herb garden, rows are less usual, except where plants are used as hedging or edging. (Note: Young evergreen hedges will need windbreak protection in their first winter.)

Salad herbs, such as winter purslane, lamb's lettuce and landcress, are planted in rows or small blocks, so cloche protection is easy to set in place. Plastic or glass cloches provide a 'tent' shelter for the plants. The sides and top of the cloches allow light through, but insulate the plants from direct contact with the weather. Cloche protection provides you with longer harvests and earlier spring crops of salad and other herbs. Sorrel and rocket survive winter in mild areas, but in extreme weather need protection.

In a herb garden where plants are not in neat uniform rows, it is simpler to protect them with a woven fleece. This can be put in place quickly and removed when weather conditions improve. It is also useful in spring to warm the soil and protect seedlings from

WARNING

■ Never apply a mulch if the ground is frozen. The mulch will thaw out the ground and the resulting cold and damp soil is the least enjoyed by herbs ■

bird and rabbit damage. Use either method to keep frost off the leaves of late-sown chervil and parsley.

PLANTING BARE-ROOT ROSES

Late autumn or early winter planting produces strong, healthy-growing roses.

■ Before the plants arrive, dig the soil well, enriching it with well-rotted compost or a proprietary bagged version.

■ Plant roses as soon as you can after receiving them from the nursery.

■ If soil or weather conditions make planting difficult, heel the roses into a temporary trench or keep them in their protective wrappings in a frost-free site until you can plant them.

■ When weather permits and the soil is neither wet nor frozen, bring the roses out of their temporary storage and take them out of the protective

wrapping, or lift them out of the temporary trench.

■ Place them in a bucket of water and wrap hessian sacking or netting around them to protect from wind damage.

■ Dig a hole large enough to accommodate the spread of the roots. Plant the roses so that the root-stock union is 2.5cm (1in) below soil level. Backfill the hole so that there are no air holes between the roots.

■ Add peat or sand if the soil is heavy.

■ Firm the plant in gently. Set stakes in place to secure standard roses as you plant them.

■ Check the roses through the autumn and winter, and firm them into the ground if they have been rocked by wind.

FORCING CHICORY

Dig up roots of chicory, cut back the leaves to just above the crown and reduce the roots to 20cm (8in). Store in a frost-proof site, then plant a few roots at a time in pots or boxes filled with damp sand. Cover with an inverted pot or box to keep out all light. Place in a dark, warm area and keep the sand just moist. If the temperature is a constant 10°C (50°F), the chicons will be ready in three to four weeks. Keep a succession going over several weeks for a steady supply for salads.

THINGS TO DO

Sow seeds
Outdoors: angelica, herb bennet

Plant out
Roses (bare-root)

Propagate
Take cuttings: echinacea (root)
Divide: ginger

Harvest
Leaves: bay, chervil, landcress, parsley, rosemary, sage, winter purslane, winter savory

Routine maintenance
■ Divide and cut back invasive plants like yarrow and comfrey, and add their nutrient-rich leaves to the compost heap
■ Continue preparing ground for new herb gardens
■ Water indoor herbs regularly but don't overwater
■ Cut back old elder stems and herb bennet

A herb garden design based on the aim of creating blends of fragrant pot-pourri mixtures, will be as aromatic and scented as the dried result. Enjoy the double pleasure of a pot-pourri garden as it grows, and later, when fragments of it hold pleasantly scented memories of the summer. The plan shows a garden designed for scent and for the pot-pourri harvest.

practical project

PLANTING AND USING HERBS FOR POT-POURRI

MAKING POT-POURRI

There are literally hundreds of different ways of combining the basic ingredients of a pot-pourri. The ingredients fall into four categories and you can pick and choose what you want to combine. First, there are the dried flowers that provide scent or colour.

— string tie

Wigwam of canes suitable for supporting jasmine or honeysuckle

2m (6½ft)

1.3m (4½ft)

bench

Wigwams connected by a long cane to make a lightweight 'pergola' suitable for fragrant sweet peas

1 *Rosa* 'Comte de Chambord'
2 lily-of-the-valley (2)
3 chives
4 lawn chamomile
5 *Rosa* 'Königin von Dänemark'
6 southernwood
7 *Lavandula angustifolia*
8 *Thymus* 'Doone Valley'
9 blue hyssop
10 pink hyssop
11 *Thymus coccineus*
12 *Thymus herba-barona*
13 *Lavandula angustifolia* 'Hidcote'
14 sweet violets and heartsease
15 sweet woodruff
16 peppermint and spearmint
17 marjoram
18 cotton lavender
19 nepeta
20 lemon balm
21 alpine strawberries
22 double-flowered chamomile
23 winter savory
24 *Dianthus* 'Hope'
25 pot marigold
26 *Dianthus* 'Mrs Sinkins'
27 *Thymus* 'Silver Queen'
28 pennyroyal
29 purple sage
30 bergamot

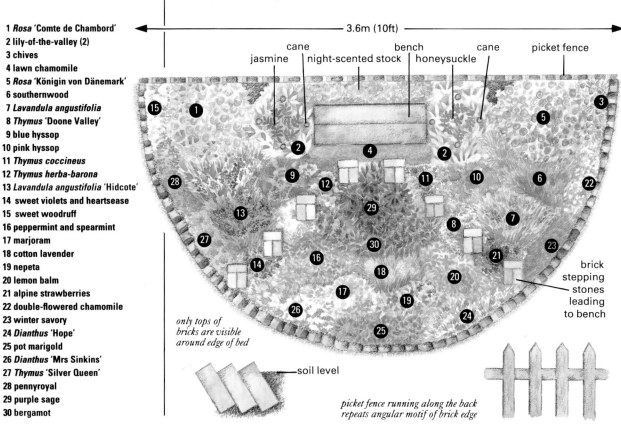

3.6m (10ft)

cane
jasmine
night-scented stock
bench
honeysuckle
cane
picket fence

only tops of bricks are visible around edge of bed

brick stepping stones leading to bench

— soil level

picket fence running along the back repeats angular motif of brick edge

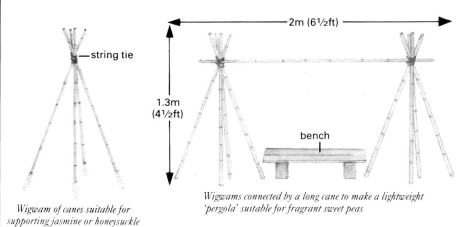

Next come dried aromatic leaves and seed pods that add scent and colour, as well as bulk. Spices and citrus peel sharpen the floral scents and may also add to the bulk. Finally, there are the fixatives that will hold the overall fragrance.

When you can, use your own material. Harvest it on dry days, after the dew has evaporated, and discard any damaged or wilted material. When it is fully dried, store it wrapped in tissue paper in cardboard boxes out of sunlight. Keep in a dry and well-ventilated place until you are ready to mix your pot-pourri.

Experiment with your dried material, spices from the kitchen and essential oils bought from health shops, until you achieve the visual and aromatic blend that pleases you most.

Fixatives

Fixatives slow down the evaporation of the fragrances of dried material and essential oils. There are many plant-derived fixatives including fennel, coriander, dill, cumin and anise seeds. Whole cloves, peppercorns and ground spices offer their own aroma and prolong the life of the pot-pourri fragrance. Traditional fixatives include gum benzoin available in a resinous form, and powdered orris root. Both are sold at craft shops and some chemists, but if you keep your own orris root dried for several years, you will be able to make your own fixative.

Essential oils

Buy these from health shops, chemists or body-care shops. They are relatively expensive and very concentrated, so use sparingly. Choose from rose, lavender, rose geranium, lemon verbena, cedarwood, citronella, eucalyptus and sandalwood.

INGREDIENTS

25g (1oz) fixative (orris root or ground gum benzoin)

25g (1oz) ground cinnamon, nutmeg or allspice

few drops essential oil of your choice

580ml (1pt) dried flowers, leaves, seeds

25g (1oz) extra lavender (or other flowers to emphasise a particular perfume)

BASIC METHOD

■ Mix the fixative and the powdered spices together in a small bowl. When well blended, add the drops of essential oil and gently combine the mixture using your fingers.

■ Place the dried material in a large china bowl. Add the blended spices, oil and fixative. Stir them into the dried material.

■ Store in an airtight container for up to six weeks. When the pot-pourri is ready to use, turn it out into a bowl or dish for display, or place it in attractive containers to offer as festive gifts.

COLOUR THEMES

Blue and pink mix
Use various coloured hyssops, lavender, rosemary, thyme and chive flowers.

Lemon-scented and gold
Combine lemon-scented, golden-leaved and variegated thymes with marigold flowers, southernwood and lemon balm leaves.

Old-fashioned mix
Combine roses, pinks and lavender to create a romantic and heavily scented mixture.

Winter spice mix
Use any of the above mixtures and add large and unusual flower heads, such as cardoon buds, echinops and small fir cones. Bundles of cinnamon sticks tied together with tartan ribbon and pieces of dried citrus peel will complete the visual and aromatic effect.

HERBS FOR INSECT-REPELLENT SACHETS

Some herbs will provide fragrance *and* practical use. They will control moths in clothes cupboards, and keep ants, fleas and flies away.

Useful herbs for this purpose include basil, bay, cotton lavender, eucalyptus, hyssop, lavender, mugwort, pennyroyal, peppermint, rosemary, rue, southernwood, sweet woodruff and tansy. Use the dried herb mixes in cotton bags to protect linen in cupboards and shelves. Hang sachets from hangers, or slip them into safe places under carpets to keep insects away.

HERBS AND SPICES FOR POT-POURRI

HERBS FOR VISUAL EFFECT
Cardoon flower heads •
Rosebuds • Sea holly flowers

SPICES FROM KITCHEN
Cinnamon sticks • Nutmeg •
Star anise •

PEEL AND SEED PODS
Aquilegia pods •
Dried lemon and orange peel •
Dried pine or spruce cones •
Fir cones • Honesty seed pods •
Holly berries •
Poppy seed pods •

HERB FLOWERS
Chamomile • Clove pink •
Jasmine • Lavender •
Lily-of-the-valley •
Night-scented stock •
Pot marigold •
Rose petals • Sage •
Sweet rocket •
Sweet violet •
Thyme

LEAVES
Alpine strawberry •
Basil • Bay •
Bergamot •
Cotton lavender •
Lemon balm •
Lemon verbena •
Marjoram •
Mint • Myrtle •
Pennyroyal
Rosemary • Sage •
Scented pelargonium

USING DRY POT-POURRI MIXES
Seal pretty writing paper in a bag with a dry mix and it will take on the predominant scent. Use pot-pourri in sachets to perfume drawers, wardrobes and linen. Place it in the inner pillow of a decorative pillow in a sitting room or bedroom

plants
OF THE
month

CHICORY
(*Cichorium intybus* – Compositae)

Chicory, or wild succory, is grown for its delicious forced chicons. The daisy-like, azure-blue blooms are clock-watcher flowers, opening only five hours a day.

type	Hardy herbaceous perennial, grown as an annual for forcing
flowers	Azure-blue or pink flowers from late spring to mid-autumn
leaves	Mid-green, pointed, toothed, bitter
height	30–120cm (12–48in)
spread	15–60cm (6–24in)
planting	Sow seed in summer, cut back leaves and lift roots in autumn for forcing. Lift and divide chicory grown for ornamental value only in spring or autumn
position	Sunny, open
soil	Light, rich, alkaline
care	Keep watered and weeded until established. For forcing, remove flower stems as soon as they appear. Dig up roots in late autumn, cut leaves back to just above the crown, and roots back to 20cm (8in). Store in a cool, frost-proof site. Plant, in boxes filled with damp sand, in a dark, warm area. Keep barely moist
propagation	Sow seed in late spring to early summer; take root cuttings of ornamental plants in late winter
species and varieties	Culinary forms include the tight-headed 'Normato' and red chicory or radicchio, 'Rosso de Verona', a non-forcing type
harvest	Pick the leaves and flowers fresh as needed. Dig up roots in autumn for forcing or drying; harvest three to four weeks after forcing
herbal value	The brittle taproot, dried, ground and roasted, is added to or substituted for coffee. Boil the young roots and eat as a vegetable; add the fresh leaves and flowers to salads. Young forced shoots or chicons can be braised and served with cheese sauces, or used fresh in salads

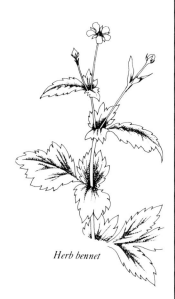

Herb bennet

GINGER
(*Zingiber officinale* – Zingiberaceae)

Grown for its spicy, underground stem, ginger can be used as an attractive indoor or conservatory plant in areas where it is not hardy.

type	Herbaceous perennial (tender in cold climates), native to the Orient
flowers	Pale yellow or white flowers in midsummer if conditions are good
leaves	Dark, glossy green, sword-shaped
height	90cm (36in) in containers; larger in natural conditions
spread	45cm (18in) or more
planting	Plant plump, fresh roots at any time of year, but best at the beginning of the growing season
position	Needs full sun and winter protection in cold climates. Grow in shade in a warm greenhouse or conservatory, with a minimum winter temperature of 13°C (55°F) and 23°C (75°F) in spring and autumn
soil	Grow in containers filled with equal parts loam-based compost, peat and sharp sand
care	Water generously from spring to autumn and mist daily in hot weather. Keep almost dry from late autumn until spring. Cut down stems in autumn
propagation	Suspend a freshly bought ginger rhizome in water until it sprouts, then plant. Or lift and divide existing rhizomes and replant in late winter
harvest	Lift and store the rhizome in autumn. Store it whole in airtight containers, or slice it into rounds and freeze it. Young roots can be crystallised or preserved in syrup. In cool climates it is unlikely that you will be able to grow sufficient to harvest, but it makes an attractive house plant
herbal value	Use ground ginger in baking and bread-making, and in Oriental cooking

HERB BENNET
(*Geum urbanum* – Rosaceae)

Use the roots of herb bennet, a wild woodland plant, to make a refreshing facial wash. In the herb garden it makes a good ground-cover and edging plant.

type	Hardy herbaceous perennial
flowers	Bright yellow flowers appear in summer and autumn, followed by bristly, reddish-brown burrs or seed cases
leaves	Bright green, toothed and divided into three sections

height	30–60cm (12–24in)
spread	20–40cm (8–16in)
planting	Plant in autumn or spring
position	Sun or light shade
soil	Fertile, moist
care	Keep weed free and watered until established. Mulch in spring and cut back in autumn
propagation	Lift and divide established plants in spring. Sow seed in autumn or spring
species and varieties	Herb bennet is also known as wood avens. Water avens (*Geum rivale*) has large, nodding pink-orange flowers with dark purple sepals. It thrives in wet soil. Garden forms include the bright orange *G.* × *borisii* and seed strains such as the semi-double, scarlet 'Mrs Bradshaw'
harvest	Lift and dry the roots in spring. When dry, slice, powder and store
herbal value	Use the clove-scented root grated to flavour apple tarts. Dried and powdered, it can be used in sachets placed in drawers to repel flies and moths

TANSY

(*Tanacetum vulgare* – Compositae)

Tough and invasive, tansy enlivens the herb garden with its button-like flowers. Use it fresh or dried to repel insects, and add to compost for its high potassium content.

type	Hardy herbaceous perennial
flowers	Yellow button-like flowers in late summer and autumn
leaves	Ferny, aromatic, deeply divided and dark green
height	60–120cm (24–48in)
spread	60–120cm (24–48in)
planting	Plant container-grown plants in autumn or spring
position	Full sun or light shade
soil	Average, well drained
care	Keep weeded and watered until established. Stake large clumps in exposed sites. Cut back in autumn
propagation	Lift and divide roots in autumn or spring. Sow seed in spring
species and varieties	*Tanacetum vulgare crispum* is a more compact form with very finely divided, but less aromatic leaves. Tansy is also known as bachelor's buttons or bitter buttons

harvest	Pick the leaves as needed and the flowers for drying before they are fully open
herbal value	Use infused tansy as a disinfectant for wiping surfaces. Leaves give a sharp flavour when cooked with meat, chopped into omelettes, pancakes and cakes. Add dried leaves to mixes for insect-repellent sachets. Use dried flowers in pot-pourri and in arrangements. Add leaves to the herbal compost heap

YARROW

(*Achillea millefolium* – Compositae)

Yarrow, or milfoil, has a soft, feathery look that disguises a tough, invasive habit. Grow it for its ornamental value and as a herbal fertiliser.

type	Hardy herbaceous perennial
flowers	Flattened heads of tiny white or pink-tinged flowers appear in early summer to early autumn
leaves	Feathery, dark green, deeply cut
height	45–60cm (18–24in)
spread	30–45cm (12–18in)
planting	Plant in autumn or spring
position	Sun or light shade
soil	Average, well drained
care	Keep weeded and watered until established. Dead head to encourage a second flush of flowers. Lift and divide regularly to maintain vigour
propagation	Lift and divide in spring or autumn; sow seed in spring
species and varieties	Garden forms include 'Cerise Queen', the rosy red 'Red Beauty' and pale yellow 'Flowers of Sulphur'. *Achillea decolorans*, or English mace, has toothed, narrow, bright green leaves and daisy-like flowers in summer and autumn. *A. ptarmica*, or sneezewort, has narrow, toothed leaves and soft, downy, white flowers
harvest	Pick leaves as needed and flowers in late summer for fresh use and for drying
herbal value	Yarrow tea made from an infusion of the leaves is soothing and relaxing. Use leaves of English mace fresh, chopped into salads, soups and stews. Sneezewort is so-called because it was used as a snuff. Use leaves, stems as a herbal activator in compost

Tansy

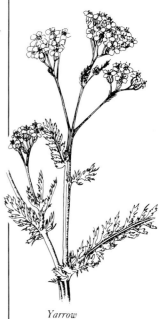

Yarrow

CAUTION
Pregnant women should avoid drinking infusions of yarrow

DECEMBER

The first month of winter drives gardeners indoors to look at seed catalogues and plan next season's garden from the comfort of an armchair. So it is for the herb gardener. But winter is also a time to reflect on the success or otherwise of the designs, features and particular plantings of the past year.

As you walk through the herb garden in winter, with memories of its busy spring, summer and autumn character in mind, you can perhaps see where change should be made for next year. You may wish to expand and develop new herb areas, or re-plan existing beds and relocate plants. Put your plans and thoughts down on paper, and wait for good weather in spring before working the soil. If weather and soil conditions do permit, let your hands, feet and spade turn to action.

Winter is not all repose for the herb gardener. Now is the time to enjoy transforming some of the herbs you have dried and prepared into attractive gifts to offer at seasonal parties. Choose unusual and ornamental bowls to hold the pot-pourri mixed from summer harvests. Use the mixtures to fill sleep and scented bedroom pillows, and sachets for clothes drawers and wardrobes. Prepare rosebud and clove pomanders to hang in wardrobes, and mix herbs for muslin bath bags. Use dried artemisia or freshly picked spruce branches as the bases for your festive door or room wreaths and garlands. Add dried red chilli peppers, bundles of cinnamon sticks and cloves of garlic as the colour and bulk accents for the wreaths of freshly picked evergreen herbs.

Not least, enjoy growing and using the herbs you have chosen for your indoor winter herb garden.

tasks

FOR THE

month

CHOOSING DECORATIVE POTS
There are a wide range of ceramic
pots available with floral themes
or in plain colours. Secondhand
china can be used effectively to
create a country look. Terracotta
is as good indoors as it is outside,
but you will need to provide
saucers with inner glazed finishes
for the pots to rest on. The
minimum size pot for healthy
indoor growing is 13cm (5in).

CHECKLIST

- Position the indoor herb collection
- Water, feed and maintain indoor herbs
- Control pests and disease
- Harvest indoor herbs and outdoor salad and
  evergreen herbs
- Make a decorative indoor landscape
- Make fresh or dried festive herbal wreaths

THE INDOOR WINTER HERB GARDEN

Since late summer you have
been preparing cuttings,
potting up suitable plants from
the garden and purchasing
herbs to grow indoors over
winter. By now they are all
accustomed to their indoor
growing site and you can
begin to use them in cooking,
to make tea and in steamy
herbal baths.

Although grown indoors for
practical use, they can have an
ornamental role, much as
herbs growing outside do. Use
attractive outer pots or *cache-
pots* to hide the plastic pots.
The outer pots will also act as
reservoirs for water, protecting
surfaces from spills.

Choose identical outer pots
for herbs on a windowsill. A
matching collection gives a
unity of design and is much
more decorative to look at
than a random collection of
pots.

POSITIONING INDOOR HERBS

The kitchen is always
associated with indoor herb
growing. It is the most practical
place from the point of view of
easy access for care of plants
and for harvesting material
from them. However, it isn't
always the best place for
herbs. Like all indoor plants,
herbs need even temperatures,
good air circulation, water,

and about five hours sunlight
per day. In the kitchen, the
dramatic rise and fall in
temperature from cooking
activities, and sudden draughts
when doors are opened, may
not suit the herbs.

Most herbs will grow well
if you can provide a daytime
temperature of 18°C (65°F),
with lower temperatures at
night. Basil, though, needs
warmer conditions, day and
night.

Air circulation
Poor air circulation encourages
fungal attack and the build-up
of insects on the plants. If you
open a window in a room
nearby, rather than in the
room where the plants are, the
air will move around without
damaging the plants. If it is
impractical to open windows
in winter, then use a small fan
to circulate air for a short time
each day. Chives, in particular,
need good air circulation
around their moist, succulent
leaves.

Aspect
Place most herbs near or in a
south- or west-facing window.
Chervil will do well in lower
light levels, and both mint and
parsley will grow well in an
east-facing site. Provide indoor
herbs with at least five hours
sunlight a day, and turn them
in their pots so that they grow
in an even shape. If indoor
winter light levels are low, you
may consider it worthwhile to
buy plant-lights that simulate
daylight.

WATERING INDOOR HERBS

Water herb plants as you
would house plants. Never let
the compost dry out
completely, but avoid
overwatering. Remember that
indoors, unless temperatures
are very high, soil dries out
more slowly than outside.
Most herbs, except mint, hate
having their roots sitting in
cold water. Rosemary, for
example, should be watered
sparingly although basil, mint
and parsley should be watered
more frequently. Water plants
in clay pots every seven to ten
days.

If possible, avoid using
water straight from the tap.
Let it stand for a while and
reach room temperature before
you water the herbs. Spray
herb plants regularly to remove
dust, unclog leaf pores and
increase humidity.

FEEDING INDOOR HERBS

As mentioned earlier, when
you pot the plants up it is best
to add a slow-release fertiliser
to the potting compost.
Watering will wash away
some of the nutrients, so if
you do not add slow-release
fertiliser at the potting stage
you should feed occasionally
to redress the balance. In the
early part of winter, when
growth is likely to be slower,
do not add fertiliser. In late
winter and early spring, when
light levels begin to increase,
feed regularly with a liquid
fertiliser.

PESTS AND DISEASES

If you are plagued with an
infestation of whitefly, try to
control it before it spreads to
all the herbs. Remove badly
affected plants and treat them
with an insecticidal soap
solution. Spray every fortnight
until the insects have
disappeared. Remove scale

from the backs of bay leaves with a piece of cotton wool dipped in the soapy solution.

HARVESTING INDOOR HERBS

Pick leaves as you need them. Turn the plant around as you cut, and don't take all your material from the same part of the plant or it will lose its shape. Don't overcut or you will have unattractive plants and, under stress, they may develop diseases and die.

Wherever you choose to site your indoor herb collection, remember that plants in containers are dependent on you for their care. You have to decide where the light, temperature and air circulation are best, and provide the plants with the right potting compost, fertiliser, pest control and correct watering. Try to keep temperatures low when daylight hours are short, so that the plants don't put on spindly, leggy growth. It is a balancing act, but the result is an extension of the harvest and a continuity of herb gardening.

INDOOR ALL YEAR

If you live in a flat or apartment and grow herbs indoors all year round, you should repot evergreen perennials each year in spring. The plants will probably need replacing after a year or two, as indoor conditions and harvesting will diminish their vigour. If you have any outdoor space put the plants out in summer to enjoy more natural conditions.

MAKING A DECORATIVE INDOOR HERB GARDEN

Instead of growing herbs in individual pots on a sunny windowsill, you may wish to combine them into a miniature landscape. The ornamental effect of this small herb garden is more important than the culinary use you might have for the herbs.

■ Use a shallow oval, terracotta bowl, complete with inner-glazed saucer, to hold the mini-garden.

■ Fill the bowl with a good potting mix and plenty of crocks for drainage.

■ Plant it up with young specimens of low-growing herbs such as creeping thyme, pennyroyal, Corsican mint and lawn chamomile to make the imitation grass, plus compact, shrubby specimens of thyme and scented pelargoniums to represent the trees.

■ Place the planted bowl on a table near a sunny window.

■ The fragrance and attractive shapes of these Mediterranean herbs will provide a little herb-garden magic for severely deprived, cold-climate winter herb gardeners.

Using herb topiaries

Some of the herbs you may have indoors are strictly 'not for kitchen use'. These are the shaped topiaries (see page 35) that you have created purely for ornamental and aromatic effect.

Place a row of conical rosemary plants on the mantelpiece to mimic a forest of festive trees. Grown into round wreaths on wire hoops, rosemary looks attractive on a hall table or in the window of a guest room.

Instead of using cut flowers on a dinner table, bring in a standard thyme or lavender plant with its aromatic leaves and stems cut to form a ball shape. Dress it up with an attractive pot cover, and conceal the soil surface with moss. Tie a few ribbons near the base of the shaped mop-head and set it on the table for a decidedly festive look.

THINGS TO DO

Harvest
Leaves: evergreens and protected salad herbs, salad burnet
Fruits: juniper berries

Routine maintenance
■ Continue to water indoor herbs but do not overwater
■ Order seeds for next year
■ Check evergreen herbs for wind rock and dislodge any snow from their branches

PLAN AHEAD
This is a good time to order seeds, sketch designs and put plans on paper – but wait for good weather before you begin working the soil.

practical project

MAKING HERBAL GIFTS AND DECORATIONS

YOU WILL NEED

bucket for soaking moss and keeping pieces of plant material fresh
secateurs
gloves (optional)

If you have herbs in abundance, turn some of the surplus into dried or fresh decorations to use in the home, or offer as original gifts when visiting friends and family.

At the simplest level, herbal decorations include fresh flower and foliage arrangements for dining room, kitchen and bedroom. Pretty, country-style displays of lady's mantle, marjoram and pot marigold flowers combine well with the aromatic leaves of marjoram, sage and mint. Dried herb flowers, such as marjoram, lavender, santolina and chamomile, look attractive with dried eucalyptus leaves and honesty seed pods.

WREATHS AND GARLANDS

Large-scale herbal decorations are useful to ornament rooms, cupboards, mantelpieces and doors on special occasions. Either make wreaths and garlands fresh in the summer – let them dry naturally while in place – or create them from a combination of dried elements in winter. There will still be sufficient fresh evergreen herbs about in winter for you to make a fresh wreath, but it will lack some of the vibrance of fresh flowers. Add bulky pods or fruits for colour and brightness.

A culinary herb wreath

A culinary wreath will look attractive as it dries. If you want to use bits of it, cut judiciously to avoid spoiling the overall effect all at once. Use sprigs of bay or sage for the base and add small bunches of leaves or, if you are making the wreath in summer, flowering sprigs of thyme, marjoram, rosemary and cumin. Also add bunches of mint and lacy flowers of cumin or aniseed. Variegated mints and thymes offer particularly good colour accents.

Scented pelargonium leaves, with their folded, mantle shapes, are useful background material. Make rosettes of leaves from one species or variety and pin them to the base. The leaves will provide fragrance for several months as they dry.

To this floral and foliage base, add the bulk and shape of various spices from the kitchen spice rack. Vanilla pods, cinnamon sticks, nutmegs, dried chilli peppers and fresh garlic cloves or small garlic bulbs provide good form and texture.

MATERIALS

round wire frame or circle of florists' foam both available from florists' or craft shops)

quantity of sphagnum moss

reel of thin gauge or florists' wire

plant material

■ Soak the sphagnum moss in a bucket of water for about ten minutes.

■ Place the wire frame on the table and fix handfuls of the damp moss in place. Bind it

NOTE

• Work on a table and in a situation where it will not matter if you make a mess. Lay newspaper down on the table to simplify the clearing up •

on to the frame with wire. Work around the frame, binding on the moss until the frame is completely covered.

■ Attach one end of the reel of florists' wire to the frame. Next, cut the stems of the plants you wish to use as background material into 7.5cm (3in) lengths and remove the lower leaves of each stem.

■ Start where the wire is attached and work around the frame. Push the stems of the background material at an angle into the sphagnum moss. Overlap them, and keep them facing in the same direction, so that all the stems are covered. Bind them in with the florists' wire as you work. Continue until the circle is completed. Loop the wire around

the frame a couple of times to hold everything in place.

■ Next attach the accent plants. They will provide colour, shape, scent and texture to add interest and variety to the wreath. Wire together small bunches of plants, cutting individual stems to 7.5cm (3in). Leave a 2.5–5cm (1–2in) length of wire hanging from each bunch.

■ Tie the small bunches in place on the base. Experiment with different colours and shapes to achieve the overall effect you want.

■ If you wish, add decorative ribbon for extra colour.

A dried flower and herb wreath

For the base use either a shop-bought straw base, a plaited raffia ring or a twisted vine twig ring. You can also make your own twig base. Choose soft, pliable twigs from dormant trees or shrubs such as birch, wisteria or willow. In summer cut artemisia stems 1m (3ft) long and, while they are still supple and flexible, shape them into rounds and wire them into place. Hang the rounds up to dry or lay them flat in a warm, well-ventilated, dark shed. When the bases are dry and you are ready to use one of them, mist it with a solution of water and fabric softener, so that it is workable and doesn't break as you pin other material to it.

Once again, you will need thin wire or sewing thread to fix the dried herbs and flowers onto the base. You will also need secateurs, sharp scissors, old newspaper to cover the working area and, of course, the dried herbs and flowers.

Make the dried ring as you would a fresh wreath. Cut the stems of the dried herbs to 5cm (2in) and make them up into small bunches. Tie the bunches together and work around the base, fixing the bunches in place. Cover stems with successive bunches so that only the flowers and foliage are visible, and the straw or other base and herb stems are completely covered.

Finally, add the accent material and fix the wreath in place.

Mini-wreaths

Use mini-wreaths as festive decorations on trees or as place markers on a dining table. Twist sprigs of curry plant, cotton lavender, wormwood, southernwood and lavender together. Tie them into place with sewing thread. Hang them to dry, or use fresh.

(Continued on page 138)

HERBS FOR WREATHS

FOR THE BACKGROUND: LEAVES AND FLOWERING STEMS OF:
Artemisia spp A. ludoviciana 'Silver King'
Bay leaves
Hop stems and female flowers
Sage purple, green and tri-colour (leaves)
Southernwood
Traveller's joy: use stems and fluffy seed heads (pick them just as the flowers fall)
Wormwood

ADD BUNCHES OF:
Borage flowers
Chive flowers
Costmary flowers
Cotton lavender leaves and flowering stems
Curry plant leaves and flowering stems
Dried everlasting flowers for extra colour
Fenugreek seed pods
Feverfew flowers
Honesty seed pods
Horehound leaves and flowering stems
Lavender flowers
Marjoram flowering stems
Monarda seed heads
Poppy seed heads
Rosemary sprigs of leaves and flowering stems
Rue sprigs of leaves and flowers
Scented pelargonium leaves made into rosettes
Tansy flowers
Thyme sprigs (especially variegated thymes 'Doone Valley' and 'Variegatus')
Winter savory sprigs of leaves and flowering stems
Yarrow leaves and flowers

ACCENTS
Anise hyssop flowers
Garlic cloves
Lacy caraway, sweet cicely and aniseed flowers
Perilla seed heads
Red chilli peppers
Rosebuds
Rosehips
Spruce and pine cones

plants
OF THE
month

Chilli pepper

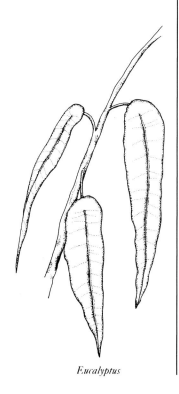

Eucalyptus

CHILLI PEPPER
(*Capsicum var. annuum* – Solanaceae)

Hot and spicy to the taste, the fruits of the chilli pepper add colour and ornament to the herb garden and, dried, to festive garlands.

type	Annual, but can be overwintered and grown as a perennial in hot climates
flowers	Small white flowers from early summer through to late summer
leaves	Mid-green, oval
height	45cm (18in)
spread	Bushes out to 35cm (14in)
planting	Sow seed indoors in spring, provide a constant temperature of 23°C (75°F) and transplant into pots for growing in the greenhouse or on a windowsill. In warm climates, sow in spring eight weeks before the last expected frosts and plant outdoors when all danger of frost is over. For fresh greenhouse peppers in winter, latest sowing time is midsummer
position	Full sun
soil	If growing in containers, use enriched potting compost. Outdoors plant in well-drained, average garden soil, enriched with well-rotted compost
care	If late frosts threaten, cover outdoor plants with woven fleece and remove it during the day. In dry weather, water well and spray plants if temperatures rise above 38°C (100°F) in the greenhouse or flowers will abort and no fruit is produced. Once flowers appear, feed regularly with high potash fertiliser
propagation	Sow seed in spring. Best germination occurs at temperatures around 27°C (80°F). Pot-grown plants can be overwintered indoors, ready to plant out again in spring
species and varieties	There are hundreds of varieties of chilli pepper, varying in degrees of spicy flavour. 'Serrano', with its short, fat peppers, is a greenhouse or indoor plant in cool climates; 'Super Cayenne' has 10cm (4in) long fruits; and 'Hero' provides a heavy crop of 15cm (6in) peppers. North American herb gardeners have a wide range to choose from, including bird or chiltepin, jalapeno and anaheim types
harvest	Harvest peppers regularly from midsummer through to autumn to encourage continuous yield. Pick them green to ripen as they dry, or leave them on the plant to redden and mature. Cut the pods off the plant with scissors. Wear gloves if you are sensitive to the compound capsicum and take care not to rub your eyes. With needle and thread, string the peppers together and hang them to dry in a sunny position. Store in airtight jars. You can freeze them too, but in small packs convenient to use at one time. Blanch large, thick-skinned peppers for two minutes in boiling water, cool, then freeze
herbal value	Use to flavour Indian, Mexican, and Thai cuisine. Add two or three to a bottle of ordinary olive oil, and use for cooking after a week or two. Use dried for pickling and chutney-making. Add clusters of dried chilli peppers to festive wreaths for colour

EUCALYPTUS
(*Eucalyptus* species – Myrtaceae)

Hard prune graceful eucalyptus, or blue gum, to form a shrub. Indoors or in a conservatory, it provides aromatic foliage to lift winter gloom.

type	Hardy and tender trees and shrubs
flowers	Small, petal-less flowers with creamy-white stamens appear on mature plants in winter, spring or summer, according to species
leaves	Leathery, evergreen, greenish-grey, aromatic. Juvenile leaves are often broad, round and more attractive than adult sickle- or lance-shaped leaves
height/spread	Potential heights and spreads range from 30 × 12m (100 × 40ft) for *E. gunnii* and *E. citriodora*, to 50 × 15m (165 × 50ft) for *E. globulus*, but all respond well to hard pruning and young plants, 30–60cm (1–2ft) high, are available. If grown in containers, indoor heights will be restricted
planting	Plant out container-grown specimens in spring or summer. Eucalyptus resent root disturbance
position	Sunny, sheltered, or cool, bright room indoors
soil	Average, dry or moist. In pots use nutrient-rich, loam-based compost

care In cold winter areas, protect young plants from cold winds. Place conservatory plants outdoors in summer. Pinch out growing tips of containerised plants to maintain bushiness, and prune outdoor forms to retain juvenile foliage

propagation Sow seed in winter or spring in heat, keep seedlings in cool, bright conditions and plant out in summer

species and varieties The tender, lemon-scented gum (*Eucalyptus citriodora*), is excellent in conservatories. The Tasmanian blue gum, (*E. globulus*), is also tender, but its silvery young leaves make it a popular annual bedding plant. The best-known species *E. gunnii*, or cider gum, is one of the hardiest, with striking, silver-blue juvenile leaves

harvest Pick and air dry leaves as needed

herbal value *E. citriodora*, with its high citronella content, is used in perfumery for its lemon, hint-of-rose fragrance. Commercially available oil of eucalyptus has antiseptic, stimulant qualities, and is used, as an inhalant, to treat respiratory illnesses, and is applied externally to cuts and burns. It is a natural insect repellent and air freshener. The fresh foliage is lovely in flower arrangements and the dried leaves can be added to pot-pourri

NORWAY OR COMMON SPRUCE

(*Picea abies* – Pinaceae)

Technically not a herb, the Norway spruce's branches are nevertheless used as the base for festive herbal wreaths and its young leaves for making spruce beer.

type Hardy conifer

flowers Insignificant male and female flowers in spring. Woody brown cones are produced in autumn on mature, tall specimens

leaves Short, needle-like, shiny dark green

height Up to 15m (50ft), but dwarf forms are much smaller

spread Up to 6m (20ft)

planting Plant container-grown plants in autumn or spring; on heavy soils, plant in spring

position Sun or light shade, shelter. Avoid frost pockets and areas of low rain

soil Rich, deep, moisture retentive but well drained. Poor, chalky, shallow and dry soils are unsuitable

care Keep weeded and watered until established. Protect young trees from late frosts. Reduce forked trees to a single leader. Feed with nitrogenous fertiliser every spring

propagation Grow species from seed sown in spring. Take cuttings of named forms in summer

species and varieties Dwarf forms include the dense, 30cm (1ft) high, bun-shaped 'Little Gem'; the flat-topped, wide-spreading 'Procumbens', 30cm (1ft) high and 1.2m (4ft) across; and the pyramid-shaped, golden-leaved 'Aurea', 3m (10ft) high and 1.5m (5ft) across

harvest Cut branches as needed

herbal value Use the cones and branches in festive decorations. Use young leaves and shoots to make spruce beer in spring

SALAD BURNET

(*Sanguisorba minor* – Rosaceae)

Charming and modestly decorative in the herb garden, salad burnet's sharp, nutty, cucumber-like taste is particularly welcome in winter salads.

type Hardy herbaceous perennial

flowers Tight clusters of tiny, crimson and white flowers appear in mid- and late summer

leaves Oval, deeply serrated, feathery leaves, evergreen in mild winters

height 30–45cm (12–18in)

spread 30cm (12in)

planting Plant in autumn or spring

position Sun or light shade

soil Well drained, average or, ideally, alkaline. In pots, use nutrient-rich, loam-based potting compost

care Water well during spring and summer. Pinch out flowering stalks for a good supply of young leaves

propagation Grow from seed, or lift and divide roots in spring. Salad burnet self seeds freely

harvest Pick fresh leaves as needed; salad burnet does not dry well

herbal value Use the leaves in winter salads, in soups, stews and herb butters, or add to wine cups and salads in summer. Flavour vinegar with the leaves or seeds

Salad burnet

SCENTED BALLS AND SACHETS

Herbs and scented flowers can be used in many ways to make gifts for the family and friends.

Rosebud and lavender ball

Use dried lavender and rosebuds harvested in early summer to make this attractive scented present.

MATERIALS

foam ball (from florists' shops)
ribbon
new terracotta pot
rosebuds
lavender flowers
cloves
bay leaves

- Cover the base of the ball with bay leaves, pinning each leaf down at top and bottom. You can cover the whole ball if you wish, but it may be difficult to push the rosebud stems through the bay leaves.

- Turn the ball the other way up, so that the bay leaves will appear to grow out of the terracotta base. Place a clove in each 'V' made by the leaf tips.

- Attach a top-knot of roses and lavender flowers. Above each bay leaf, insert a rosebud, with lavender flowers at intervals.

- When the ball is completely covered, tie a decorative ribbon just below the rim of the terracotta pot.

Pot-pourri sachets

- Use fragments of pretty fabrics to make fragrant sachets of pot-pourri to give as gifts. (See page 126 for recipes.)

- Lay the fabric flat and place the scented dried herbs in the centre. Swirl the material together like the ends of a sweet paper, and hold in place with an elastic band. Tie a pretty ribbon around the neck of the sachet to hide the elastic band.

additional
plants

In addition to those in the plant profiles, there are many more herbs that have a traditional place in the herb garden because of their medicinal, cosmetic, culinary or aromatic properties. This is a list of just some of those herbs and their uses.

AGRIMONY *(Agrimonia eupatoria* – Rosaceae)
Sweetly scented, tall and tapering spires of small yellow flowers are the decorative features this hardy herbaceous perennial. *Cultivation* Grow in full sun in average, well-drained soil. *Uses* Use leaves, stalks and flowers fresh to provide a yellow dye.

ALOE *(Aloe vera* – Liliaceae)
An evergreen succulent, tender in cool climates, aloe forms rosettes of fleshy leaves, valued for the healing properties of their gelatinous sap. *Cultivation* Grow outdoors in hot climates; in cool climates choose frost-free sites, usually indoors. *Uses* Pick leaves and apply sap to burns, sunburn and skin wounds.

COMFREY *(Symphytum officinale* –
 Boraginaceae)
A real garden 'thug', this hardy herbaceous perennial is as invasive as it is valuable. *Cultivation* Grow it only if you have space, in sun or light shade. Cut back frequently. *Uses* Add cut leaves to herbal compost heap several times during the year. Leaves are traditionally used with nettles and water, to make an unpleasant-smelling spray, to kill aphids.

COMMON FLAX *(Linum usitatissimum* –
 Liliaceae)
A hardy annual with thin, feathery leaves and saucer-shaped, sky-blue flowers in summer, flax is now grown as a decorative plant in herb gardens and commercially, for linseed oil. *Cultivation* Grow in full sun in average soil. It combines well with grey-leaved herbs such as sage. *Uses* Mainly ornamental, but the seed can be toasted for use in salads or in stuffings. Use dried seed heads in arrangements.

ELDER *(Sambucus nigra* – Caprifoliaceae)
A hardy deciduous tree or shrub, elder is essentially a hedgerow plant. The attractive golden, purple and cut-leaved forms are useful in large informal herb gardens. *Cultivation* Plant in spring or autumn in sun or shade in moist, fertile soil. *Uses* Harvest leaves at any time to air dry for use in insect-repellent sachets. Use fresh flowers and berries to make wine, vinegars and to flavour tarts. Use berries to make jams and jellies.

EVENING PRIMROSE *(Oenothera biennis* –
 Onagraceae)
A hardy biennial, evening primrose, has large yellow flowers that open towards evening in summer and autumn. *Cultivation* Grow in full sun in moist or well-drained soil. *Uses* Harvest roots in second year, before it flowers to use as a vegetable; similar in taste to salsify or scorzonera. Use young leaves in salads. Commercially, evening primrose seed is much in demand for its medicinal properties.

FOXGLOVE *(Digitalis purpurea* –
 Scrophulariaceae)
A hardy biennial or short-lived perennial, it has stately pink, mauve or white flowers. Used only as an ornamental in a modern herb garden, it is a traditional medicinal herb. *Cultivation* Plant or sow in spring or autumn in open sunny or part-shaded sites in average, well-drained soil. *Uses* Foxglove is poisonous, so is best enjoyed for its ornamental beauty only.

JASMINE *(Jasminum officinale* – Oleaceae)
A hardy, deciduous climber, with delicate ferny leaves and fragrant, pink-tinged, white, trumpet-shaped flowers in summer and autumn. *Cultivation* Grow in sun or partial shade in well-drained fertile soil. *Uses* Pick flowers as they open to dry for pot-pourri or to add to tea. Freeze them in ice-cube trays to use in summer drinks, or use fresh to decorate cakes and desserts. In the herb garden jasmine offers fragrance and height.

JUNIPER *(Juniperus communis* – Cupressaceae)
A hardy coniferous shrub or tree, with many dwarf columnar forms that add shape and height to the herb garden. *Cultivation* Grow in sun or shade in average, well-drained soil. Both male and female forms are needed for berry production. *Uses* Add crushed dried berries to marinades and stuffings. Use fresh leaves, in muslin, to add aroma to soothing baths.

LAMB'S LETTUCE *(Valerianella locusta* –
 Valerianaceae)
A hardy annual, it is grown for its leaves that provide edging in the winter herb garden and fresh salad material in winter. *Cultivation* Sow in late summer in rows and thin to 15cm (6in). Protect with cloches in severe seasons.

Mullein

Sweet woodruff

Wild strawberry

Grow in sun or partial shade. *Uses* Pick leaves as needed to use in salads, or blanch for a spinach substitute.

MUSTARD *(Brassica* species – Cruciferae)
A hardy annual with small yellow flowers in summer and spicy, hotly-flavoured leaves, mustard is a useful salad crop. Grow white mustard *(Sinapis alba)* and black mustard *(Brassica nigra)* for their seed and Chinese mustard greens *(B. juncea)* for spicy leaves. *Cultivation* Sow in rows in spring or in pots for a quick leaf crop. Grows best in full sun in well-drained and well-manured soil. *Uses* Pick leaves as you need them; flowers as they open, to use in salads; and seed late in summer to use for pickles, marinades and, ground, in hot footbaths.

MULLEIN *(Verbascum thapsus –* Scrophulariaceae)
Tall and stately mullein, a hardy biennial, adds spires of bright colour to the herb garden. Its downy, grey leaves form attractive rosettes and in its second year it has long stems of cup-shaped yellow blooms. *Cultivation* Grow in full sun, sheltered from wind, in well-drained average soil. Stake, if necessary. *Uses* Dry individual flowers or whole spikes for pot-pourri or dried arrangements.

PEONY *(Paeonia officinalis –* Paeoniaceae)
A hardy herbaceous perennial with single crimson or white flowers in spring and summer, and deeply divided, dark green leaves. *Cultivation* Grow in a sunny site in well-drained fertile soil. Water well and mulch in spring. Cut plants back in autumn. *Uses* Pick flowers as they open and air dry or place in boxes with a proprietary dessicant. Dry individual petals on drying frame. Add flowers or petals to pot-pourri.

PRIMROSE *(Primula vulgaris –* Primulaceae)
A hardy herbaceous perennial with a rosette of bright green leaves, the primrose's pale yellow flowers are among the earliest edible spring flowers to appear. *Cultivation* Grows well in partial shade in moist, average soil. Protect leaves from slugs and flowers from birds. Divide mature plants after flowering or propagate from seed given cold treatment outside. *Uses* Harvest home-grown plants only. Use flowers fresh in salads, crystallised for cake decorations, steeped in water to make a fragrant handwash or dried in pot-pourri.

RUE *(Ruta graveolens –* Rutaceae)
A hardy evergreen sub-shrub, rue has softly textured blue-grey leaves, making it useful as a neat edging or hedge. Its leaves may cause an allergic reaction. *Cultivation* Grow in full sun or partial shade in average, well-drained soil. Keep it compact by cutting out flowering stems. *Uses* Pick leaves to dry for insect-repellent sachets.

SWEET WOODRUFF *(Galium oderatum –* Rubiaceae)
A low-growing and fragrant, hardy herbaceous perennial, it has elegant ruff-like whorls of leaves and dainty, starry, white spring blooms. *Cultivation* Grow in cool semi-shade under trees in average, but moist loamy soil. Sow seed in late summer to provide cold treatment over winter or lift and divide in spring. *Uses* Pick flowers as they open to dry for pot-pourri or to make flower garlands to dry. Use leaves in sachets as moth repellents.

TRAVELLER'S JOY *(Clematis vitalba –* Ranunculaceae)
A hardy deciduous climber, with deeply lobed leaves and creamy white flowers in summer and autumn. *Cultivation* Grow in full sun, with roots in shade in rich, well-drained soil. *Uses* Pick long stems with flowers and twirly seed heads to dry for decorative wreaths. Leaves were once used to relieve blister's on travellers' feet.

WILD STRAWBERRY *(Fragaria vesca –* Rosaceae)
Hardy evergreen perennial that spreads to form clumps. It's creamy white spring and summer flowers are followed by fragrant dark red fruits. It has downy green, lemon-scented leaves. *Cultivation* Grow in sun or shade in moist, but well-drained and fertile soil. Divide large clumps in spring or autumn. *Uses* Use leaves in pot-pourri and fruit in summer drinks or as garnish for salads and sweets.

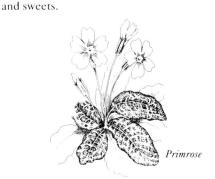

Primrose

USEFUL ADDRESSES

SPECIALIST NURSERIES, PLANT AND SEED SUPPLIERS

A range of basic culinary herbs is available in spring from most garden centres and larger nurseries. There are also specialist herb nurseries with display gardens, where both usual and unusual herbs are sold. Please contact nurseries for opening times.

Arne Herbs
Limeburn Nurseries
Limeburn Hill
Chew Magna
Avon BS18 8QW

Mail order service available.

Barwinnock Herbs
Barrhill
Ayrshire KA26 0RB

Organically grown culinary, medicinal, pot-pourri and dye plants. Mail order service, send two 2nd class stamps for catalogue.

Blackbrook Herb Gardens
Blackbrook Cottage
Alderley Road
Wilmslow
Cheshire SK9 1PZ

Small specialist nursery offering plants by mail order or direct from nursery.

Caroline Holmes Herbs
Denham End Farm
Denham
Bury St Edmunds
Suffolk IP29 5EE

Send three 2nd class stamps for catalogue list of over 200 species and varieties of herb plants.

Cheshire Herbs
Fourfields, Forest Road
Little Budworth
Nr Tarporley
Cheshire CW6 9ES

Specialist herb nursery with display garden. Seeds and plants.

Chiltern Seeds
Bortree Stile
Ulverston
Cumbria LA12 7PB

Unusual aromatic plants and wildflowers. Catalogue packed with information.

Daphne ffiske Herbs
Rosemary Cottage, Bramerton
Norwich, Norfolk NR14 7DW

Sells unusual herbs, including some of her own cultivars.

David Austin Roses Ltd
Bowling Green Lane
Albrighton
Wolverhampton, WV7 3HB

Specialist rose grower with a wide range of old roses.

Henry Doubleday Association
Ryton-on-Dunsmore, Coventry
Warwickshire CV8 3LG

Organic gardening organisation, with herb display garden. Catalogue available.

Herb and Heather Garden Centre
Main Road, West Haddlesey
Near Selby
North Yorkshire YO8 8QA

Organically grown herbs and display gardens.

Hexham Herbs
The Chesters Walled Garden
Chollerford, Hexham
Northumberland NE46 4BQ

Organically grown herbs, old roses, wildflowers. Holders of the National Thyme and Marjoram Collections.

Hill Farm Herbs
Park Walk, Brigstock
Northamptonshire NN14 3HH

Herbs and cottage garden plants. Also sell dried herbs in bunches. Mail order catalogue available.

Hollington Nurseries Ltd
Woolton Hill, Newbury
Berkshire RG15 9XT

Specialist nursery with display gardens and tearoom. Catalogue available.

Iden Croft Herbs
Frittenden Road
Staplehurst
Kent TN12 0DN

Send SAE for plant list. Extensive herb gardens next to acres of herbs grown for catering trade. Walled garden and shop. Holders of National Origanum Collection.

Jekka's Herb Farm
Rose Cottage, Shellards Lane
Alveston, Bristol
Avon BS12 2SY

Mail order herbs available between June and November.

Laurel Farm Herbs
Main Road
Kelsale, Saxmundham
Suffolk IP17 2RG

Large selection of rosemary, lavender and sage, as well as other herbs.

Lower Severalls Herb Nursery
Crewkerne
Somerset TA18 7NX

Herbs and cottage garden plants.

Mills Farm Plants and Gardens
Norwich Road, Mendlesham
Suffolk IP14 5NQ

Specialist nursery selling old and modern pinks, shrub roses and herbaceous perennials, including many aromatic plants.

Mr Fothergill's Seeds Ltd
Gazeley Road
Kentford, Newmarket
Suffolk CB8 7QB

Seed merchant with good range of basic culinary herb seeds. Catalogue available.

Norfolk Herbs
Blackberry Farm
Dereham Road
Dillington, Dereham
Norfolk NR19 2QD

Send SAE for catalogue of herbs and scented pelargoniums.

Norfolk Lavender
Caley Mill
Heacham, King's Lynn
Norfolk PE31 7JE

Holders of National Lavender Collection. Display gardens.

Peter Beales Roses
London Road
Attleborough
Norfolk NR17 1AY

Specialist rose grower, with wide range of old roses.

# USEFUL ADDRESSES

Southwick Country Herbs
Southwick Farm
Nomansland, Tiverton
Devon EX16 8NW

Herbs and aromatic plants. Display gardens. Send SAE for plant list and prices.

Suffolk Herbs
Monks Farm
Pantlings Lane
Kelvedon
Essex CO5 9PG

Organic herb seeds by mail order. Catalogue available.

Suttons Seeds Ltd
Hele Road
Torquay
Devon TQ2 7QJ

Seed merchant with good range of basic culinary herb seed. Catalogue available.

The Cottage Herbery
Mill House
Boraston Ford, Boraston
Nr Tenbury Wells
Worcestershire WR15 8LZ

Display herb garden and specialist nursery. Open on Sundays only. Send four 2nd class stamps for catalogue.

The Herb Nursery
Thistleton
Oakham
Rutland LE15 7RE

Herbs, herbaceous and wildflowers, scented pelargoniums. Display gardens. SAE for plant list.

The Herbary Prickwillow
Ely
Cambridgeshire CB7 4SJ

Fresh cut, organically grown, culinary herbs and container-grown plants. Display gardens.

Thompson & Morgan Ltd
Poplar Lane
Ipswich
Suffolk IP8 3BU

Seed merchant with good range of basic culinary herb seed. Catalogue available.

HERB SOCIETIES

The Herb Society
134 Buckingham Palace Road
London SW1W 9AS

The Herb Society of America
9019 Kirtland Chardon Road
Mentor
Ohio 44060
United States of America

The Australian Herb Society
PO Box 110
Mapleton 4560
Australia

Herb Federation of New Zealand
PO Box 007
Christchurch
New Zealand

The Herb Society of South Africa
PO Box 37721
Overport 4067, Natal
South Africa

The Herb Association of South Africa
PO Box 1831
Estcourt 3310, Natal
South Africa

FURTHER READING

Herbal Delights Mrs C. F. Leyel (Faber & Faber 1937). A delightful compilation by the founder of the Society of Herbalists (now The Herb Society) of tisanes, syrups, confections, electuaries, robs, juleps, vinegars and conserves, demonstrating the pleasure herbs impart.

Herb Gardening Claire Lowenfeld (Faber & Faber 1964). One of the first 20th-century books to provide 'hands on' growing and using information about herbs. Claire Lowenfeld was founder of Chiltern Herbs.

The Herb Garden Charles Lyte (Oxford Illustrated Press 1986) describes a journey of discovery through the herb garden, one that Charles Lyte, gardening correspondent of the Daily Mirror, began when he was six.

A Modern Herbal Mrs M. Grieve (Dover 1971, with an updated Index of Scientific names in the 1982 edition. An unabridged version of the encyclopedia first published in 1931).

Mrs Grieve's work marked a milestone in the revival of interest in herbalism in the 20th century.

The Complete Book of Herbs Lesley Bremness (Dorling Kindersley 1988). An A-Z reference on identifying and using herbs.

Using Herbs in the Landscape Debra Kirkpatrick (Stackpole Books, USA 1992). A manual on using herbs ornamentally in the garden.

Herb Garden Design Faith Swanson and Virginia Rady (University Press of New England 1984). A wonderful collection of real herb-garden designs from the eastern United States.

A Dyer's Manual Jill Goodwin (Pelham Books 1982) offers detailed and expert information on growing, collecting and using dye plants.

INDEX